Studies in the History of Medieval Religion

VOLUME XI

MONASTIC REVIVAL AND REGIONAL IDENTITY IN EARLY NORMANDY

The rulers of Normandy performed a complex juggling act: starting from a pagan Norse military power base round Rouen, they built an accepted political entity within the boundaries of the Christian state their ancestors had invaded. Successfully reconciling Viking, Frankish and Breton elements within their realm, the Norman rulers made 'one people out of the various races', in the words of one eleventh-century writer. As part of that effort, they revived and reformed monasteries in the region, enlisting the aid of prestigious abbots from reform centres beyond Normandy. By the early eleventh century there was a consciousness within the region that a new people as well as a new principality had taken shape over the course of the past century. In this process of state-building and ethnogenesis, the revival and reform of monasticism played a crucial role.

This book evaluates the relationship between Norman lords and monastic communities and demonstrates how that relationship contributed to the political and social evolution of the duchy. Through this regional focus, *Monastic Revival and Regional Identity in Early Normandy* adds to our understanding of the part monasticism played in tenth- and eleventh-century society, and, more broadly, in the formation of political and cultural entities in medieval Europe. The conclusions presented here are based on an analysis of published sources as well as over two hundred unpublished charters located in Norman archives and libraries.

Dr CASSANDRA POTTS teaches at Middlebury College, Vermont.

Studies in the History of Medieval Religion

ISSN 0955-2480

General Editor Christopher Harper-Bill

MONASTIC REVIVAL AND
REGIONAL IDENTITY IN EARLY NORMANDY

CASSANDRA POTTS

THE BOYDELL PRESS

First published 1997
The Boydell Press, Woodbridge

ISBN 0 85115 702 5

The Boydell Press is an imprint of Boydell & Brewer Ltd
PO Box 9, Woodbridge, Suffolk IP12 3DF, UK
and of Boydell & Brewer Inc.
PO Box 41026, Rochester, NY 14604–4126, USA

A catalogue record for this book is available
from the British Library

Library of Congress Cataloging-in-Publication Data
Potts, Cassandra, 1958–
   Monastic revival and regional identity in early Normandy /
Cassandra Potts.
      p.   cm. – (Studies in the history of medieval religion, ISSN
0955-2480 ; v. 11)
   Includes bibliographical references and index.
   ISBN 0–85115–702–5 (alk. paper)
   1. Monasticism and religious orders – France – Normandy – History.
2. Normandy (France) – Church history. I. Title. II. Series.
BX2613.P68 1997
271'.00944'20902 – dc21   97–12256

This publication is printed on acid-free paper

Printed in Great Britain by
St Edmundsbury Press Ltd, Bury St Edmunds, Suffolk

Contents

To Todd with love

Abbreviations

ADSM	Archives départementales de la Seine-Maritime
ADCalva	Archives départementales du Calvados
ADEure	Archives départementales de l'Eure
ADOrne	Archives départementales de l'Orne
AN	*Annales de Normandie*
BHL	*Bibliotheca hagiographica latina.* Brussels: 1898–1911
BN	Bibliothèque nationale
BSAN	*Bulletin de la société des antiquaires de Normandie*
Dudo	Dudo of Saint Quentin, *De moribus et actis primorum Normanniae ducum*, ed. Jules Lair. Paris: 1865.
EHR	*English Historical Review*
Fauroux	Fauroux, Marie. *Recueil des actes des ducs de Normandie de 911 à 1066. Mémoires de la société des antiquaires de Normandie.* vol. 36. Caen: 1961.
Gallia	*Gallia Christiana.* Paris: 1715, rpt. 1967.
GND	*Gesta Normannorum Ducum of William of Jumièges, Orderic Vitalis, and Robert of Torigni.* Ed. and trans. Elisabeth M. C. van Houts. 2 vols. Oxford: 1992–1995
Instr.	*Instrumenta*
MGH	*Monumenta Germaniae Historica*
ms. lat.	Bibliothèque nationale, fonds latin
Neustria	*Neustria Pia.* Ed. Arthur du Monstier. Rouen: 1663.
nouv. acq. fr.	Bibliothèque nationale, fonds français, nouvelle acquisition
nouv. acq. lat.	Bibliothèque nationale, fonds latin, nouvelle acquisition
Orderic	Orderic Vitalis. *The Ecclesiastical History of Orderic Vitalis.* Ed. and trans. Marjorie Chibnall. 6 vols. Oxford: 1969–1980.
PL	Migne, J. P. *Patrologiae cursus completus: series latina.* Paris: 1844–1864.
Regesta	*Regesta Regum Anglo-Normannorum.* Ed. H. W. C. Davis. vol. 1. Oxford: 1913.
RHDFE	*Revue historique de droit français et étranger*
TRHS	*Transactions of the Royal Historical Society*

Preface

I began this book with a single question in mind: why would the Vikings who settled in France and founded the duchy of Normandy restore the monasteries that their predecessors had destroyed? While it seemed straightforward at the outset, this question led to a multitude of controversial issues. Historians debate with considerable force the degree of destruction caused by the Vikings, as well as the degree to which those who settled assimilated and preserved Frankish institutions. The question as I posed it assumed that there was disruption in the first place, and that the Vikings who settled went to the trouble to repair the damage. These assumptions had to be re-evaluated during the course of my research, and my original question has been revised on two points. First, the original settlers at the beginning of the tenth century were Vikings, but their descendants at the end of the century were not: they were Normans, and that meant something new in their day. Monasticism was therefore revived not by Vikings but by Normans, by the children and especially the grandchildren of the original settlers.

The second point is that monastic life in this region was restored in place; it was not rebuilt from scratch. We owe our view of the ninth and tenth centuries largely to ecclesiastical writers of the eleventh and twelfth centuries who had their own reasons for exaggerating the extent of Viking destruction. The vision that they present of the ruin of monasticism during the period of Viking raids, however, is undermined by evidence of continuity on several levels. The Normans were responsible for a revival of monastic life, not in the sense of a resurrection, but rather in terms of a rejuvenation, imparting new vigor and strength to existing traditions. The question therefore became why did the Normans encourage this revival of monastic life in the lands they called Normandy?

In searching for answers to this question, I found myself continually drawn to broader issues of regionalism and political consolidation. I have concluded that the revival and reform of monasticism in Normandy were inextricably linked to a broader process of regional and cultural identification that was going on at the same time. Monasticism in Normandy was an important facet of this process – not merely a symptom or sign, but a causative factor. It had a direct role in the creation of Normandy. This book is therefore about monasticism in early Normandy, but the central problem it addresses is how that movement contributed to Normandy's regional identity. While my focus is on a single region, the processes at work in Normandy contribute to our understanding of the role that monasticism played in other regions of tenth- and eleventh-century European society, and more broadly, in the formation of political and cultural entities in medieval Europe.

The first chapter of the book discusses the origins of Normandy and introduces the evidence, setting out some of the practical and theoretical constraints presented by the sources. The second chapter offers an overview of monasticism in the region from the early tenth century to the Conquest of England in 1066, focusing on the transformation of western Neustria into Normandy. The third and fourth chapters trace the stages of the development of monastic patrimonies, analyzing the methods of acquisition, the composition and the geographical configuration of monastic holdings. The emphasis here is on the contributions that monasteries made to the social, economic and political cohesion within the duchy, at the local level in the third chapter and at the regional level in the fourth. The fifth chapter focuses specifically on Mont-Saint-Michel and its lands in order to evaluate this community's position in early Normandy. Because of its situation, the case of Mont-Saint-Michel highlights the dynamics at play in the definition of the boundaries of the duchy, especially in the west. The sixth chapter then considers the relationship of ducal to non-ducal houses and their patrons, revealing the ties between men, lands and customs binding the monasteries of Normandy into a cohesive order. Finally, the conclusion sums up the contributions of Norman monasticism to the strength, organization and identity of the duchy on the eve of the Conquest of England.

Over the years I have received assistance from many people. I would like to thank in particular C. Warren Hollister, Jeffrey Burton Russell, and Harold Drake, for their unflagging support during graduate school and afterwards. They read several chapters of this book in earlier versions and offered many helpful comments. This is true as well for Robin Fleming, Katie Mack Roberts, Lauren Helm Jared, Michael Burger and Marylou Ruud. To David Bates I owe a great debt for years of advice and direction, especially with respect to the charter material; I am particularly grateful for his guidance during the year I spent researching unpublished sources in the Norman archives. I am also grateful to Simon Keynes for his many suggestions and for having shared with me his enthusiasm for and expertise in charter evidence. François Gay, professor emeritus at the University of Rouen, provided valuable assistance with positional data and broader questions of Norman geography that arose over the course of this project. I would also like to thank Professor Gay for his and his family's warm hospitality in Normandy. And to Alva Bennett I owe special thanks for the long hours we spent laughing and cursing our way through Dudo of Saint Quentin.

I have benefitted from conversations and correspondences with many other scholars whose insights have helped me clarify my thoughts on issues related to this topic: most notably, Eleanor Searle, Lucien Musset, Michel Bouvris, David Spear, Paul Hyams, Felice Lifshitz, Emily Albu, Rosamond McKitterick, and Elisabeth van Houts. Most recently, Robin Fleming and Marjorie Chibnall have read the entire text, offering many valuable insights and criticisms. My research assistant John Turner has helped enormously in the final stages of manuscript preparation. I would also like to express my gratitude to the the Fulbright Commission, the Social Science Research Council, the University of California, and the Huntington Library for providing funds and resources that supported this research, to Middlebury College for providing a year's leave to complete the book, and to the Interlibrary Loan Departments of University of California, Santa Barbara and Middlebury College for tracking down hundreds of articles and volumes.

This book could not have been written without the support of my family. I would like to thank my parents, Allen and Ruth Potts, and my sister Rebecca, for their love and support. My daughter Gillian brightened up the final stages of manuscript production. And finally, this book is dedicated to Todd Hannahs, for his willingness to discuss each and every aspect of my work at a moment's notice, and his uncanny ability to see the forest through the trees.

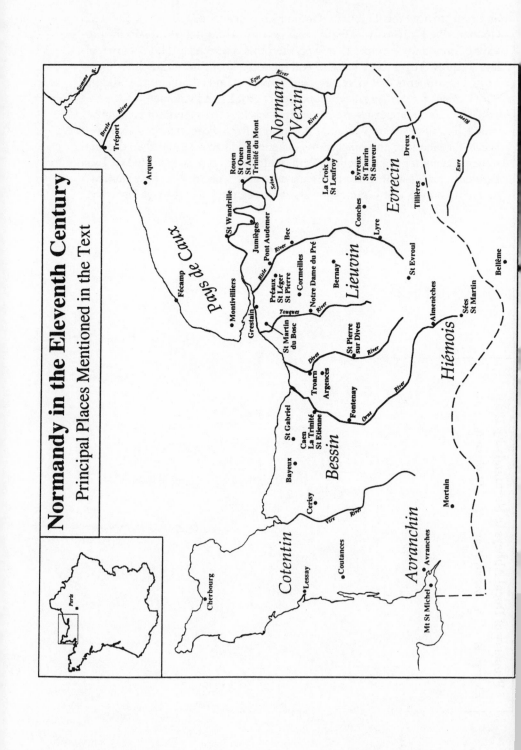

Normandy in the Eleventh Century

Principal Places Mentioned in the Text

Paris

Somme R.

Bresle River

Tréport

Arques

Fécamp

Pays de Caux

Montivilliers

St Wandrille

Grestain

Rouen
St Ouen
St Amand
Trinité du Mont

Jumièges

Risle River

Pont Audemer

Bec

Préaux
St Léger
St Pierre

Cormeilles

Notre Dame du Pré

St Martin du Bosc

Touques River

Bernay

St Pierre sur Dives

Troarn

Argences

Fontenay

Dives River

Orne River

Norman Vexin

Epte River

River

Seine

Eure River

Dreux

La Croix
St Leufroy

Evreux
St Taurin
St Sauveur

Tillières

Conches

Lyre

Evrecin

Lieuvin

St Evroul

Bellême

Almenèches

Sées
St Martin

Hiémois

St Gabriel

Caen
La Trinité
St Etienne

Bayeux

Cerisy

Bessin

Vire River

Mortain

Cotentin

Cherbourg

Lessay

Coutances

Avranchin

Avranches

Mt St Michel

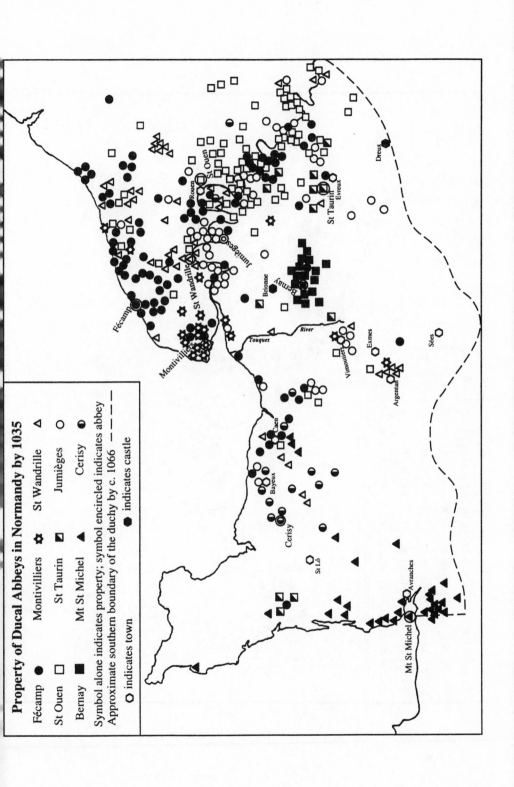

Property of Ducal Abbeys in Normandy by 1035

Fécamp ●	Montivilliers ●
St Ouen ☐	St Taurin ◨
Bernay ■	Mt St Michel ▲
St Wandrille △	
Jumièges ○	
Cerisy ◐	

Symbol alone indicates property; symbol encircled indicates abbey
Approximate southern boundary of the duchy by c. 1066 — — —
⬡ indicates castle
⬠ indicates town

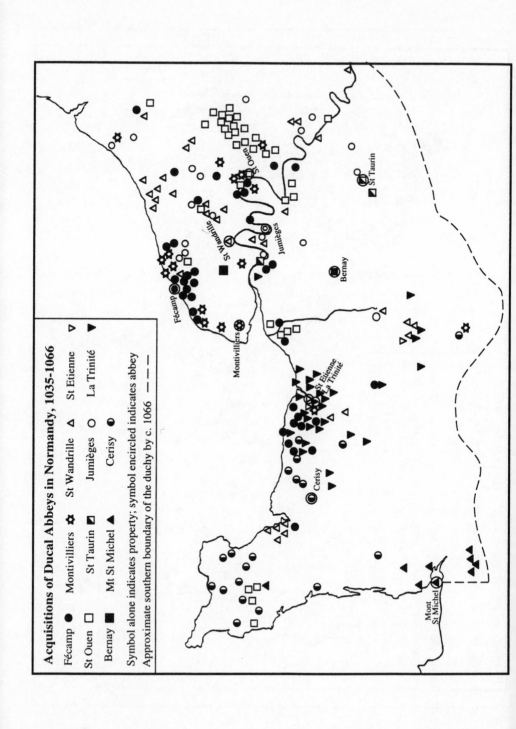

Acquisitions of Ducal Abbeys in Normandy, 1035–1066

Fécamp ●   Montivilliers ✿   St Wandrille △   St Etienne ▽

St Ouen □   St Taurin ◩   Jumièges ○   La Trinité ▶

Bernay ■   Mt St Michel ▲   Cerisy ◐

Symbol alone indicates property; symbol encircled indicates abbey

Approximate southern boundary of the duchy by c. 1066   — — —

St Taurin

St Ouen

St Wandrille

Jumièges

Bernay

Fécamp

Montivilliers

St Etienne
La Trinité

Cerisy

Mont
St Michel

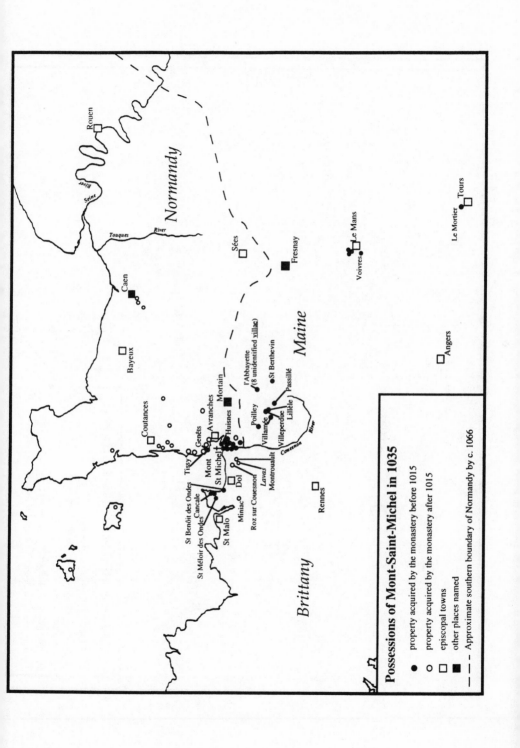

Rouen

Seine River

Normandy

Touques River

Caen

Bayeux

Coutances

Tissy
Genêts
Avranches
Mont
St Michel
Huisnes
Montrouault

St Benoît des Ondes
St Méloir des Ondes
Cancale
St Malo
Miniac
Roz sur Couesnof
Dol
Lavas

Sées

Mortain

l'Abbayette
(8 unidentified villae)
Poilley
Villamée
Villeperdue
Lillele
Passillé
St Berthevin

Fresnay

Voivres
Le Mans

Angers

Le Mortier
Tours

Maine

Cesnonn River

Brittany

Rennes

Possessions of Mont-Saint-Michel in 1035

●   property acquired by the monastery before 1015

○   property acquired by the monastery after 1015

□   episcopal towns

■   other places named

– – –   Approximate southern boundary of Normandy by c. 1066

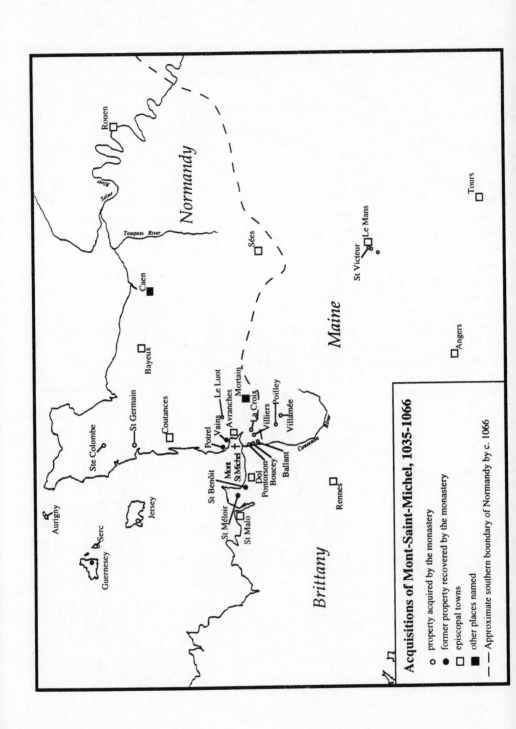

Acquisitions of Mont-Saint-Michel, 1035-1066

○ property acquired by the monastery
● former property recovered by the monastery
▢ episcopal towns
■ other places named
--- Approximate southern boundary of Normandy by c. 1066

Normandy

Maine

Brittany

Rouen

Seine River

Touques River

Caen

Bayeux

Coutances

St Germain

Ste Colombe

Aurigny

Guernesey

Serc

Jersey

St Méloir

St Malo

St Benôit

Mont St Michel

Dol

Pontorson

Boucey

Ballant

Rennes

Potrel

Vains

Le Luot

Avranches

La Croix

Villiers

Poilley

Villamée

Mortain

Sées

St Victeur

Le Mans

Tours

Angers

Couesnon River

1

Origins and Evidence

The revival and reform of monastic life in early medieval Normandy was led by a circle of monks who had been influenced, directly and indirectly, by the great Burgundian abbey of Cluny. They came to a land where ecclesiastical life had been disrupted by civil wars and Norse raids, where Vikings and descendants of Vikings had settled, seized the reins of power, and carved a new realm from the larger body of Carolingian Neustria. Within a generation or two, the newcomers had abandoned the Norse language and religion and accepted much that was Frankish. However, these *northmanni* were not assimilated in the tenth or eleventh centuries: they did not 'become' Franks by accepting certain traditions and customs in the land. Instead, over the course of a century of acculturation, this corner of northern Francia witnessed the creation of a new collective identity. Normandy emerged during the tenth and eleventh centuries through a process of ethnogenesis and state-building which extended gradually and unevenly from the Norman capital of Rouen.[1]

By the early eleventh century, there was a consciousness within Normandy that a new people, as well as a new principality, had taken shape over the course of the past century. This recognition was expressed by the earliest historian of the realm: a canon from Vermandois named Dudo of Saint Quentin. Dudo crafted his tale of Normandy's past to please his audience, members of the Norman ducal court, in the first decades of the eleventh century. According to him, Rollo, the tenth-century Viking founder of Nor-

---

[1] On the distinction between assimilation and acculturation, see Raymond H. C. Teske, Jr. and Bardin H. Nelson, 'Acculturation and Assimilation: a Clarification', *American Ethnologist* 1 (1974), pp. 351–67. Scholarship on the subject of regional and ethnic identity is vast, crossing time-periods, cultures and disciplines. For an introduction to the literature, see Fredrik Barth, ed., *Ethnic Groups and Boundaries: The Social Organization of Culture Difference* (Boston, 1969); Paul Cloke, Chris Philo and David Sadler, *Approaching Human Geography: An Introduction to Contemporary Theoretical Debates* (New York, 1991); George H. T. Kimble, 'The Inadequacy of the Regional Concept', in *London Essays in Geography*, ed. Rodwell Jones (Cambridge, Ma., 1951), pp. 151–74; David A. Chappell, 'Ethnogenesis and Frontiers', *Journal of World History*, 4 (1993), pp. 267–75. For a recent case study on the relationship between religious traditions and the formation of ethnic identity, see David Harry Miller, 'Ethnogenesis and Religious Revitalization beyond the Roman Frontier: The Case of Frankish Origins', *Journal of World History*, 4 (1993), pp. 277–85.

mandy, received a vision of his future while he was still a pagan wanderer.[2] In his dream, Rollo saw himself transported to a mountain in Francia, washed in a clear and fragrant fountain, and joined there by thousands of birds of all types who came from every direction to build their nests around the mountain. A Christian, whom he had captured in battle, interpreted the dream for Rollo: the mountain symbolized the Christian church; the fountain, the baptism which Rollo would receive; and the birds represented the 'men of different realms' who would make their homes with Rollo, yielding obedience to him.[3]

Origin-stories, such as Dudo's, were widespread in medieval Europe. Common to many other cultures and periods, the purpose of these tales is to create a viable past which reinforces collective identity and values.[4] To be effective, they must ring true at some level, and although this point is usually overlooked, Dudo's origin-story reflects the reality of Normandy's origins. When Rollo and his companions settled in the area around Rouen, they initiated a century-long process by which their heirs would bring Franks, Bretons and rival Viking groups – birds of all types – under their authority. By recognizing the different origins of the people of Normandy, Dudo broke from tradition. A standard feature of medieval origin stories was the assumption of single descent: the people who comprised a cultural and political unit were generally thought to be biologically homogeneous; this common ancestry was indeed often the point of the story.[5] Given his training, Dudo was undoubtedly aware of this tradition, yet he chose instead to offer a truer account, one that underlined a message of inclusion which was central to his patrons. The

---

[2] Dudo of Saint-Quentin, *De Moribus et actis primorum Normanniae Ducum*, ed. Jules Lair (Caen, 1865), pp. 146–47.

[3] Dudo, p. 147: 'Tibi aves diversarum specierum obtemperabunt; tibi homines diversorum regnorum serviendo accubitati obedient'.

[4] Susan Reynolds, 'Medieval *origines gentium* and the Community of the Realm', *History*, 68 (1983), pp. 375–90; R. W. Southern, 'Aspects of the European Tradition of Historical Writing, 1. The Classical Tradition from Einhard to Geoffrey of Monmouth', *TRHS*, 20 (1970), pp. 173–96, especially pp. 188–92.

[5] Reynolds, 'Medieval *origines gentium*', p. 379. For background on the development of Normandy's collective identity, see R. H. C. Davis, *The Normans and their Myth* (London, 1976), pp. 7–17, 49–69; G. A. Loud, 'The "Gens Normannorum" – Myth or Reality?' *Anglo-Norman Studies*, 4 (1982), pp. 104–16, 204–09. Loud argues that Norman historians conformed to the traditional view of common descent, and it is true that Dudo and his successors described Rollo and his followers as Danes/Dacians/Danaans, who descended from the Trojan exile Antenor (Dudo, p. 130: 'Igitur Daci nuncupantur a suis Danai, vel Dani, glorianturque se ex Antenore progenitos . . .'). Loud's argument, however, misses the broader picture. The dominant theme of Dudo's work is that Normandy was the product of a difficult but ultimately successful union between these newcomers and natives. For a fuller development of this argument, see Cassandra Potts, '*Atque unum ex diversis gentibus populum effecit*, Historical Tradition and the Norman Identity', *Anglo-Norman Studies*, 18 (1996), pp. 139–52. On the tradition of Trojan ancestry in medieval historical writing see Southern, 'Aspects', pp. 189–90.

Norman achievement, as it was recognized and celebrated in the region's own mythology, was the successful incorporation of various peoples from different backgrounds into one community, thereby creating a new people, a new ethnicity and identity.

Dudo of Saint Quentin is notorious for his willingness to subordinate fact to fancy, but his work stands at the beginning of Norman historiography.[6] He offers the fullest narrative description of Norman history written before 1066, and Dudo himself tells us he wrote at the express command of the Norman duke.[7] He therefore sheds light on how early eleventh-century Normans interpreted the first century of their rule, or at least how Dudo imagined they did. Later chroniclers and historians of the region repeated his account of Normandy's past over and over, and their repetition attests to Dudo's success at striking a common and resonant chord.[8] Had Dudo's version rung false in the ears of later Normans, it would not have been so avidly plagiarized. The central message of Rollo's dream became an integral part of Norman self-perception. It was repeated by later historians and summarized in the second half of the eleventh century by a monk at the abbey of Saint Wandrille who wrote simply that Rollo reconciled 'the men of all origins and different professions in little time, and he made one people out of the various races'.[9]

This point, that within a century of their conquest and settlement the Normans saw themselves as a new people born of the synthesis of several groups, is easily lost in the longstanding historiographical debate concerning Normandy.[10] As Michel de Boüard wrote forty years ago, the study of early

---

6   The most comprehensive study of Dudo's *De moribus* remains Henri Prentout, *Etude critique sur Dudon de Saint-Quentin et son histoire des premiers ducs normands* (Caen, 1915). More recently, see Leah Shopkow, 'The Carolingian World of Dudo of Saint-Quentin', *Journal of Medieval History*, 15 (1989), pp. 19–37; Eleanor Searle, 'Fact and Pattern in Heroic History: Dudo of Saint-Quentin', *Viator*, 15 (1984), pp. 75–86; Felice Lifshitz, 'Dudo's Historical Narrative and the Norman Succession of 996', *Journal of Medieval History*, 20 (1994), pp. 101–20; Pierre Bouet, 'Dudon de Saint-Quentin et Virgile: L'Enéide au service de la cause normande', in *Recueil d'études en hommage à Lucien Musset* (Caen, 1990), pp. 215–36; Victoria B. Jordan, 'The Role of Kingship in Tenth-Century Normandy: Hagiography of Dudo of Saint Quentin', *Haskins Society Journal*, 3 (1992), pp. 53–62; Emily Albu Hanawalt, 'Dudo of Saint-Quentin: The Heroic Past Imagined', *Haskins Society Journal*, 6 (1995), pp. 111–18.

7   Dudo, p. 119.

8   Elisabeth M. C. van Houts, 'The *Gesta Normannorum Ducum*: a history without an end', *Anglo-Norman Studies*, 3 (1981), pp. 106–18; Elisabeth M. C. van Houts, ed. and trans., *The Gesta Normannorum Ducum* of William of Jumièges, Orderic Vitalis, and Robert of Torigni, vol. 1 (Oxford, 1992), pp. xix–xciv; Gerda C. Huisman, 'Notes on the Manuscript Tradition of Dudo of St Quentin's *Gesta Normannorum*', *Anglo-Norman Studies*, 6 (1984), pp. 122–35.

9   Jean Laporte, ed., *Inventio et miracula Sancti Vulfrani* (Rouen, 1938), p. 21: 'Obtima denique iura legesque equissimas domi militieque prudenter instituit, quibus omnis generis diversarumque artium homines brevi tempore sibi conciliavit, atque unum ex diversis gentibus populum effecit'.

10 Published research concerning the history of early Normandy is extensive. Useful

medieval Normandy has been dominated by a dispute between those who see discontinuity in the Viking heritage of the early Normans, and those who stress continuity by focusing on the Normans' capacity to assimilate and absorb Frankish customs.[11] The main problem with this debate is that it tends to polarize discussion as both sides garner evidence to support their respective claims. This is unfortunate because it obscures the broader picture and leads us to overlook the fact that discontinuity at the upper levels of society did not mean discontinuity at the lower levels. The important issue after all is not whether Normandy was more Viking or more Frankish at a given date but rather how it evolved, melding these divergent traditions into a new and dynamic synthesis.

Above all, the men who seized control of this region were opportunists, and in this they were true to their Viking heritage. Rollo and his descendants recognized quite swiftly the importance of broadening the basis of their support, both internally and externally. While central to all effective leadership, this goal held particular urgency for these former Vikings as they sought to settle in a land whose people were inclined to consider them the scourge of God.[12] Both within the area they sought to control and outside in neighbor-

surveys are found in David Bates, *Normandy Before 1066* (London, 1982); Eleanor Searle, *Predatory Kinship and the Creation of Norman Power, 840–1066* (Berkeley, 1988); Jean Renaud, *Les Vikings et la Normandie* (Ouest-France, 1989); Emily Zack Tabuteau, *Transfers of Property in Eleventh-Century Norman Law* (Chapel Hill, 1988); David C. Douglas, *William the Conqueror: the Norman Impact upon England* (Berkeley, 1964); John Le Patourel, *The Norman Empire* (Oxford, 1976); Karl Ferdinand Werner, 'Quelques observations au sujet des débuts du 'duché' de Normandie', in *Droit privé et institutions régionales: Etudes historiques offertes à Jean Yver* (Paris, 1976), pp. 691–709; Lucien Musset, 'Naissance de la Normandie (Ve–XIe siècles)', in *Histoire de la Normandie* (Toulouse, 1970), pp. 75–130. A useful collection of primary sources translated from Latin into French is available in Michel de Boüard, ed., *Documents de l'histoire de la Normandie* (Toulouse, 1972).

11 Michel de Boüard, 'La Hague, camp retranché des vikings?' *Annales de Normandie*, 3 (1953), pp. 3–14, at p. 3. De Boüard discussed this historiographical debate in greater detail in his later article, 'De la Neustrie carolingienne à la Normandie féodale: continuité ou discontinuité?' *Bulletin of the Institute of Historical Research*, 28 (1955), pp. 1–14. He sided firmly with the 'Scandinavistes', describing Normandy in the tenth century as 'un appendice méridional du monde nordique' (p. 7). With the exception of Eleanor Searle's *Predatory Kinship*, more recent scholarship has generally supported the continuity model. See, for instance, Bates, *1066*; Tabuteau, *Transfers of Property*; Jean Yver, 'Les Premières institutions du duché de Normandie', in *I Normanni e la loro espansione in Europa nell'alto medioevo* (Spoleto, 1969), pp. 299–366. Most recently on the side of continuity, see Felice Lifshitz, *The Norman Conquest of Pious Neustria: Historiographic Discourse and Saintly Relics, 684–1090* (Toronto, 1995). For a fuller discussion of this historiographical debate, see below, Chapter Three, note 8.

12 While recent scholarship has tended to emphasize the Vikings' more constructive attributes, it is worth remembering the terror they inspired for contemporary Europeans. On this point in particular, see J. M. Wallace-Hadrill, 'The Vikings in Francia', in *Early Medieval History* (New York, 1975), pp. 217–36. Simon Coupland points out that although the Vikings were not engaged in a 'consciously anti-Christian crusade', to

ing regions, *northmanni* were viewed with considerable suspicion and alarm, and Frankish sources throughout the tenth century continued to paint the Normans in lurid colors.[13] The assassination of Rollo's son William Longsword in 942 and the attack on Rouen that followed must have left no doubt in the minds of the Normans that they were not wanted.

In the face of such hostility, the new lords of Rouen had to seize every opportunity to strengthen their position. On one hand, they preserved and maintained to a significant degree Carolingian legal and administrative institutions which helped to centralize the realm.[14] At the same time, they expanded their network of alliances and neutralized potential threats through a practice of selective marriages, both internally and externally.[15] They also enriched their treasury by controlling the currency, collecting revenues based on Carolingian taxes, and encouraging general economic growth under their authority.[16] And finally, another institution which they encountered in the region that became Normandy and which they reshaped to their advantage was the church.

Historians generally consider the revival of the church in the tenth and eleventh centuries among the most important aspects of the rise of Normandy. Many scholars ascribe William the Conqueror's success in securing and administering the Anglo-Norman realm at least in part to the assistance he received from ecclesiastical communities and churchmen. What has not received sufficient attention, however, is the role that the church played in the establishment of Normandy before 1066. From a political point of view,

their victims they appeared as both 'the rod of God's wrath' and 'the people of God's wrath'. And Carolingian charters often referred to Vikings simply as the enemies of Christianity. See, for example, Georges Tessier, ed., *Recueil des actes de Charles II le Chauve, roi de France*, vol. 2 (Paris, 1952), p. 157; Simon Coupland, 'The Rod of God's Wrath or the People of God's Wrath? The Carolingian Theology of the Viking Invasions', *Journal of Ecclesiastical History*, 42 (1991), pp. 535–54.

13 Olivier Guillot, 'La Conversion des normands peu après 911: des reflets contemporains à l'historiographie ultérieure (Xe–XIe s.)', *Cahiers de civilisation médiévale*, 24 (1981), pp. 101–16, 181–219.

14 Yver, 'Premières institutions'. Yver's analysis is taken further by Lucien Musset, 'Origines et nature du pouvoir ducal en Normandie jusqu'au milieu du XIe siècle', in *Les Principautés au moyen-âge: communications du congrès de Bordeaux en 1973* (Bordeaux, 1979), pp. 47–59.

15 This is a central thesis of Searle, *Predatory Kinship*; see chapters 3 and 4 in particular.

16 This subject has been explored in depth by Lucien Musset. Among his many articles, see in particular Musset, 'A-t-il existé en Normandie au XIe siècle une aristocratie d'argent?' *Annales de Normandie*, 9 (1959), pp. 285–99; Lucien Musset, 'Foires et marchés en Normandie à l'époque ducale', *Annales de Normandie*, 26 (1976), pp. 3–23; Lucien Musset, 'Recherches sur le tonlieu en Normandie à l'époque ducale', in *Autour du pouvoir ducal normand, Xe–XIIe siècles*, ed. Lucien Musset, Jean-Michel Bouvris, and Jean-Marie Maillefer (Caen, 1985), pp. 61–76. Yver also discusses the continuity of economic structures in 'Premières institutions', pp. 339–43. For an excellent analysis of Norman coinage, see Françoise Dumas-Dubourg, *Le Trésor de Fécamp et le monnayage en Francie occidentale pendant la seconde moitié du Xe siècle* (Paris, 1971).

there were several reasons why it made good sense for the Norman rulers to promote and support religious traditions and ecclesiastical institutions in Normandy. For one thing, it helped mollify their subjects: the Viking settlers represented for the most part a warrior elite; they were a minority ruling over Christian subjects.[17] Ecclesiastical patronage on the part of this military aristocracy helped establish their credibility as legitimate lords over the Frankish population; it helped convince their subjects to accept these Viking sons as rulers.[18]

Not surprisingly, Dudo devoted a characteristically florid section of his work to this theme of predator turned patron, promising in hindsight that the church in Normandy would be elegantly clothed by those by whom she had been left in tatters.[19] The contrast between Vikings who attacked the church and those who rebuilt it did not escape the attention of people outside the duchy. Ralph Glaber, for instance, writing in Burgundy in the early eleventh century, made a point of distinguishing between the bad Northmen who destroyed churches and towns, and the good Northmen who settled around Rouen, and 'made generous gifts to the churches of almost the whole world'.[20] Having settled in Francia, these 'good' Northmen wanted to play in the brutal game of Frankish power politics: their growing reputation in the tenth and early eleventh centuries as generous Christian lords facilitated their acceptance as members, an advantage they deliberately sought.

Through benefactions to the church, the Normans helped shake off their image as bloodthirsty Vikings. But even more importantly, the church provided an infrastructure for the Norman rulers to expand their authority geographically and socially. Dudo of Saint-Quentin flattered his audience by claiming that Rollo received all the lands of later Normandy, as well as rights over Brittany, from the Frankish king in 911.[21] In truth, his rule was consid-

---

17 For a summary of scholarship on the question of Viking settlement in Normandy, see Davis, *Normans*, pp. 20–27; Renaud, pp. 67–74; Gillian Fellows-Jensen, 'Viking Settlement in Normandy: The Place-Name Evidence as seen from the Danelaw', *Souvenir Normand* (Copenhagen, 1979), pp. 15–24. The majority of Vikings appear to have settled along the Seine near Rouen, in the pays de Caux, and in the northern section of Cotentin. Bates, *1066*, provides some helpful maps of Scandinavian place-names in Normandy, pp. 266–67.

18 It is telling that in the second half of the eleventh century, the *Liber de revelatione* from Fécamp explained that the broader population was reconciled to rule of the Northmen by divine intervention: 'Divinitus itaque conciliatis populis, pax mundo redditur'. *Neustria Pia*, p. 202. Lemarignier, *Etude sur les privilèges d'exemption et de juridiction ecclésiastique des abbayes normandes depuis les origines jusqu'en 1140* (Paris, 1937), pp. 259–62, discusses this text and places the most probable date for its composition between 1090–1094.

19 Dudo, p. 141: '. . . quorum praedatu pannosa, horum dono compte palliata'.

20 *Rodulfus Glaber Opera*, ed. and trans. John France, Neithard Bulst, and Paul Reynolds (Oxford, 1989), pp. 36–37.

21 Dudo, pp. 165–71, in particular p. 169: 'Dedit itaque rex filiam suam, Gislam nomine, uxorem illi duci, terramque determinatam in alodo et in fundo, a flumine Eptae usque

erably more circumscribed, and it took over a century for Rollo's heirs to assert effective control over the area that eventually became lower Normandy, west of the Risle River. Both Viking raids and civil wars had taken a toll on ecclesiastical organization in this region, but nevertheless the church provided a skeletal bureaucracy for administering these lands. Restoring and co-opting that structure was one way that the Norman rulers of Rouen extended their influence into areas they sought to bring more firmly under their rule. The lords of Rouen thus restructured and strengthened the surviving ecclesiastical organization to help link the peripheries of their realm to the center. Consequently, it was no coincidence that the boundaries which the new principality assumed conformed closely to the archiepiscopal boundaries of Rouen.

Medieval historians have frequently noted secular rulers using the church to advance lordship.[22] Foremost among the advantages usually mentioned in this connection is access to a literate administration, to advisors who know how to marshal economic resources, and to landholders who prefer peace and stable government. In an age when delegation too often led to the rise of rival lineages, ecclesiastical landlords were generally easier to dislodge than secular lords, and in the eleventh century they were increasingly expected to die without heirs. In early Normandy, these benefits were all important, but the church's role in the developing sense of regional identity in the duchy extended beyond this aristocratic level. As they recovered from the disruptions of the previous century, ecclesiastical communities helped bind the province together socially and politically. The church was the ideal institution for achieving this goal since it functioned at the most elite level of society; yet its chain of command reached deep into local communities, operating on a popular level to which the Norman lords had little access. This hierarchy did not necessarily work smoothly or systematically: no doubt there were parish priests in tenth- and eleventh-century Normandy who never heard from their local bishops.[23] But the records indicate that many did, and their connection to a wider church network increasingly in favor of the Normans broadened the basis of local support for these rulers. As the duchy expanded, the church therefore served as a valuable vehicle for regional identity. It provided a multi-layered structure making possible the successful creation of 'one people out of all the races' in Normandy.

---

ad mare, totamque Britanniam de qua posset vivere.' It could perhaps be interpreted that the land, from the Epte River to the sea, signified only upper Normandy, north of the Epte, but this interpretation would conflict with Dudo's claim that the churches of Evreux and Bayeux and the abbey of Mont-St-Michel all lay within Rollo's realm. On this point, see David Douglas, 'Rollo of Normandy', *EHR*, 57 (1942), pp. 417–36, at p. 430, note 1.

[22] See below, Chapter Four, notes 8 and 9.

[23] On this subject, see Imbart de la Tour, *Les Paroisses rurales du 4e au 11e siècle* (Paris, 1900, rpt. 1979), pp. 300–45.

While the argument summarized above could apply to either the secular or the regular clergy, this book concentrates on the revival of monasticism in the duchy. The main reason for this is the timing of reform movements. Monastic communities reacted earlier than the episcopal hierarchy to the negative effects on the church which accompanied the dissolution of Carolingian authority: Cluny was founded almost a century and a half before the pontificate of Leo IX. The Normans who ruled Rouen sought to improve their credibility, to gain respect from the Franks by their dealings with the church. That goal was harder to attain with regard to monasticism than secular orders since the standards for the monastic communities were already higher in the tenth century. Perhaps the dukes realized that their primary method of co-opting the episcopal hierarchy – appointing kinsmen as key prelates – was too obvious for them to apply to their monasteries. It was too obvious, that is, if they sought the status and respect that were associated with patronage of the highest quality of monks. And so, instead of merely appointing their relatives and vassals as abbots, the Norman dukes went out of their way to recruit aggressive, reform-minded abbots from neighboring provinces to restore monasticism in the duchy.

Scholarship on the subject of early Norman monasticism is rich and varied, but widely scattered in articles, chapters within broad surveys, and monographs on individual abbeys. Collections of articles have been gathered to celebrate the anniversaries of specific monasteries, and a few volumes combine articles by various authors on Norman monasticism in general.[24] No synthesis reconciles the conclusions offered by these disparate works, and no single study considers the main issue addressed here: the contribution of monasticism to Normandy's regional identity. The limitations of evidence greatly restrict our view of the early duchy and in part explain the uneven treatment which monasticism in Normandy has received in the past. The fullest contemporary source was Dudo of Saint Quentin, who tailored his story to flatter his patrons. Dudo's tale, albeit colorful, often strays from the few facts which are known about the first century of the Viking settlement. Later Norman and Anglo-Norman historians, Frankish chronicles, monastic annals and occasional house histories offer some correction to Dudo's version, but the broad outline of Norman history in the tenth and early eleventh

---

[24] Collections of essays on Norman monasticism are found in the following works: *Aspects du monachisme en Normandie (IVe–XVIIIe siècles): actes du colloque scientifique de l'Année des Abbayes Normandes*, ed. Lucien Musset (Paris, 1982); *Les Abbayes de Normandie: actes du XIIIe congrès des sociétés historiques et archéologiques de Normandie*, ed. Lucien Andrieu et al. (Rouen, 1979); *La Normandie bénédictine au temps de Guillaume le Conquérant*, ed. L. Gaillard and J. Daoust (Lille, 1967). Anniversary volumes have been compiled for Fécamp, Jumièges and Mont-St-Michel: *L'Abbaye bénédictine de Fécamp: ouvrage scientifique du XIIIe centenaire*, 3 vols. (Fécamp, 1959–1961); *Jumièges: congrès scientifique du XIIIe centenaire*, 2 vols. (Rouen, 1955); *Millénaire monastique du Mont Saint-Michel*, 2 vols. (Paris, 1967).

centuries remains uncertain, since these sources are often narrow in their outlook and distant from the events they describe.

Since reliable political narratives of pre-Conquest Normandy are lacking, historians must find answers from other types of evidence. These include saints' lives, liturgical manuscripts and ecclesiastical charters, all of which can provide insights which archaeological, onomastic and numismatic evidence supplement. From hagiographical and liturgical sources we gain specific information concerning the internal affairs of individual monasteries, relations between houses and outside ties.[25] Sacramentaries, breviaries and missals, for example, offer insights on the dissemination of saints' cults within the region.[26] But for the intersection of monastic and political goals in the region, ecclesiastical charters represent a more important body of evidence.[27] Transfers of property and agreements between lay individuals in early Normandy left no written testimony, but transactions involving ecclesiastical institutions began to be recorded in charters during the second half of the tenth century.[28] In the eleventh century, these records proliferated and hundreds survive, both originals and later copies.

---

[25] For an overview of Norman saints, see Jean Fournée, Le Culte populaire des saints en Normandie (Paris, 1973). With the exception of Lifshitz' recent book, Norman Conquest, there are no extended studies on Norman hagiography or liturgy in this period, although it is a field of rich potential. Scholars working on other regions, however, have demonstrated how these sources can be used to shed light on political and social movements. Particularly insightful in this area are works by Sharon Farmer, Communities of Saint Martin: Legend and Ritual in Medieval Tours (Ithaca, 1991); Thomas Head, Hagiography and the Cult of Saints: The Diocese of Orléans, 800–1200 (Cambridge, 1990); and on the role of liturgy, Frederick S. Paxton, Christianizing Death: The Creation of a Ritual Process in Early Medieval Europe (Ithaca, 1990). For an introduction to the literature, see Julia M. H. Smith's review article 'Early Medieval Hagiography in the Late Twentieth Century', Early Medieval Europe, 1 (1992), pp. 69–76; John M. McCulloh, 'Historical Martyrologies in the Benedictine Cultural Tradition', in Benedictine Culture, 750–1050, ed. W. Lourdaux and D. Verhelst (Leuven, Belgium, 1983), pp. 114–31.

[26] This subject is explored in Cassandra Potts, 'When the Saints go Marching: Religious Connections and the Political Culture of Early Normandy', in Anglo-Norman Political Culture and the Twelfth Century Renaissance: Proceedings of the Borchard Conference on Anglo-Norman History, ed. C. W. Hollister (Woodbridge, 1997), pp. 17–31.

[27] Several studies illustrate the insights monastic charters offer to Frankish social and political history after the Viking invasions. For example, see Constance B. Bouchard, Sword, Miter, and Cloister: Nobility and the Church in Burgundy, 980–1198 (Ithaca, 1987); Stephen D. White, Custom, Kinship, and Gifts to Saints: The Laudatio Parentum in Western France, 1050–1150 (Chapel Hill, 1988); Barbara H. Rosenwein, To Be the Neighbor of Saint Peter: The Social Meaning of Cluny's Property, 909–1049 (Ithaca, 1989).

[28] On Norman and Anglo-Norman charters, see Fauroux, pp. 41–66; Lucien Musset, Les Actes de Guillaume le Conquérant et de la reine Mathilde pour les abbayes caennaises (Caen, 1967), pp. 25–41; David Bates, 'The Conqueror's Charters', in England in the Eleventh Century: Proceedings of the 1990 Harlaxton Symposium, ed. Carola Hicks (Stamford, Lincolnshire, 1992), pp. 1–15; Cassandra Potts, 'The Early Norman Charters: A New Perspective on an Old Debate', in England in the Eleventh Century,

Unlike their counterparts in Anglo-Saxon England, Norman charters served mainly as memoranda or aids to oral memory rather than as legal conveyances or title-deeds.[29] As a result, they tend to be varied in form and content and quite descriptive, providing a great deal of information regarding the types of agreements that took place, the parties involved, their motives and their resources. Included in these charters were mnemonic aids ranging from descriptions of how the duchess's hair looked that day (*sparsis capillis* – it was messy), to anecdotes recalling what a boy was wearing when he was thrown into the lake following his father's donation to an abbey.[30] Such incidental information can often prove quite illuminating, in particular with respect to the relations between monasteries and lay communities.

As the number of documents rose, the eleventh century saw these charters evolve gradually from a formal Carolingian style modeled on the royal chancery to a simpler, more stream-lined record.[31] This evolution signified the wider use of written documents in general. As ecclesiastical communities became increasingly accustomed to using charters to confirm donations and transactions, we also find more and more individuals placing their marks on a given document. While a single ducal cross frequently served as the only validation during the reign of Richard II, it was more common by the middle of the century to have a series of crosses scattered along the bottom of the parchment, representing the authentication of multiple attestors. In the second half of the century, we even find witnesses adding their *signa* to charters at different stages of a transaction. These changes in diplomatic style mean

pp. 25–40; Tabuteau, *Transfers*, pp. 211–22; François Burckard, 'Chartes, cartulaires et archives des abbayes', in *Trésors des abbayes normandes* (Rouen, 1979), pp. 59–83; R. Allen Brown, 'Some Observations on Norman and Anglo-Norman charters', in *Tradition and Change: Essays in Honour of Marjorie Chibnall presented by her friends on the occasion of her seventieth birthday*, ed. Diana Greenway, Christopher Holdsworth and Jane Sayers (Cambridge, 1985), pp. 145–63; Joseph R. Strayer, 'On the Early Norman Charters, 911–1066', in *Medieval Statecraft and the Perspectives of History* (Princeton, 1971), pp. 39–43; Simon Keynes, 'Regenbald the Chancellor (sic)', *Anglo-Norman Studies*, 10 (1988), pp. 185–222. Facsimiles of Norman charters appear at the back of Charles Homer Haskins, *Norman Institutions* (New York, 1918), plates 1–7, and in *Recueil de fac-similés de chartes normandes*, ed. J. J. Vernier (Rouen, 1919). A detailed study of the diplomatic forms and paleography of Norman ducal charters remains unpublished and lies mouldering in the tiny municipal library of Evreux: Armand Bénet, 'Etude sur la diplomatique des ducs de Normandie', Thesis of l'Ecole des Chartes, 1881.

29 This point is made by Tabuteau, *Transfers*, pp. 212–20.

30 Tabuteau, *Transfers*, p. 151; Fauroux, no. 224, p. 432. In contrast, for Anglo-Saxon charters, see Frank M. Stenton, *The Latin Charters of the Anglo-Saxon Period* (Oxford, 1955), in particular p. 67 where he writes, 'But unless compelled by special circumstances, the clerks of the king's writing-office avoided all except the necessary minimum of factual detail.'

31 The evolution of Norman diplomatic styles in the eleventh century receives fuller discussion in Potts, 'Early Norman Charters'.

that valuable information was often recorded concerning who was present at a given ceremony and how they participated in the ritual itself.

These documents reveal much concerning how Norman ecclesiastical lands were acquired and developed, and they offer the clearest view available on the internal organization of monastic patrimonies. The charters make it possible to determine the sorts of property monasteries acquired, how they administered their possessions and how they consolidated their holdings. All this offers insight into the social and economic roles of monasteries as land-lords and neighbors at the local level. The charters also make it possible to map the abbeys' patrimonies at different stages in order to trace the expansion of monastic lands through the duchy. This offers a better understanding of the tenurial geography of pre-Conquest Normandy, helping to clarify the relationship between lands acquired by ducal abbeys, the ducal demesne and the lands of other lay lords. The structure and composition of the charters reveal connections between monastic *scriptoria* as well as outside influences. And finally, the attestation lists of these records provide valuable prosopographical evidence concerning monastic communities and their patrons.

Monastic charters are, therefore, among the richest sources available for the history of Normandy and Norman monasticism before the Conquest of England. Unfortunately, many remain unpublished. Only the charters issued or confirmed by the dukes and those of a handful of monasteries have been systematically edited and published.[32] The great majority of non-ducal monastic charters from this period exist only as manuscripts in the departmental archives and municipal libraries of Normandy, in private collections or at the Bibliothèque Nationale and the National Archives in Paris. The conclusions presented in this study are based on an analysis of published sources as well as approximately two hundred unedited charters, with special emphasis placed on records involving monasteries which were founded, refounded or reformed by direct orders of the dukes.[33] These ducal houses were the most important

---

[32] The ducal charters appear in the excellent edition by Fauroux. Musset, *Abbayes caennaises*, edited the Conqueror's *acta* for the abbeys of St Etienne and La Trinité, Caen. The charters of Jumièges and Trinité-du-Mont, Rouen are published in J. J. Vernier, *Chartes de l'abbaye de Jumièges (v. 825 à 1204)*, 2 vols. (Rouen, 1916), and A. Deville, ed., *Cartulaire de l'abbaye de la Sainte-Trinité du Mont de Rouen*, in *Cartulaire de Saint Bertin*, ed. B. Guérard (Paris, 1841), respectively. Most of St Wandrille's charters have been edited by Ferdinand Lot, *Etudes critiques sur l'abbaye de Saint-Wandrille* (Paris, 1913). More charters can be found in *Neustria* and *Gallia*, 11. For background on these collections, see David Knowles, 'Great Historical Enterprises, I. The Bollandists', *TRHS*, 8 (1958), pp. 147–66 and Knowles, 'Great Historical Enterprises, II. The Maurists', *TRHS*, 9 (1959), pp. 169–87. Various other *acta* are scattered in specific works on local history, periodical articles and antiquarian studies on specific noble families. Unless the editions are modern and accessible, I will provide both published and archival references.

[33] There were eleven ducal monasteries in Normandy by 1066: Fécamp; St Ouen; St Wandrille; Jumièges; Mont-St-Michel; St Taurin; Bernay; Cerisy; Montivilliers; St Etienne, Caen; La Trinité, Caen.

in the expansion of monastic life in Normandy; their charters, therefore, tell us the most about the role that the revival of monasticism played in the creation of Normandy. To establish the broader context in which to place our analysis of that evidence, however, it is necessary to turn now to an overview of monasticism in the region from the time of the Viking settlement to the Conquest of England.

2

Monasticism and the Norman Rulers

Rollo, you will grasp the mystic meanings of your dream:
you will stand at the lofty peak of the mountain of the church.
The leprosy of your sins will be cleansed in the font of salvation.
Now men in the place of birds, bearing shields for you,
climbing the mountain of the church,
will redeem themselves in the fountain . . .
Freed of sins, they will consecrate the mystic holy rites,
and they will make nest-homes near the heights of the mountain,
and they will erect churches, supported by diverse gifts.
Good duke, pious duke, and patrician most venerable,
all things are at hand for you which in sleep your soul drank in.

Dudo of Saint Quentin[1]

Dudo of Saint Quentin builds up slowly to the Treaty of Saint Clair sur Epte in his account of the Viking rulers of Normandy. He tells first of the destruction wrought in Francia by the ruthless Dane Hasting before Normandy existed. Only after the audience has fully appreciated the desolation of the Frankish realm by the raiders from the North is Rollo, the founder of Normandy, introduced, and Dudo greatly embellishes this Viking's early career. In Dudo's hands, Rollo becomes a noble son unjustly disinherited in Denmark who leads a band of youths from Scandinavia to seek a new home. After a series of spectacular victories in England, Rollo hesitates between returning to Denmark and proceeding to Frankish territory. It is during this period of

---

[1] Dudo, p. 169:
> Rollo, tui visus capies en mystica sensa.
> Ecclesiae stabis praecelso vertice montis.
> Fonte salutifero scelerum purgabere lepra.
> Nunc homines, volucrumque loco, tibi scuta gerentes,
> Se, Ecclesiae montem scandentes, fonte piabunt,
> Extremum quorum capies nunquam quoque visu.
> Immunes scelerum, libabunt mystica sacra,
> Nidorumque domos facient montis juga circa,
> Ecclesiasque struent diverso munere fultas.
> Dux bone, Dux pie, Patrici semperque verende,
> Adsunt cuncta tibi, quae somno animus tuus hausit.

indecision that Rollo receives his vision of the fountain on the mountaintop with the birds gathering around. He leaves England to fulfil his dream in Francia, eventually accepting baptism, pledging homage to Charles the Simple at Saint Clair sur Epte and receiving from the king all the lands between the Epte River and the sea, as well as rights over Brittany for himself and his men.[2]

Immediately after his baptism, Rollo demands to know which churches were considered the most venerable in his realm. 'Before the land is distributed to my lords, I wish to give a portion to God and Holy Mary and to the named saints, that they might deem it worthy to come to my assistance.'[3] Dudo goes on to describe Rollo's generosity to monasteries and churches throughout his new realm, from Rouen on the Seine, to Bayeux in the west – even as far as Mont-Saint-Michel in the south-west corner of the Avranchin next to Brittany. Like so much else that Dudo wrote, his description of Rollo's farflung generosity to ecclesiastical institutions across Normandy is generally dismissed as unreliable. Historians doubt Rollo's actual commitment to Christianity, and they point out that many of the churches which supposedly enjoyed Rollo's patronage stood outside the limits of his authority.[4] While Dudo's depiction of Rollo as such a generous ecclesiastical patron across the whole of the later duchy is exaggerated, the author was nevertheless right to link the destinies of the Viking dynasty and ecclesiastical revival within the province of Rouen. If Rollo did not deserve such high praise as a patron of the church, his successors clearly did – and Dudo knew that they wanted to be seen in this light.

From Dudo's time to our own, historians have agreed that the partnership forged between the Norman rulers and their church helps account for the remarkable successes of the duchy in the eleventh century. Orderic Vitalis' description of Anglo-Norman monks as cowled champions 'armed with the power of virtue against Satan and taught to fight unremittingly in the Lord's battles' perhaps sums up best the benefits of clerical support from the medi-

---

2   Rollo's precise relationship to the king is left deliberately ambivalent in Dudo's account, p. 169. The Viking renders homage to the king (manus suas misit inter manus regis), but performs the kiss of fealty only by proxy, with the result that the king is flipped on his back. Dudo obviously added this detail to amuse his audience – Norman lords who were proud of their Viking heritage and independence vis à vis the king. On this alleged meeting between Rollo and Charles the Simple in 911, see Douglas, 'Rollo', pp. 427–29; Prentout, Etude critique, pp. 196–203; Jean-François Lemarignier, Recherches sur l'hommage en marche et les frontières féodales (Lille, 1945), pp. 74–85; Lucien Valin, Le Duc de Normandie et sa cour (912–1204): étude d'histoire juridique (Paris, 1910), pp. 21–37.

3   Dudo, pp. 170–71: 'Antequam dividatur terra meis principibus, Deo et sanctae Mariae, sanctisque denominatis, desidero partem istius terrae dare, ut dignentur mihi in auxilium subvenire.'

4   According to Dudo, the cathedrals of Rouen, Bayeux and Evreux as well as the monasteries of Jumièges, Mont-St-Michel and St Ouen all received gifts from Rollo. See David Douglas, 'The Rise of Normandy', in Time and the Hour: Some Collected Papers of David C. Douglas (London, 1977), pp. 95–119, at p. 103; Jean Laporte, 'Les Origines du monachisme dans la province de Rouen', Revue Mabillon, 31 (1941), pp. 1–13, 25–41, 49–68, p. 51, note 3; Orderic, 2, pp. 8–9 and note 5.

eval point of view.[5] Modern historians tend to be more worldly, but no less emphatic.[6] The strength and the vigor of the Norman church on the eve of the Conquest of England provide a striking contrast with its condition at the time of the Norman settlement. Although Dudo's statement of a land devastated by Viking rapacity and stripped of its population by Hasting and his band is another exaggeration set up to contrast with the peace and prosperity he describes in Normandy under Rollo and his successors, the disruption of ecclesiastical life is nevertheless well attested.[7] Gaps in episcopal lists, accounts of monks fleeing with their relics, and the disappearance of many Frankish abbeys all bear witness to the violence suffered by the church in the ninth and tenth centuries.[8]

---

[5] Orderic, 2, pp. 244–45.

[6] In England, David Douglas has argued that William the Conqueror's success in 1066 depended very much on the support of the Norman church, which 'gave special direction to Norman policy'. Elizabeth Hallam calls the Norman church at the time of the Conquest of England 'a pillar of ducal authority', and David Knowles stresses the contributions of the Norman monasteries to the organization and solidarity of the early duchy. Douglas, *William the Conqueror*, p. 84; Elizabeth M. Hallam, 'The King and the Princes in Eleventh-Century France', *Bulletin of the Institute of Historical Research*, 53 (1980), pp. 143–56, at p. 147; David Knowles, *The Monastic Order in England* (Cambridge, 1940, 2nd edition, 1963), pp. 87–99. Also see Douglas, 'Rise', pp. 106–07; Bates, *1066*, pp. 218–25; Davis, *The Normans and their Myth*, pp. 38–44; Le Patourel, *Norman Empire*, pp. 279–318. This view is also found in scholarship across the channel. For instance, Olivier Guillot writes, 'In the description of the remarkable take-off which Normandy experienced during the thirty years of William's government before the Conquest, one must always attribute an important part to the church.' And Lucien Musset notes that there was, 'spontaneously and very early, a sort of symbiosis between the Norman ducal state and Benedictine monasticism'. Olivier Guillot, 'La Libération de l'église par le duc Guillaume avant la conquête', in *Histoire religieuse de la Normandie*, ed. Guy-Marie Oury (Chambray, 1981), pp. 71–85, at p. 73. Lucien Musset, 'Monachisme d'époque franque et monachisme d'époque ducale en Normandie: le problème de la continuité', in *Aspects du monachisme en Normandie (IVe–XVIIIe siècles): Actes du Colloque Scientifique de l''Année des abbayes Normandes'*, ed. Lucien Musset (Paris, 1982), pp. 55–74, at p. 74.

[7] Dudo, p. 165.

[8] For general background on the impact of Viking raids on Frankish monasticism, see Pierre Riché, 'Consequences des invasions normandes sur la culture monastique dans l'occident franc', in *I Normanni e la loro espansione in Europa nell'alto medioevo* (Spoleto, 1969), pp. 705–26; Jacques Dubois, 'Les Listes épiscopales témoins de l'organisation ecclésiastique et de la transmission des traditions', *Revue d'histoire de l'église de France*, 62 (1976), pp. 9–23. For more specific work that focuses on the diocese of Rouen, see Canon Legris, 'L'Exode des corps saints au diocèse de Rouen (IXe–XIe siècles)', *Revue Catholique de Normandie*, 28 (1919), pp. 125–36, 168–74, 209–21; Fournée, *Cult populaire*, pp. 47–51; Douglas, 'Rise', pp. 103–04; Annie Renoux, 'Le Château des ducs de Normandie à Fécamp (Xe–XIIe s.): quelques données archéologiques et topographiques', *Archéologie médiévale*, 9 (1979), pp. 5–35; Jean Laporte, 'La Date de l'exode de Jumièges', in *Jumièges: congrès scientifique*, 1, pp. 47–48; Lucien Musset, 'Les Destins de la propriété monastique durant les invasions normandes (IXe–XIe s.): l'exemple de Jumièges', in *Jumièges: congrès scientifique*, 1, pp. 49–55; Lucien Musset, 'L'Exode des

The Vikings themselves, however, do not deserve all the blame for the disruption and violence in pre-Norman Neustria. As rival territorial lords vied with each other over the fragmented pieces of the Carolingian realm, civil wars broke out throughout Francia. Under these conditions, the Vikings were not the only ones engaged in plunder and tribute-taking. The Franks themselves had a long tradition of such activities: indeed, Einhard recalls that the Byzantines had a saying, 'If a Frank is your friend, then he is not your neighbor.' [9] Internal violence undermined efforts to keep the invaders at bay, and in their petty wars Franks were quite willing to employ Vikings to fight against other Franks, despite the outraged objections of clerical observers. According to the Annals of Saint Bertin, an aristocratic conspiracy formed in Neustria against the king in 856, the same year that saw Vikings setting up a winter camp along the Seine, just south of Rouen.[10] Three years later, when 'some of the common people living between the Seine and the Loire' attempted to organize their own defense against the Vikings, they were cut down by their own lords.[11] Distracted by internal quarrels, the Frankish counts failed to provide protection against the Vikings, yet they were unwilling to allow peasants to defend themselves. The chronicler notes with sympathy that these commoners, killed by their own aristocracy, had nevertheless 'fought bravely against the Danes of the Seine'.[12]

The ruin of churches in the ninth and tenth centuries is usually attributed to Viking raids, but it is clear that the Franks themselves had a hand in the destruction. Orderic Vitalis, writing in the twelfth century, demonstrates this impulse to blame Vikings for deeds done by Franks. On one hand, Orderic spends considerable space describing Hugh the Great's at-

reliques du diocèse de Sées au temps des invasions normandes', *Bulletin de la société archéologique et historique de l'Orne*, 83 (1970), pp. 3–33. Felice Lifshitz has recently made an argument for a re-evaluation of the evidence for this disruption, specifically of the evidence for relics being taken out of the province by monks on the run from Vikings. Her argument is discussed below, note 19.

9   Timothy Reuter, 'Plunder and Tribute in the Carolingian Empire', *TRHS*, 35 (1985), pp. 75–94, p. 91, note 83. Reuter's comment preceding that footnote is worth noting in this context: 'We have heard much about the destructive effects of the Vikings on Frankish society in the ninth century: we forget that for most of Europe in the eighth and ninth century it was the Franks who were the Vikings.' In response to Reuter's article, see Niels Lund, 'Allies of God or Man? The Viking Expansion in a European Perspective', *Viator*, 20 (1989), pp. 45–59. A more recent discussion of the relative brutality of Franks and Vikings appears in Coupland, 'Rod of God's Wrath', pp. 545–46.

10   *The Annals of St-Bertin, Ninth-Century Histories, Volume I*, ed. and trans. Janet L. Nelson (Manchester, 1991), pp. 82–83.

11   *Annals of St-Bertin*, p. 89. For background on the events of this year, see Ferdinand Lot, 'La Grande Invasion normande de 856–862', *Bibliothèque de l'école des chartes*, 69 (1908), pp. 5–62.

12   *Annals of St-Bertin*, p. 89, note 1. Nelson's interpretation of this passage is preferable to Lot's, 'Grande Invasion', pp. 32–33, note 2.

tack on the region of Ouche in the mid-tenth century, placing orders in the Frankish lord's mouth to sack the whole province in retaliation against the king:

> Wreck churches, burn houses, destroy ovens and mills, drive away flocks and herds, carry off for ever booty of all kinds, and, laden with plunder, turn your backs on these faithless men.[13]

The monastery of Saint Evroul fell victim to Hugh's rage. His men broke into the sanctuary, seized whatever they found worth stealing, including the community's relics, and left the monks 'not knowing what to do or where to go since they had lost everything'. They decided finally to go into exile, as had so many of their compatriots. Orderic states emphatically that this monastery was levelled 'to the ground by the hands of Hugh and the Franks'.[14] Yet earlier in the same book, Orderic attributed the devastation of Ouche to the Danes, even though the Vikings rarely carried their raids to that region. As Orderic's recent editor explains, it was probably just 'a slip of the pen', but a telling slip, since it shows how natural it seemed to a later writer like Orderic to attribute destruction of the region to the Vikings, even when he knew better.[15]

The theft of Saint Evroul's relics brings up another loss sustained by Neustrian monasteries which is also usually attributed to the Vikings. Medieval and modern historians of early Normandy have told and retold dramatic tales of monks fleeing the ecclesiastical province of Rouen in the face of Viking incursions, carrying the relics of their saints with them to safety further inland.[16] In several cases, there is no reason to doubt the records that describe the flight of monks and relics from the Vikings. Charters and annals from the ninth century make explicit reference to burned monasteries, monks seeking refuge from the Norse and the bodies of saints being relocated to safer locations. The desperate journey of the monks of Noirmoutier, carrying their relics of Saint Philibert, is one of the better known accounts, thanks to the ninth-century Ermentarius. Less well-known is the passage which

---

13 Orderic, 3, pp. 314–15.

14 Orderic, 3, pp. 316–17.

15 Orderic, 3, pp. 276–77 and note 2. Orderic describes the *devastationem Danorum* in the region of Ouche. Also see Orderic, 2, pp. 16–17, where he writes that St Evroul's monastery was destroyed by pagans: *cœnobium. . . quod destructum est a paganis*.

16 The classic study of this exodus is Legris, 'L'Exode des corps saints'. Also see Fournée, *Cult populaire*, pp. 47–52; Laporte, 'La Date de l'exode de Jumièges'; Musset, 'L'Exode des reliques du diocèse de Sées'. Simon Coupland, 'Rod of God's Wrath', p. 551, points out the irony of this situation: saints were supposed to provide protection, yet 'religious communities time and again fled their houses with the bodies of their patrons, thereby seeking to safeguard the very objects which were supposed to guarantee their protection.' Not surprisingly, local populations resented having their saints carried off, especially in these times of crisis; their complaints occasionally made it into hagiographical writings.

appears in the *vita* of Saint Romain, written by Fulbert of Jumièges in the first half of the tenth century.[17] Fulbert came to Rouen from the monastery of Saint Cyprian of Poitiers to participate in the reform of the Merovingian monastery of Jumièges during the reign of Rollo's son William Longsword. He is therefore a key witness to the state of monasticism in the early stages of Norman rule. In his *Vita Romani* Fulbert describes the seventh-century bishop defeating a demon. The evil one tries to frighten the saint with a grim view of the future:

> So will I also rouse against you a nation from the extreme ends of the sea and the unknown islands, which will compel your people, ejected as well from their own dwellings, to seek seats in an outer region, or to serve foreign lords in their own homes. But that will not be the end of this calamity. For I will also bring it about that your bones and those of other slaves of God, removed from their own seats for fear of that overcoming nation, will assume an unwilling pilgrimage of exile and, carried all through alien territories, seek new seats for themselves.[18]

Thus the demon threatens the saint with a future which was to Fulbert and his audience the recent past – invasion from the north and the exile of saints, including the 'unwilling pilgrimage' of the bones of Saint Romain himself.

In some cases, however, the exodus of relics had nothing to do with Viking attacks. Indeed, some were simple thefts perpetrated by other Franks described by later writers as desperate measures to safeguard the holy treasures from Vikings, as in the case of the relics from Saint Evroul.[19] The impulse to

---

17 The sources for the *vita* of St Romain and other documents relevant to his cult are identified in BHL 7313. Felice Lifshitz has recently discovered an earlier manuscript of this life. An edition and translation is found in her dissertation: 'The Dossier of Romanus of Rouen: The Political Uses of Hagiographical Texts', Columbia University, 1988.

18 Lifshitz, 'Dossier', pp. 196, 257–58. The translation is from Lifshitz. It is important to note that Fulbert wrote this in the first half of the tenth century; it thereby demonstrates that the flight of relics during the Viking raids was not merely an eleventh- or twelfth-century topos.

19 This point is made by Felice Lifshitz in her article, 'The "Exodus of Holy Bodies" Reconsidered: The Translation of the Relics of St. Gildard of Rouen to Soissons', *Analecta Bollandiana*, 110 (1992), pp. 329–40. Lifshitz takes this argument much further in her more recent article, 'The Migration of Neustrian Relics in the Viking Age: the Myth of Voluntary Exodus, the Reality of Coercion and Theft', *Early Medieval Europe*, 4 (1995), pp. 175–92. Indeed, she turns the evidence on its head, asserting that hagiographers who claimed that relics were taken from monasteries in the ecclesiastical province of Rouen for fear of the Normans often did so in order to cover up the fact that the relics had in fact been stolen. Why were so many relics stolen from this province? In Lifshitz's view, 'the desirability of the relics of the ecclesiastical province of Rouen arose precisely because it was recognized how well those relics had protected their own homelands from depredation during the ninth century' ('Migration', p. 178). Thus, relics were taken from this region, not in the ninth or tenth centuries to save them from the Vikings, but in the eleventh and twelfth centuries, because they were thought to have done such a good job protecting their communities from the Vikings.

attribute to Norse raids the movement of all relics out of Neustria derives from and reinforces the assumption that ruined churches were always the work of Vikings. In both cases later writers, especially in the late eleventh and twelfth centuries, seemed more comfortable blaming the Vikings. Perhaps destruction wrought by the Vikings simply made a better story. It was certainly simpler than untangling the confusing web of alliances and broken faith that comprised ninth- and tenth-century Frankish politics. It also complemented Dudo's version of the past: terrible destruction of the Neustrian church by the Vikings under Hasting only sharpened the contrast with the supposed restoration of order and godliness under Rollo and his successors.

Whether churches were attacked by Franks or Vikings, whether relics were stolen or transported to safety, religious life in the ecclesiastical province of Rouen was clearly shaken in the century before the Viking settlement. The existence of bishops for each of Normandy's seven dioceses is not certain until 990, and even then not all were able to reside at their sees.[20] Five bishops of Coutances in a row, from Rollo's time until 1025, remained in exile in Rouen. And when Bishop Herbert braved a return to Coutances in 1025, both he and his successor held out instead in the naturally fortified town of St Lô.[21] New cathedral churches began rising only in the 1020s, and the dukes' practice of granting Norman abbeys freedom from episcopal jurisdiction consistently undermined the authority of bishops.[22] Only in the second half of the reign of William the Conqueror do the Norman bishops appear to have established ecclesiastical hegemony within their dioceses.

Although the argument is ingenious, I find it difficult to imagine so many eleventh- and twelfth-century hagiographers engaged in a collective endeavor to fool their audiences. Moreover, the ecclesiastical province of Rouen is the one area of France where the Vikings obviously settled and held sway: I cannot see how Franks in neighboring provinces would have seen this as a testament to the power of the indigenous saints 'to protect their homelands'. In sum, while I accept that there were some cases of relic thefts disguised as voluntary transfers by later hagiographical writers, and I am grateful to Lifshitz for identifying those specific cases, I am not willing to accept her broader conclusions. On this subject, also see Patrick J. Geary, *Furta Sacra: Thefts of Relics in the Central Middle Ages* (Princeton, 1978, revised edn 1990), pp. 131, 141–42, 150.

[20] The experience of Adelmus bishop of Sées offers one example of the hardships which the secular clergy endured. Adelmus was captured by the Northmen in the late ninth century and taken to England where he was sold as a slave. At length he escaped and returned to Neustria where he composed the *Sacramentaria ad usum Parisiensem* for Franco, the archbishop of Rouen who allegedly baptised Rollo c. 911. In this *Sacramentaria*, Adelmus called himself, perhaps with a note of pride, the *captivus episcopus*: BN, ms. lat. 2294, fols. 71–86. The 990 document showing bishops in all seven of Normandy's sees appears in Fauroux no. 4.

[21] *Gallia*, 11, *Instr.* cols. 217–18.

[22] Lemarignier, *Etude sur les privilèges*, especially pp. 64–83; Jean-François Lemarignier, 'Une église de premier âge féodal', in *Histoire des institutions françaises au moyen âge*, ed. Ferdinand Lot and Robert Fawtier, 3 (Paris, 1962), pp. 49–77, at pp. 70–72.

Until that time, the revival of religious life in Normandy was carried out primarily through the agency of monasteries closely allied to the duke.[23]

Although the regular church tended to recover more quickly than the secular church, monastic life in the region had suffered significant damage during the ninth and tenth centuries. Out of approximately forty-five monasteries active in the ecclesiastical province of Rouen before the invasion period, at least twenty disappear from our sources entirely.[24] Those that survived or were revived would later recall the loss of buildings, holy treasures, lands and rich libraries, especially at Jumièges and Fontenelle, which was later called Saint Wandrille.[25] It is impossible to know precisely the extent of the destruction. Eleventh- and twelfth-century sources paint grim scenarios which later writers elaborated, leading some historians to conclude that there were no monasteries left standing in the region when Rollo met Charles the Simple.[26] However, the formulaic nature of these description raises doubts concerning their accuracy. And it is difficult to see how either Viking raids or Frankish wars, disorganized and random as they were, can be reconciled with systematic and universal destruction. Later writers no doubt simplified the confusion of the past by positing the annihilation of monasticism at the hands of the Vikings, a view which offered dramatic appeal and provided a clean slate on which to describe the later reforms. But the fact that eight of the nine ducal abbeys active in Normandy before 1060 were former Merovingian monasteries in itself belies this abrupt and complete break with the past.[27]

As elsewhere in Europe, most Neustrian monasteries suffered a series of attacks rather than a single, definitive disaster. Church authorities frowned

---

23 This case is presented most convincingly by Jean-François Lemarignier, 'Le Monachisme et l'encadrement religieux des campagnes du royaume de France situées au nord de la Loire, de la fin du X à la fin du XI siècle', Settimana internazionale di studio, 6, (1974), pp. 357–98. Also see Douglas, 'Rise', pp. 106–07.

24 Lucien Musset, 'Les Abbayes normandes au moyen âge, position de quelques problèmes', in Les Abbayes de Normandie: actes du XIIIe congrès des sociétés historiques et archéologiques de Normandie, ed. Lucien Andrieu et al. (Rouen, 1979), pp. 13–26, at pp. 15–16. Laporte, 'Origines', p. 33.

25 Geneviève Nortier, Les Bibliothèques médiévales des abbayes bénédictines de Normandie (Caen, 1966), pp. 1–3, 98–103, 143–46, 164–75.

26 David Knowles writes, 'Indeed, c. 930 no monastery existed in the land of the Normans', and David Douglas likewise considers it 'probable that not a single monastery remained in the Norman land' in the third decade of the tenth century. Knowles, Monastic Order, p. 84; Douglas, 'Rise', p. 104. Also see the overview of Norman monasticism in the tenth and eleventh centuries by Joseph Daoust, 'Normandie bénédictine', in Normandie, ed. Gaillard, pp. 25–53. More recently, Jean Renaud, pp. 79–80, has concurred with this view: 'Aucune abbaye n'a survécu et les moines ont fui, dans le plus grand désordre, emportant reliques et documents qui, dans la plupart des cas, ne furent jamais restitués'.

27 Those eight monasteries were: Fécamp, Jumièges, Saint Wandrille, Saint Ouen, Montivilliers, Mont-St-Michel, Saint Taurin and Cerisy. Bernay was the exception, founded by Duke Richard II in the first quarter of the eleventh century.

on flight, and the clergy tried to resume their vocations between incursions.[28] The ninth-century annals of Fontenelle, for example, record that the monastery of Jumièges, along with the town of Rouen, was burned in 841 by Vikings who returned in 851 and in 855.[29] Yet in 849 and in 862 the king confirmed the possessions of this community in charters which make no reference to the Vikings.[30] The monks apparently recovered from the fire and continued to manage their landed interests despite these recurring attacks. At some point after 862, a group of monks from Jumièges fled east to Haspres, but it is uncertain whether the entire community abandoned the site.[31] Writing a century and a half later, Dudo describes Jumièges as an active monastery in Rollo's day – Jumièges was one of the abbeys which Rollo allegedly endowed.[32] But William of Jumièges, writing still later in the eleventh century, depicts the monastery as abandoned and overgrown with bushes and brambles until two monks from Haspres returned after Rollo's death.[33]

There is no way of knowing whether Dudo or William of Jumièges was correct about the monastery's status in the early tenth century, although the latter's access to local legends might lend greater weight to his account. Regardless of whom we decide to follow, the uncertainty regarding Jumièges is symptomatic of the difficulty historians have pinpointing what happened to monasteries in the region throughout the ninth and early tenth centuries. The general confusion of our sources mirrors the uncertainty of the age, and it seems in some cases that the monks themselves could not decide whether it was safer at home or abroad. The relics of Saint Ouen provide a case in point. An extant original charter from 872 records that Saint Ouen's remains were taken from the Merovingian monastery of Saint Ouen in Rouen and brought to the town of Gasny on the Epte River 'because of fear of the Normans'.[34] But they remained there less than four years, since another charter, dated 876, confirms the estates of the abbey of Saint Ouen in Rouen, 'where the body of Saint Ouen rests'.[35] The monks must have decided that the threat

---

[28] The same point is made by Albert d'Haenens regarding the impact of Viking attacks in Flanders in *Les Invasions normandes en Belgique au IXe siècle: le phénomène et sa répercussion dans l'historiographie médiévale* (Louvain, 1967), especially pp. 125–43.

[29] '. . . Gemmeticum monasterium igne cremarunt'. *Chronicon Fontanellense: les premières annales de Fontenelle*, ed. Jean Laporte in *Mélanges: documents, société de l'histoire de Normandy*, 15 (Rouen, 1951), pp. 63–91, at pp. 75, 87, 89–91.

[30] Vernier, no. 3 and 4, pp. 5–14.

[31] Laporte proposes a 'partial dispersion' of the monks of Jumièges in 866. Laporte, 'La Date de l'exode de Jumièges', p. 48.

[32] Dudo, p. 170.

[33] Jumièges, *GND*, 1, pp. 84–87.

[34] ADSM 14H 156, published by F. Pommeraye, *Histoire de l'abbaye royale de St-Ouen de Rouen* (Rouen, 1662), pp. 399–400: '. . . causa metus Nordmannici'.

[35] ADSM 14H 143, published by Pommeraye, pp. 401–03 and by Tessier, *Charles le Chauve*, 2, no. 407, pp. 406–11: '. . . ubi praeciosissimus confessor Christi Audoinus corpore requiescit'.

had subsided and that Rouen was again safe for their saint. This hope was apparently premature, however, since the bones were then carried further to Condé-sur-Aisne, only to be returned to Rouen yet again around 918.[36] The overall impression of this period is one of confused disorder and uncertain fear as monks like those of Saint Ouen, Saint Evroul and Jumièges fled and returned, with or without the bones of their saints, while Franks and/or Vikings preyed on their communities.

One final factor which needs to be taken into account when gauging the impact of the Viking raids on monasteries in this region is the Benedictine bias of the extant sources: to later monks, if a community did not function according to regular Benedictine customs, it did not deserve to be considered a monastery. At Mont-Saint-Michel and Saint Evroul, for instance, there is evidence to suggest that remnants of the earlier communities had survived, but later Benedictine monks were eager to disavow any connection with these predecessors. Eleventh-century sources from the Mont describe the 'clerks' who preceded the Norman monks as debauched voluptuaries who had to be expelled, although there is no contemporary evidence that this expulsion actually took place.[37] In his history of the monastery of Saint Evroul the twelfth-century Orderic Vitalis simply ignored the mention of canonici at the monastery in a royal charter dated 900.[38] In both cases, these so-called canons had probably followed an earlier, mixed rule, perhaps based on that of Saint Columbanus. The same prejudice against non-Benedictine observance can be seen at a later date at Fécamp. Manuscript evidence indicates that the 'canons' who lived at Fécamp in the late tenth century remained there after the Benedictine reform at the turn of the century, despite later claims that their decadence and disorder had forced the reformed monks to kick them out.[39] This bias against canons and monks who followed other rules appears in sources outside of Normandy in the eleventh and twelfth centuries, where monastic writers likewise decry the alleged decadence of non-Benedictines to justify their take-over of communities.[40] Like the tendencies to exaggerate

36 Philippe Lauer, 'Les Translations des reliques de Saint Ouen et de Saint Leufroy du IXe au Xe siècle et les deux abbayes de La Croix-Saint-Ouen', Bulletin philologique et historique du comité des travaux historiques et scientifiques (1921), pp. 119–36.

37 Jacques Hourlier, 'Le Mont Saint-Michel avant 966', in Millénaire 1, pp. 13–28, at pp. 26–27. See below, Chapter Five, pp. 85–87.

38 Marjorie Chibnall, 'The Merovingian Monastery of St Evroul in the Light of Conflicting Traditions', Studies in Church History, 8 (1972), pp. 31–40, at pp. 38–39. As Chibnall points out, there is no question that Orderic knew of this charter, since he had copied it himself.

39 The eleventh-century source that says the Fécamp canons were expelled is the Liber de revelatione, in Neustria, p. 210. On their continued existence at Fécamp, see Betty Branch, 'Inventories of the Library of Fécamp from the Eleventh and Twelfth Century', Manuscripta, 23 (1979), pp. 159–72, at p. 163.

40 See, for example, Francis X. Hartigan, 'Reform of the Collegiate Clergy in the Eleventh Century: The Case of Saint-Nicholas at Poitiers', Studies in Medieval Culture, 6 and 7 (1976), pp. 55–62. Ademar of Chabannes provides a striking example of this

and attribute all destruction to the Vikings, it has encouraged historians to draw too sharp a line between Neustrian and Norman monasticism.

Contemporary accounts from outside the region suggest that the Viking settlers of Rouen switched gradually from plundering the monasteries of northern Francia to patronizing them, over the course of two or three generations.[41] During the first half of the tenth century Frankish writers were uncertain whether the *northmanni* of the Seine would ever become Christian. They viewed their fellow churchmen who attempted this conversion with sympathy and respect, almost as if they were missionaries in a foreign, pagan, land. In one letter of encouragement to the archbishop of Rouen, Hervey of Rheims in the first quarter of the tenth century offered suggestions on how to deal with the problem of Vikings reverting to paganism 'like dogs to their own vomit'.[42] Among the various sources which Hervey cited was Gregory the Great's advice to the missionaries in England: move slowly, and do not expect a complete break with the past.[43] Rouen is simply called the 'city of the Danes' in a tenth-century manuscript from Soissons, a reference which the later copies omit.[44] And while Frankish sources considered Rollo's son William Longsword a good Christian, the pagan reaction after his death is well documented.[45]

In most areas, however, the Viking settlers represented only an aristocratic minority: Christianity remained firm in the land and among the people whom they ruled, and deeper traditions eventually prevailed. Moreover, the Scandinavian immigration was predominantly male. Intermarriage with Christian women facilitated the Vikings' acceptance of the Frankish relig-

bias when he gloats over the death of canons who had eaten meat (Hartigan, pp. 60–61). The dangers of accepting later Benedictine views which exaggerate the line between secular and monastic clergy is discussed more broadly in *Pastoral Care Before the Parish*, ed. John Blair and Richard Sharpe (Leicester, 1992), a collection of essays which focuses on the British Isles.

[41] The most important article on contemporary Frankish views of the conversion of the Normans is Olivier Guillot, 'La Conversion des Normands peu après 911', *Cahiers de civilisation médiévale*, 24 (1981), pp. 101–16, 181–219.

[42] *PL*, 132, cols. 659–74, at c. 663: 'Ut rogastis humilitatem nostram quaerere divinis in oraculis qualiter consulendum vobis foret his qui rebaptizati sunt, et aeque ut ante baptismum juxta paganismi morem, quemadmodum sues suum reversi ad volutabrum, et canes ad vomitum, ludicras voluptates nefando paganorum ritu exercuere.'

[43] *PL*, 132, col. 665.

[44] Albert Poncelet, 'Vita Sancti Gildardi episcopi Rothomagensis et ejusdem translatio Suessiones, anno 838–840 facta', *Analecta Bollandiana* 8 (1889), pp. 389–405, at pp. 396–97 and note 5: '... Rotomagensium metropolis Danorum archipraesulem'.

[45] The most important source on William Longsword's Christianity is the *Planctus de morte Guillelmi*, written between 942 and 963, most likely at Jumièges. For an edition and discussion, see J. Lair, *Etude sur la vie et la mort de Guillaume Longue-Epée, Duc de Normandie* (Paris, 1893). More recently, see van Houts' introduction to Jumièges, *GND*, 1, pp. xxviii–xxix. On the general uproar which followed Longsword's assassination, see Bates, *1066*, pp. 13–14.

ion.[46] By the middle of the tenth century contemporaries outside the region were considering the conversion of the *northmanni* of Rouen a conceivable goal. And by the end of the century the Christianization of the Normans had become a new trend in Frankish historiography, a success story on which the Franks congratulated themselves for bringing the Vikings into the church.[47] Norman historiography, quite naturally, preferred the view provided by Dudo that they had been converted directly by God, rather than by the Franks.

Eleventh-century Norman writers support this chronology of conversion, suggesting that conditions in the first half of the tenth century were too unsettled for monasticism to flourish within the region. William of Jumièges notes that although William Longsword had supported the monks' efforts to restore the abbey of Jumièges around 940, the community suffered a setback when the Norman leader was assassinated in 942. King Louis IV appointed a governor named Rodulf Torta to administer the province:

> This man, worse than all the heathens, razed to the ground all the monas-
> teries around the shores of the Seine which they had set on fire, and took
> all the stone to Rouen to repair the city. When he came to Jumièges he
> broke into the monastery of St Mary and destroyed it. He would have
> demolished it right to its foundations had not a priest called Clement
> ransomed from the workmen two towers . . .[48]

Thus, William of Jumièges records that it was a Frank who sabotaged the monks' first attempt to restore Jumièges in the 940s. As the Normans tried to recover from the death of their leader, both Hugh the Great and the king vied for control of Rouen. Rudolf Torta apparently considered fortification of the city sufficiently urgent to warrant dismantling monastic buildings.

Another attempt to recover a former monastery met with disappointment shortly after Longsword's death when Gerard of Brogne led a group of monks from the Flemish abbey of Saint Pierre of Ghent, where members of the Fontenelle community had found refuge, to Rouen.[49] The eleventh-century *Inventio et miracula Sancti Vulfranni* describes Gerard and his followers coming before William Longsword's son, Richard I, equipped with a collection of

---

46 Renaud, pp. 65–82. On intermarriage with Frankish women, Rollo's descendants set the example: C. W. Westrup, 'Le mariage de trois premiers ducs de Normandie', *Normannia*, 6 (1933), 411–26.

47 See Guillot, 'Conversion'.

48 Jumièges, *GND*, 1, pp. 108–11.

49 For a discussion of the extant sources on Fontenelle's flight from the Vikings, relations with St Pierre of Ghent and its reestablishment in Normandy as St Wandrille, see Elisabeth M. C. van Houts, 'Historiography and Hagiography at Saint-Wandrille: the 'Inventio et miracula sancti Vulfranni', *Anglo-Norman Studies*, 12 (1990), pp. 233–51. Also see Lot, *Etudes critiques*, pp. xxx–xlvi; Laporte, 'Origines', pp. 50–51; Jean Laporte, 'Gérard de Brogne à Saint-Wandrille et à Saint-Riquier', *Revue Bénédictine*, 70 (1960), pp. 142–66; E. Sabbe, 'Etude critique sur la biographie et la réforme de Gérard de Brogne', in *Mélanges Félix Rousseau* (Brussels, 1958), pp. 497–524.

charters and the relics of Saint Wandrille, hoping to reclaim the abbey's site and former lands. According to this account, young Richard ordered Gerard to read the charters publicly before an assembly of his great lords. When the abbot had finished, murmurs and protestations broke out among the Normans who were unwilling to hand over former monastic lands which, they argued, 'their forefathers had won through blood and battle'.[50] Since these monks were from Flanders, it is possible that Richard and his men looked upon them with particular suspicion since Richard's father had been recently murdered at the instigation of their count and patron. Blocked by their resistance, Gerard and his band of monks returned to Flanders in discouragement. The general lesson conveyed by the accounts of Gerard's aborted recovery of Fontenelle and Rodulf Torta's destruction of monastic buildings is that during the first half of the tenth century conditions were not yet favorable for Benedictine life.

Although Gerard's attempt to revive the abbey of Fontenelle had failed, a second expedition led by Gerard's disciple Mainard I some twenty years later enjoyed greater, albeit brief, success.[51] The Flemish monks received from the duke the ruined site of the Merovingian abbey which he helped them to rebuild, and the restored abbey was renamed Saint Wandrille, although the saint's body remained in Flanders.[52] More monks from Saint Pierre of Ghent joined the original colonists, bringing books, ornaments and charters.[53] The monastery of Saint Wandrille, however, appears to have suffered yet another setback around 966 when Richard I transferred Mainard to the post of abbot of the newly reformed abbey of Mont-Saint-Michel. For forty years after his departure no word is heard from Saint Wandrille, a period of time in which the community appears to have fallen into the hands of lay proprietors again.[54]

Like the fate of Saint Wandrille after his translation, Mainard I's sub-

---

[50] *Inventio*, pp. 23–24: 'Quo facto murmur et contradictio fieri cepit ab omnibus qui se dicebant nequaquam posse carere propriis honoribus quos sibi armis et sanguine predecessorum suorum pepererat bellicosa virtus, sive quos sibi ipsi diuturno adquisierant servitio multisque sudoribus.' Although none of the Merovingian or Carolingian charters for the abbey of Fontenelle survive in original form, several exist as later copies and are edited by Lot, *Etudes critiques*, nos. 1–6.

[51] *Gallia*, 11, c. 176. According to the *Inventio*, pp. 24–26, the duke and his court were persuaded to support the monks' endeavor by a miracle at the site of the former abbey which was reported by the Norman lord, Turstin the Rich. While Turstin was hunting one day, he followed a deer to the ruins of the former abbey of Fontenelle. At the place of the altar, the deer suddenly stopped, apparently sensing that he was safe there. Turstin's dogs, miraculously, were unable to touch him, held back by an invisible power. Realizing that this must be a holy place, Turstin fell down on his knees and prayed. Then he collected his dogs and departed, leaving the deer in peace. This Turstin might be the same man who appears in Fauroux nos. 42 and 53.

[52] Fauroux, no. 52.

[53] *Inventio*, pp. 26–27; *Gallia*, 11, c. 176.

[54] Van Houts, 'Historiography'; Lot, *Etudes critiques*, p. xlv.

sequent career at Mont-Saint-Michel remains largely cloaked in silence. So
too is Duke Richard's enterprise to replace the community that had weath-
ered the Viking invasions at the Mont with Benedictine monks from upper
Normandy. Mont-Saint-Michel's ambivalent relationship with the Norman
rulers of Rouen is the subject of a later chapter.[55] It should be noted here,
however, that although the Mont was officially reformed by Richard I and is
traditionally thought to have been a Norman ducal monastery, the community's actual commitments lay more with its neighbors to the south in Brittany and Maine than with the Viking principality during the first half
century after its reformation in 966. Mont-Saint-Michel did not in fact
constitute a 'Norman' monastery until after Robert the Magnificent's war
with Alan of Brittany in the 1030s, and even thereafter its loyalties were
mixed.[56]

Efforts to restore and reform in melius monastic life at Saint Wandrille and
Mont-Saint-Michel during the reign of Richard I therefore found only limited success. More certain progress was achieved, however, at the abbeys of
Fécamp, Saint Ouen, Saint Taurin, and Jumièges. The most influential of
these communities was Fécamp, which had been a community of nuns in the
late ninth century.[57] It was located on the northern coast of the Pays de
Caux, an area that experienced heavy Scandinavian settlement, and Fécamp
was within the perimeter of the lands controlled by William Longsword, if
not Rollo himself.[58] A castle was constructed there, traditionally attributed

---

55 See below, Chapter Five.
56 Cassandra Potts, 'Normandy or Brittany? A Conflict of Interests at Mont Saint Michel
   (966–1035)', Anglo-Norman Studies, 12 (1990), pp. 135–56. To this day, Mont-St-
   Michel's position is ambivalent. The Michelin guides to Normandy and Brittany both
   include Mont-St-Michel among their principle sights, and there is no direct train route
   from Normandy to this famous monastery. Coming from Rouen, it is necessary to
   change trains in Le Mans.
57 Annie Renoux, 'Le Monastère de Fécamp pendant le haut moyen âge (VIIe–IXe
   siècle): quelques données historiques et archéologiques', in Abbayes de Normandie, ed.
   Andrieu, pp. 115–33, at p. 126. The following works are useful for general background
   on the monastery of Fécamp: J. M. Besse, Province ecclésiastique de Rouen, vol. 7 of
   Abbayes et prieurés de l'ancienne France (Paris 1914), pp. 34–40; Gallia, 11, cols. 201–07;
   Léon Fallue, Histoire de la ville et de l'abbaye de Fécamp (Rouen, 1841, rpt. 1975); H.
   Gourdon de Genouillac, Histoire de l'abbaye de Fécamp et de ses abbés (Paris, 1875);
   Robert Soulignac, Fécamp et sa campagne à l'époque des ducs de Normandie (911–1204)
   (Fécamp, 1987); Lucien Musset, 'Notules fécampoises', BSAN, 54 (1959), pp. 584–98;
   Micheline Mabille, 'Le temporel de l'abbaye de Fécamp des origines à la fin du XIIIe
   siècle', Thesis of l'Ecole des Chartes, 1953. Also see the assorted articles in L'Abbaye
   bénédictine de Fécamp.
58 The degree of Viking settlement is determined largely by the concentration of personal
   and place names which include Scandinavian elements. For a helpful bibliography on
   this difficult subject, see Christiane Vandeventer, 'Bibliographie de la toponymie normande', Cahiers Léopold Delisle, 18 (1969), pp. 87–119. For personal names, see Jean
   Adigard des Gautries, Les Noms de personnes scandinaves en Normandie de 911 à 1066
   (Lund, 1954). Adigard des Gautries is also responsible for the fundamental scholarship

to Longsword, which remained an important ducal residence for over a century.[59] According to Dudo, Richard I was born at Fécamp; he certainly was buried there, along with his sons, Robert and Richard II, as well as Richard II's son, William, who had been a monk at Fécamp.[60] It was therefore with good reason that the abbey of Fécamp has been called the 'Saint Denis of the dukes of Normandy'.[61]

From Richard I to William the Conqueror, the Norman dukes favored the monastery of Fécamp and fostered this house as a center of monastic reform throughout the province. In the late eleventh century the monastery recorded its past in the *Liber de revelatione*, which recalls that William Longsword rebuilt the church and his son Richard I installed canons there.[62] A charter records the consecration of the church in 990, in the presence of all the bishops of the province.[63] Sometime during the next few years Richard I appealed to the most important monastic reformer in Francia, Mayeul abbot of Cluny, to come to Normandy and rule Fécamp. The *Liber de revelatione* claims that the canons had grown decadent and lax, and that Richard felt the need to reform the community.[64] But negotiations with Mayeul fell through, allegedly because the abbot demanded the right to

on Norman toponymic evidence, which he published in a series of articles: Jean de Adigard de Gautries, 'Les Noms de lieux de l'Orne attestés entre 911 et 1066', *Société historique et archeologique de l'Orne*, 65 (1947), pp. 95–119; Jean Adigard des Gautries, 'Les Noms de lieux de la Manche attestés entre 911 et 1066', AN, 1 (1951), pp. 9–44; Jean Adigard des Gautries, 'Les Noms de lieux du Calvados attestés entre 911–1066', AN, 2 (1952), pp. 209–28; 3 (1953), pp. 22–36, 135–148; Jean Adigard des Gautries, 'Les Noms de lieux de l'Eure attestés entree 911–1066', AN, 4 (1954), pp. 39–59, 237–55; 5 (1955), pp. 15–33; Jean Adigard des Gautries, 'Les Noms de lieux de la Seine-Maritime attestés entre 911 et 1066', AN, 6 (1956), pp. 119–34, 223–44; 7 (1957), pp. 135–58; 8 (1958), pp. 299–322; 9 (1959), pp. 151–67, 273–83. For syntheses of this material, see Renaud, pp. 153–98; François de Beaurepaire, 'La Toponymie de la Normandie: méthodes et applications', *Cahiers Léopold Delisle*, 18 (1969), pp. 1–86; Gillian Fellows-Jensen, 'Viking Settlement in Normandy: The Place-Name Evidence as seen from the Danelaw', *Souvenir Normand: Annuaire* (Copenhagen, 1979), pp. 15–24; Map 3 in Bates, *1066*, p. 266.

59 Annie Renoux, 'Le Palais des ducs de Normandie à Fécamp: bilan récent des fouilles en cours', in *Académie des inscriptions et belles-lettres: comptes rendus des séances de l'année 1982* (Paris, 1982), pp. 6–30; Annie Renoux, 'Fouilles sur le site du château ducal de Fécamp (Xe–XIIe siècle): bilan provisoire', *Anglo-Norman Studies*, 4 (1982), pp. 133–52, 221–23; Soulignac, *Fécamp*, pp. 73–112.

60 Dudo, p. 191; Lucien Musset, 'Les Sépultures des souverains normands: Un aspect de l'idéologie du pouvoir', in *Autour du pouvoir ducal normand, Xe–XIIe siècles*, ed. Lucien Musset, Jean-Michel Bouvris and Jean-Marie Maillefer, *Cahier des Annales de Normandie*, no. 17 (Caen 1985), pp. 19–44. The Robert, son of Richard I, who was buried at Fécamp was a different son from the Robert who held the archbishopric of Rouen, 939–1037. See Musset, 'Sépultures', pp. 22–23.

61 Prentout, *Etude critique*, p. 326.

62 *Liber de revelatione*, in *Neustria*, pp. 193–214, at pp. 204–06.

63 Fauroux, no. 4.

64 *Neustria*, p. 210.

collect for his monks the pasture tax which Richard collected throughout his lands.[65] A more likely reason is that Mayeul simply did not consider monastic reform in a realm ruled by *northmanni* a viable enterprise. But after Richard I's death in 996, his son Richard II continued the search for a worthy abbot of Fécamp, and in 1001 he found his man: William of Dijon, an Italian reformer who had been Mayeul's disciple at Cluny before becoming abbot of Saint Bénigne of Dijon.[66] Widely respected as an administrative and spiritual leader, William of Dijon was responsible for the reform of over forty monasteries throughout Francia and Lotharingia by the time of his death.[67]

Like Mayeul, however, William of Dijon initially refused the invitation to come to Fécamp, protesting that the Normans were 'barbaric and savage men, who destroy rather than build up the holy temples'.[68] The eleventh-century *Liber de revelatione* follows Dudo's lead in playing up the contrast between the dangerous Viking reputation of the Normans and their transformed Christian piety at the turn of the millennium. But whatever reservations he had, William of Dijon eventually accepted Richard II's offer and came to Normandy with a group of his monks in 1001. So pleased at their arrival, Richard II is said to have waited on them himself at the dinner table.[69] The canons whom Richard I had installed were supposedly evicted, accused of carnality. Artistic and palaeographical evidence from the scriptorium, however, argues that at least some remained to become part of the newly reformed community.[70]

William of Dijon ruled Fécamp until 1028, and from that base he estab-

---

65 Neithard Bulst, *Untersuchungen zu den Klosterreformen Wilhelms von Dijon (962–1031)*, in *Pariser Historische Studien*, 11 (Bonn, 1973), pp. 147–48; Lemarignier, *Etude sur les privilèges*, pp. 30–31; Laporte, 'Origines', pp. 52–53; Neithard Bulst, 'La Réforme monastique en Normandie: étude prosopographique sur la diffusion et l'implantation de la réforme de Guillaume de Dijon', trans. Victor Saxer, *Etudes Anselmiennes: les mutations socio-culturelles au tournant des XIe–XIIe siècles*, 4 (1984), pp. 317–30.

66 William of Dijon, otherwise known as William of Volpiano, is the subject of a contemporary biography by Ralph Glaber, *Vita domni Willelmi abbatis*, in *Rodulfus Glaber Opera*, 254–99. According to Glaber, when William arrived at Fécamp, he found the house much in need of new discipline: 'In that place there was an inconsequential little congregation of clerics living in a carnal manner unfettered by the burden of the Rule.' (pp. 272–73). The bibliography on this saint is extensive. The most important secondary works include: Bulst, *Untersuchungen*; René Herval, 'Un Moine de l'an mille: Guillaume de Volpiano, 1er abbé de Fécamp', in *Abbaye bénédictine de Fécamp*, 1, pp. 27–44; Watkin Williams, 'William of Dijon: a Monastic Reformer of the Early XIth Century', *Downside Review*, 52 (1934), pp. 520–45; M. Chaume, 'Les Origines paternelles de Saint Guillaume de Volpiano', *Revue Mabillon*, 14 (1924), pp. 68–77.

67 Glaber, *Vita*, pp. 286–87.

68 *Neustria*, p. 212: 'Quibus B. memoriae Guillelmus Abbas primum respondisse fertur "Charissimi filii, audivimus duces Normannos, homines barbaros et truculentos, subvertere et non aedificare sancta Templa." ' Glaber says nothing of these reservations of William of Dijon.

69 *Neustria*, p. 212.

70 Branch, 'Inventories', p. 163.

lished the foundation for the reform of monasticism in the region controlled by the Normans.[71] While accepting direct control of several abbeys, he also trained a generation of monks whose reforms would eventually extend throughout the region and the century. This network of reform radiating from Fécamp is the key to the cohesiveness of Norman monasticism before 1066, and it is primarily responsible for the role which Norman abbeys played in the expansion of ducal authority. It was a gradual process, since neither William nor his successors attempted to oust reigning abbots or monks. Instead, like the Norman churchmen who infiltrated the English church after 1066, they waited for opportunities opened by the deaths of older abbots. After fourteen years as abbot of Fécamp, William of Dijon accepted from the duke the additional responsibility of becoming abbot of Jumièges after the former abbot died in 1015.[72] He ruled Jumièges for only two years before passing it on to Thierry, one of his original disciples from Dijon who had followed him to Normandy.[73] The monastery of Bernay likewise came under William of Dijon's direct influence, since Richard II simply entrusted the new community to him in 1025.[74] Bernay remained essentially a daughter-house of Fécamp, with Thierry as its second *custos*, until another monk from Fécamp became the first abbot of Bernay around mid-century.[75]

According to the Chronicle of Saint-Bénigne, William of Dijon was also personally responsible for the reform of Saint Ouen, a commission which he fulfilled between 1006 and 1011.[76] While we do not know if the next two

---

[71] Bulst, *Untersuchungen*, pp. 147–85; Robert of Torigny, *De Immutatione ordinis monacho-rum*, in *Chronique de Robert de Torigni abbé du Mont-Saint-Michel*, ed. Léopold Delisle, 2 vols. (Rouen, 1872–73), vol. 2, pp. 184–206, at pp. 192–93.

[72] Bulst, *Untersuchungen*, pp. 163–67. Also see Jean Chazelas, 'Jumièges au XIe siècle', in *Normandie*, ed. Gaillard, pp. 107–16.

[73] Jean Laporte, 'Les Listes abbatiales de Jumièges', in *Jumièges: congrès scientifique*, 1, pp. 435–66, at pp. 443–44; H. Chanteux, 'L'Abbé Thierry et les églises de Jumièges du Mont-Saint-Michel et de Bernay', *Bulletin Monumental*, 98 (1939), pp. 67–72.

[74] Fauroux no. 35: 'Cujus ego animi conscius confestim servorum Dei assiduam ibi consti-tui habitationem, tradens illud Fiscannensi sanctæ Trinitatis æcclesiæ perpetuo reti-nendum, commitens venerabili Vuillelmo abb'ati perficiendum et cunctis ejus successoribus monastice ordinandum.' On the monastery of Bernay also see Besse, pp. 196–97; *Gallia*, 11, cols. 830–34; Patrice Cousin, 'L'Abbaye Notre-Dame de Bernay au XIe siècle', in *Normandie*, ed. Gaillard, pp. 141–51; G. Bouet, 'L'Abbaye de Bernay', *Bulletin monumental*, 31 (1865), pp. 95–100; John Bilson, 'Nouvelles Observations sur l'église abbatiale de Bernay', *Bulletin Monumental*, 75 (1911), pp. 396–422. The *villa* of Bernay had belonged to Jumièges in 849 (Vernier, no. 3, p. 8, note 12).

[75] *Gallia*, 11, cols. 830–31; Torigny, *De immutatione*, p. 194.

[76] Bulst, *Untersuchungen*, pp. 161–63. On the abbey of St Ouen, see Besse, 29–34; F. Pommeraye, *Histoire de l'abbaye royale de St-Ouen de Rouen* (Rouen, 1662); Paul le Cacheux, 'La Baronnie de Saint-Ouen de Rouen', *BSAN*, 47 (1940), pp. 63–81; Lauer, 'Translations des reliques'; Lucien Musset, 'Actes inédit du XIe siècle, l'abbaye de Saint-Ouen de Rouen et la ville de Caen', *BSAN*, 58 (1968), pp. 119–26; *Gallia*, 11, c. 140 reads: 'Hildebertus a Guillelmo Divionensi, ut credere est, institutus, utrique Richardo Normannorum duci carus fuit.' The fonds of St Ouen, ADSM 14H, are

abbots of Saint Ouen were connected with Fécamp, Nicholas, who ruled the monastery from c. 1036 to 1092, had been trained at Fécamp by William of Dijon's disciple and successor, John of Ravenna.[77] Nicholas was also the son of Duke Richard III, further demonstrating the close association between the Fécamp circle of reform and the ducal family. From Saint Ouen, a group of monks was sent out to the former abbey of La Croix Saint Leufroy, which was ruled by abbots from Saint Ouen through the eleventh century.[78]

William of Dijon's disciple Thierry was not only abbot of Jumièges and the second *custos* of Bernay; he was also Richard II's choice to rule Mont-Saint-Michel when its abbot died in 1023. That appointment was problematic, however, since the monks at the Mont resisted being pulled into Fécamp's orbit. After Thierry, Mont-Saint-Michel received, with some reluctance, two more of William of Dijon's students as its abbots before the middle of the century.[79] Consequently, despite the Mont's ties and interests outside of Normandy, there were clear links between it and Fécamp which were reflected in its leadership, liturgy, art and intellectual life.[80] John of Ravenna, who was also trained by William of Dijon, succeeded him as abbot of Fécamp

---

unusually rich with original charters, including several original Carolingian *acta* that survived the Viking incursions.

77 *Gallia*, 11, c. 141; Bulst, *Untersuchungen*, p. 163; Orderic, 4, p. 308, note 1.

78 In 918 Charles the Simple had placed La Croix St Leufroy in the possession of St Germain des Prés, citing the need to restore churches which had been destroyed by the pagans and assure the veneration of saints who had been expelled: '. . . idcirco oportet nos non modo praeesse, verum potius sanctis prodesse ecclesiis ac praesertim derutis, quibus feritate paganorum pulsa existunt corpora sanctorum hactenus debita veneratione carentium.' This charter survives in original form and is published in *Recueil des actes de Charles III le Simple, roi de France (893–923)*, ed. Ferdinand Lot and Philippe Lauer (Paris, 1949), no. 92, pp. 209–12. Interpretations of this document vary widely, with the central question being whether Saints Ouen and Leuffroy should be considered among those saints banished from their churches. Compare Lifshitz, 'Migration', with Jean Letort, 'L'Abbaye de la Croix-Saint-Leufroy au XIe siècle', in *Normandie*, ed. Gaillard, pp. 187–89; Lauer, 'Translations'; Laporte, 'Origines', pp. 49–50. On St Ouen's reform, see Pierre-François Lebeurier, *Notice sur l'abbaye de la Croix-Saint-Leufroy* (Rouen, 1866), pp. 1–40; M. Renault, 'Essai historique sur la paroisse et l'abbaye de la Croix-St-Leufroi', *Mémoires de la société des antiquaires de Normandie*, 25 (1863), pp. 652–98; M. Charpillon, *Dictionnaire historique de toutes les communes du département de l'Eure* (Les Andelys, 1868–79), pp. 901–6; *Gallia*, 11, cols. 632–37. Pope Alexander II confirmed St Ouen's pre-eminence over the community between 1061 and 1073: ADSM 14H 140.

79 *Gallia*, 11, c. 515; Bulst, *Untersuchungen*, p. 170; Jean Laporte, 'Les séries abbatiale et priorale du Mont Saint-Michel', in *Millénaire*, 1, pp. 267–81, at pp. 272–73.

80 R. Le Roux, 'Guillaume de Volpiano: son cursus liturgique au Mont Saint-Michel et dans les abbayes normandes', in *Millénaire*, 1, pp. 417–72; Michel Le Pesant, 'Les Relations du Mont Saint-Michel avec les autres abbayes normandes', in *Millénaire*, 1, pp. 743–50; Henri Tardif, 'La Liturgie de la messe au Mont Saint-Michel aux XIe, XIIe et XIIIe siècles', in *Millénaire*, 1, pp. 353–77; François Avril, 'La Décoration des manuscrits au Mont Saint-Michel (XIe–XIIe siècles)', in *Millénaire*, 2, pp. 203–38, especially pp. 235–38.

from 1028–1078. Under his long administration Fécamp flourished and remained at the center of the growing network of monasteries in Normandy. Even more than William of Dijon, John of Ravenna was renowned for his spiritual writings.[81] Together, these two men were largely responsible for bringing a new asceticism to Norman monastic life, inspired by the eremitical movement of their native Italy and later reflected in the works of their fellow Italian Anselm of Bec.[82]

In 1034 Fécamp received the abbey of Saint Taurin from Robert the Magnificent in exchange for the ancient house of Montivilliers, which Richard II had placed in Fécamp's hands.[83] At Montivilliers, Robert the Magnificent granted the request of John of Ravenna and re-established there a house of nuns, choosing his father's half-sister to be abbess.[84] Duke Robert also restored the former Merovingian abbey of Cerisy between 1030 and

---

81 Jean Leclercq and Jean-Paul Bonnes, Un Maître de la vie spirituelle au XIe siècle: Jean de Fécamp (Paris, 1946), remains the best study of this abbot's spirituality. On his mysticism specifically, see A. Wilmart, 'La Complainte de Jean de Fécamp sur les fins dernières', in Auteurs spirituels et textes dévots du moyen âge latin (Paris, 1932), pp. 126–37. Wilmart ranks John of Fécamp's spiritual works with those of Saint Bernard, Augustine and Gregory the Great. John of Fécamp's administrative and financial skills are discussed by Lucien Musset, 'La Vie économique de l'abbaye de Fécamp sous l'abbatiat de Jean de Ravenne (1028–1078)', in Abbaye bénédictine de Fécamp, 1, pp. 67–79, 345–49.

82 The connections which exist between the works of John of Fécamp and Saint Anselm are discussed by Gillian R. Evans, 'Mens Devota: The Literary Community of the Devotional Works of John of Fécamp and St. Anselm', Medium Ævum, 43 (1974), pp. 105–15. Evans points out the similarities in thought and style between the two writers, concluding that they belong to a common genre. William of Dijon was probably influenced by his friend Romuald, Peter Damian's role model and the leader of the eremitical movement of his day. Romuald is portrayed as 'the father of reasonable hermits who live by the law', in Bruno of Querfurt's Life of Five Brethren, as cited by Leyser, p. 32. Henrietta Leyser, Hermits and the New Monasticism: A Study of Religious Communities in Western Europe, 1000–1150 (London, 1984), pp. 31–33.

83 As Fauroux no. 5 reveals, St Taurin had been rebuilt by Richard I between 962 and 996; its refoundation is discussed in more detail below, Chapter Four, pp. 65–69. For a general history of St Taurin, see Louis Debidour, Essai sur l'histoire de l'abbaye bénédictine de St-Taurin d'Evreux (Evreux, 1908). A useful but unpublished study is the joint work by Martine Chapron and Véronique Vecile, Le Temporel de l'abbaye de St-Taurin d'Evreux du Xème siècle au XVème siècle (vers 965–1400), UER des lettres et sciences humaines, Rouen, 1979. Also see Besse, pp. 173–74; Gallia, 11, cols. 626–32. This exchange is described in Fauroux no. 87.

84 Gallia, 11, cols. 281–86. On Montivilliers, most recently, see Jacques Le Maho, 'L'abbaye de Montivilliers et l'aristocratie locale aux XIe et XIIe siècles', in L'Abbaye de Montivilliers à travers les ages: actes du colloque organisé à Montivilliers le 8 mars 1986, vol. 46 of Recueil de l'association des amis du vieux Havre (Le Havre, 1988), pp. 1–16; Jean-Michel Bouvris, 'La Renaissance de l'abbaye de Montivilliers et son développement jusqu'à la fin du XIe siècle', in L'Abbaye de Montivilliers, pp. 17–84. The following studies are also useful: Georges Priem, 'L'Abbaye royale de Montivilliers', in Normandie, ed. Gaillard, pp. 153–77; Ernest Dumont, L'Abbaye de Montivilliers (Le Havre, 1876); Paul le Cacheux, L'Exemption de Montivilliers (Caen, 1929).

1032, appointing a former monk from Saint Ouen as its first abbot.[85] By 1035, the only revived Norman abbey that stood outside the reforms generated from Fécamp was Saint Wandrille, which had been reformed c. 1007 by a former schoolfellow of Fulbert of Chartres, Gerard abbot of Crépy, who came to Normandy like William of Dijon at Richard II's urging.[86] Unlike William of Dijon's reforms, Gerard of Crépy's reform of Saint Wandrille appears to have been based predominantly on customs from Fleury and Chartres.[87]

Eight monasteries, then, were active in the ecclesiastical province of Rouen by the first quarter of the eleventh century: Fécamp, Jumièges, Saint Ouen, Saint Wandrille, Montivilliers, Mont-Saint-Michel, Bernay, and Saint Taurin. With the exception of Richard II's foundation of Bernay, every one of these abbeys traced its origins back to Merovingian times. While we need not accept eleventh-century claims that monastic life in the region was completely destroyed by the Vikings, these communities clearly suffered during the ninth and tenth centuries. Buildings were destroyed, libraries were lost, and relics were scattered throughout Francia. But by Robert the Magnificent's death in 1035, these monasteries were all flourishing again, richly endowed by the Norman rulers and under the direct or indirect influence of abbots whom the dukes had invited to Normandy to help in the revival of monastic life in the duchy. Although the half-century between 1030 and 1080 witnessed the rise of over twenty private monasteries, these new communities were integrated into the monastic network loyal to the ducal house and centering on Fécamp.[88] Whereas in other areas of the former Carolingian empire the appearance of private abbeys signalled the fragmentation of central authority over the church, in Normandy this was not the case.

The relationship of Fécamp to the other Norman monasteries has led to the suggestion that the abbots of Fécamp and the dukes of Normandy hoped to create a system of reform in conscious imitation of the Cluniac model.[89] Certainly the charter of Richard II which places William of Dijon at the head of Fécamp implies that reform along Cluniac lines was intended. Preserved at Fécamp in the original, the document promises that the monks of Fécamp

---

85   Fauroux no. 64. For brief overviews of the history of Cerisy, see Georges Duval, 'L'Abbaye de Cerisy', in *Normandie*, ed. Gaillard, pp. 179–85, and John Howe, 'The Date of the "Life" of St. Vigor of Bayeux', *Analecta Bollandiana*, 102 (1984), pp. 303–12. The most thorough study of the monastery of Cerisy remains Paul de Farcy, *Abbayes de l'évêché de Bayeux*, vol. 1 of 3 vols. (Laval, 1887–88), a work which is particularly useful because of the number of documents it includes. On the appointment of abbots at Cerisy, see de Farcy, pp. 1–3; 76–87; *Gallia*, 11, cols. 408–13.

86   *Inventio*, pp. 31–32.

87   Jean Laporte, 'Gérard de Brogne à Saint-Wandrille et à Saint-Riquier', *Revue Bénédictine*, 70 (1960), pp. 142–66, at p. 164.

88   See below, Chapter Six.

89   Jean Laporte, 'Un Diplôme pour Romainmôtier dans les archives de Fécamp', *BSAN*, 56 (1963), pp. 415–29, in particular pp. 423–24.

would enjoy the liberty to manage their own affairs and elect their own abbot according to the customs of Cluny, which the document praises as 'the fountain of holy piety whose rule, having now been distributed through many places far and wide, flowed forth by God's providence to this place'.[90] These were high-sounding phrases which celebrate the prestige which William of Dijon's reform brought to the duchy, but they should not to be taken too literally. Fécamp enjoyed freedom from episcopal and seigniorial authority by virtue of its close ties to the Norman rulers, but that protection had its own price. Neither William of Dijon nor his successors could operate independently of the Norman rulers. Indeed, the monastery was so closely associated with Richard II's policy that it served as his chancery during William of Dijon's reign.[91] Even the pope referred to Fécamp as Richard II's church: in 1017 when Benedict VIII sanctioned the privileges of Fécamp, he addressed his bull to the duke, referring to the monastery as *ecclesiam tuam*.[92] And despite the promise of free abbatial elections in Fécamp's charter, Richard II and his successors reserved the right to decide who would be abbot at Fécamp, as they did for all their monasteries.

Most importantly, the network which evolved from these reforms was a loose association based on human relationships rather than institutional ties. Like the monasteries of Saint Bénigne in Burgundy and Gorze in Lotharingia which William of Dijon also ruled, Fécamp's influence spread naturally as her monks and others trained by former Fécamp monks accepted positions of authority in the flourishing monasteries of the duchy.[93] Connections between houses are apparent in their liturgy and products of their *scriptoria*,

---

[90] Fauroux no. 9, p. 80: '. . . a nobis juste collata utantur libertate, ita dumtaxat ut, in ipsa electione vel ordinatione abbatis, illa per omnia servetur consuetudo quae hactenus in Cluniaco cenobiorum servata est illustrissimo (*sic*), unde fons sanctae monastice religionis per multa jam longe lateque dirivatus loca ad hunc usque Deo profluxit propicio, cujus sanctae religionis observatio ut magis ac magis ad profectum tam mee quam genitoris ac genitricis omniumque fidelium proficiat animarum'.

[91] Fauroux pp. 41–43; Brown, 'Some Observations', p. 151. Recent scholarship has shown that the traditional assumptions about a Cluniac 'Order' in the tenth and eleventh century must also be revised. For Cluny, as elsewhere, monastic reform in these centuries should be understood as a process which had more to do with personal interactions than institutional categories. On this subject, see in particular, Barbara H. Rosenwein, *Rhinoceros Bound: Cluny in the Tenth Century* (Philadelphia, 1982); Constance B. Bouchard, 'Merovingian, Carolingian and Cluniac Monasticism: Reform and Renewal in Burgundy', *Journal of Ecclesiastical History*, 41 (1990), pp. 365–88.

[92] BN, coll. Moreau, vol. 19, fols. 111r–12r = nouv. acq. fr. 21819, fols. 6rv. The key section of this bull is edited in Jean-François Lemarignier, *Etude sur les privilèges*, pp. 37–38, note 38.

[93] For a discussion of St Bénigne and Gorze as centers of monastic reform under William of Dijon, see Bulst, *Untersuchungen*, pp. 30–53, 86–90; Hubert Dauphin, 'Monastic Reforms from the Tenth Century to the Twelfth', *The Downside Review*, 70 (1952), pp. 62–74; Dominique Iogna-Prat, 'Le Monachisme autour l'an mil en quelques questions', in *Religion et culture autour de l'an mil: royaume capétien et Lotharingie*, ed. Dominique Iogna-Prat and Jean-Charles Picard (Auxerre, 1990), pp. 13–15.

especially at Fécamp, Jumièges and Mont-Saint-Michel, but each monastery remained legally independent and proud of its separate traditions.[94] Gerard of Crépy's influence at Saint Wandrille reminds us that William of Dijon was not the only reforming presence in the duchy. To assure that the quality of observance within the duchy was high, and that the monks remained their faithful servants, the Norman rulers were willing to draw from more than one source of monastic reform.

Eric John has written that during the tenth century every reformed monastery in England could be considered a 'royal *eigenkloster*' serving as 'a *foyer* of royalist propaganda'.[95] A similar case could be made for Normandy, but this partnership between rulers and monks was not unusual in western Europe during this period. As several studies have recently underlined, reforming abbots of the tenth century were accustomed to seeking the support and the company of kings and rulers to achieve their goals.[96] And there were many advantages to prompt rulers in the tenth and eleventh centuries to support monasticism. As repositories of administrative and economic expertise, monasteries served as powerful landholders. Yet they posed less of a threat than secular lords, especially since the dukes could exercise their prerogative to move and remove abbots. For rulers who governed through itineration, monasteries provided valuable stopping places, providing shelter and provisions for a court on the move. The existence of monasteries, especially along frontiers or in areas which were in dispute, also helped to reinforce territorial claims.[97] Patrons and protectors of monastic life, moreover, enjoyed the spiritual benefits of constant prayers said on their behalf.

Beyond these benefits, however, the Norman rulers gained status with two main audiences which were particularly important to them: the population within the region they ruled and those in neighboring provinces. By taking under special protection monasteries ravaged during the Viking raids, the Norman lords placed emphasis on their own transformation from pagan conquerors to Christian lords. This sent an important message to their subjects, helping to heal the rift and blur the line between Northman and Frank. By linking their present with the religious past of the region, the Norman

---

94 For liturgical connections between these abbeys and Saint Bénigne, see R. Le Roux, 'Guillaume de Volpiano: son cursus liturgique au Mont Saint-Michel et dans les abbayes normandes', in *Millénaire*, 1, pp. 417–72.

95 Eric John, 'The King and the Monks in the Tenth-Century Reformation', in *Orbis Britannaie and Other Studies* (Leicester, 1966), pp. 154–80, at pp. 178–79.

96 See for example Marco Mostert, *The Political Theology of Abbo of Fleury* (Hilversum, 1987); *St Dunstan: His Life, Times and Cult*, ed. Nigel Ramsay, Margaret Sparks and Tim Tatton-Brown (Woodbridge, 1992); Françoise Coutansais, 'Les Monastères du Poitou avant l'An Mil', *Revue Mabillon*, 53 (1963), pp. 1–21; Constance B. Bouchard, 'Laymen and Church Reform around the Year 1000: the Case of Otto-William, Count of Burgundy', *Journal of Medieval History*, 5 (1979), pp. 1–10

97 Marjorie Chibnall, *The World of Orderic Vitalis* (Oxford, 1984), pp. 50–51. This point is discussed in greater detail below, Chapter Four.

rulers took advantage of inveterate traditions within the region to enhance their own credibility. At the same time, by appealing to Mayeul of Cluny Richard I had set his sights at the top, and his son followed his example by bringing William of Dijon and Gerard of Crépy to the duchy. The successful recruitment of these prestigious reformers won respect outside of Normandy and linked Norman monasticism to wider currents of reform. At the local and the international level therefore, the revival and reform of monasticism in Normandy contributed to the prestige of the rulers and the coherence of the realm.

3

Local Ties:
Monastic Lands and Lay Communities

> We admonish lest any reader shudder because of the shame of
> disastrous misfortunes which happened to the Frankish people, not to
> destroy them but to correct them, because of the accumulation of
> their sins.
>
> Dudo of Saint Quentin[1]

Ecclesiastical writers in the ninth and tenth centuries saw the Viking attacks
on western Europe as God's punishment for the collective sins of the people.[2]
This theme provides the backdrop to Dudo of Saint Quentin's first book in
which he describes the actions of the bloodthirsty Hasting and his Vikings in
lurid and dramatic detail. As long as they were perceived as penance imposed
from above, the Vikings were a temporary affliction, a trial which would end
once the people had suffered sufficiently to pay for their sins. Dudo, at the
end of Book One, urges his readers not to despair – the destruction which
Francia suffered at the hands of Hasting and his band was merely a painful
interlude. The holy church and the community of saints were eternal and
undying and would continue to exist in heaven and on earth after the Viking
scourge had passed. The Vikings who came to stay in western Neustria,
however, rewrote their part in God's plan. These former agents of God's
wrath associated their rule with the traditional saints and religious communities of the region, thereby tapping into deeply rooted and enduring sources of
spiritual pride and local loyalty. In so doing, they assumed a permanent place
within the Christian world.

Generosity toward churches and monasteries was understood at the time
as rendering service to the saints who were honored and whose relics were
venerated at each community. Consequently, anyone who acted against the
interests of a church by stealing its treasures or invading its lands became the

---

[1] Dudo, p. 137: 'Ne quis lector abhorreat monemus, ob adversorum ignominiam casuum,
qui non ad interitum, sed ad correctionem, propter exagerationem scelerum, Fran-
cigenis acciderunt.'

[2] This theme has been most recently examined in Coupland, 'Rod of God's Wrath'.

enemy of that community's saints, subject to their punishment. Thus, when Robert the Magnificent confirmed the possessions of the cathedral of Rouen, he did so 'in the bodily presence of the holy confessors Romain, Ouen, Lo, [and] Cande, whom we earnestly request be adjutants of this testimonial and avengers of those tempted to oppose or diminish this bequest or take anything away from the use of the brothers serving there'.[3] The saints were physically and spiritually present in their relics, and they would reward those who were good to their communities on earth with blessings in this world and the next. The old monasteries which were reformed and enriched by the dukes therefore served as focal points for local piety, tangible symbols which testified to this new alliance of holy saints and former Vikings. The inhabitants of the duchy could see that past and present guardians of the province joined forces in these places, an alliance which underscored the transformation of the Normans from temporary agents of divine retribution to the newest members of God's eternal city.

Working in monastic *scriptoria*, hagiographers of the eleventh century added flattering stories involving the Norman dukes to their collections of saints' lives. The new tales told of the honors which the rulers extended to the saints as well as miracles performed in their presence, symbolizing heaven's support for the new regime.[4] This was a compelling means of endorsing ducal governance, and as these stories circulated beyond the monastery walls they strengthened the perception of legitimate authority which was (and remains) crucial to political success. While promoting the spiritual links between rulers and saints, monastic communities also contributed to the development of the region economically and socially. To appreciate their role in these areas, it is best to begin by analysing the material foundations of Norman abbeys, since the origin, location and extent of their lands largely determined their position in local society.[5]

---

3   Fauroux no. 67, p. 203: 'Hec sunt igitur que privilegii nostri jure firmamus, sub testimonio Christi et corporali presentia sanctorum confessorum Romani, Audoeni, Laudi, Candidi, quos nostri hujus testimonii adjutores esse deposcimus et ultores de his esse precamur qui huic testamento contraire aut ex his aliquid ab usu fratrum inibi servientium subtrahere aut minuere temptaverint.'

4   See, for example, *Historiae Fiscannensis Fragmentum*, in 'Catalogus Codicum Hagiographicorum Latinorum Bibliothecae Publicae Rotomagensis', ed. Albert Poncelet, *Analecta Bollandiana*, 23 (1904), pp. 251–75. For a survey of saints and saints' lives in early Normandy, see Jean Fournée, *La Spiritualité en Normandie au temps de Guillaume le Conquérant* (Flers, 1987), and Fournée, *Culte populaire*. Lifshitz provides a detailed study of specific hagiographical narratives in *Norman Conquest*.

5   Lucien Musset, Jean Yver and Robert Carabie have all touched upon this topic in their efforts to gauge the impact of the Viking settlement on pre-Norman customs and institutions. Lucien Musset, 'Les Domaines de l'époque franque et les destinées du régime domanial du IXe au XIe siècle', *BSAN*, 49 (1946), pp. 7–97; Lucien Musset, 'Aux Origines d'une classe dirigeante: les Tosny, grands barons normands du Xe au XIIIe siècle', *Francia*, 5 (1977), pp. 45–80; Lucien Musset, 'Les Fiefs de deux familles vicomtales de l'Hiémois au XIe siècle, les Goz et les Montgommery', *RHDFE*, 48

This is a subject which has already received considerable attention by scholars, and their findings point to a single conclusion: much of the property that monasteries, especially ducal monasteries, received during the late tenth century and early eleventh century comprised former monastic lands which had fallen into the ducal patrimony at the time of the Norman settlement and were subsequently returned to the monasteries.[6] The fact that these lands had been taken over by the Norman lords warns against underestimating the disruptions of the ninth and tenth centuries. Clearly, ecclesiastical institutions lost control of their estates during the transition from Frankish to Norman rulership. At the same time, however, their recovery points to a strong measure of continuity at the local level in Norman territory. Property boundaries must have survived the Viking settlement if tenth and eleventh-century monks could regain monastic lands dating back to the Merovingian and Carolingian periods.[7] Thus, disruption at the top of society when the Northmen assumed control should not be equated with a levelling of society. The Norman leaders appropriated ecclesiastical estates during the invasion period, but they did not dismantle local institutions or erase local boundaries.[8] Indeed, it was not in their interests to do so, since the value of land depended largely on people to work it. For the most part, peasant life simply

(1970), pp. 342–43; Lucien Musset, 'Recherches sur la consistance géographique des patrimoines monastiques normands: Iles Britanniques et Continent de l'époque Franque au XIIIe siècle', AN, 8 (1958), pp. 185–86; Yver, 'Premières institutions', especially pp. 306–09; Robert Carabie, La Propriété foncière dans le très ancien droit normand (XIe–XIIIe siècles) (Caen, 1943), in particular pp. 118–28.

6   Musset, 'Domaines', in particular, pp. 42–52; Musset, 'Problème de la continuité', pp. 73–74; Musset, 'Consistance géographique', pp. 185–86. As Musset writes: 'We therefore consider ourselves correct in thinking that the distribution of Neustrian lands did not occur haphazardly, and that to a certain degree, the memory of the former borders had been respected.' Musset, 'Domaines', p. 49.

7   Musset's position is consistent with the conclusions presented in Robert Carabie's detailed study of landed property in Normandy. Like Musset, Carabie argues that 'the Norman invasion did not bring about the fundamental upheaval that is commonly attributed to it. Without doubt estates changed masters. But the agrarian organization hardly felt this change.' Carabie, Propriété foncière, pp. 122–23.

8   The points raised here are directly related to the historiographical debate between continuity and discontinuity in early Normandy. The classic argument in favor of continuity of Frankish institutions appears in Yver, 'Premières institutions'. Bates qualifies but generally continues this case for Frankishness and continuity in 1066, pp. 1–38. Searle, on the other hand, rejects Yver's argument, especially with regard to the Vikings' assumption of Carolingian forms of governance: Predatory Kinship, pp. 3–11, and 'Frankish Rivalries', p. 198, note 2. She states in Predatory Kinship, p. 126, 'The land they settled could have retained, in any case, few living traditions, and it is going too far to suppose that by the turn of the eleventh century the Norse-Norman warleaders required or desired Frankish traditions that would curb their independent expansion.' In sharp contrast to Searle's view of discontinuity, Lifshitz has most recently asserted, 'The Norman princes, alone among late Carolingian potentates, kept the institutional hierarchies inherited from the Empire absolutely intact' (Norman Conquest, p. 107). The significance of this historiographical dispute fades when we take

continued under the new masters.[9] The Viking invasions in Flanders provide a useful comparison. There too, the breakdown of ecclesiastical organization did not mean that farms and villages were abandoned, and the continuity of domainal organization argues against an exodus of rural populations.[10]

The dukes appear in the charters as the greatest benefactors of Norman abbeys, and consequently the majority of recorded lands that monasteries received before the reign of William the Conqueror was located in upper Normandy and the territory around Rouen where early ducal lordship was strongest.[11] Those communities which had lost property outside of this area during the invasion period generally had to wait until the rulers of Rouen had spread their authority beyond upper Normandy. The failed attempt of the Flemish monks to restore Fontenelle during Richard I's reign shows the difficulties facing those who sought to take back lands from unwilling lords. Tattered charters from the past were not enough: old claims had to be backed by stronger arguments to persuade people to relinquish their rights to lands. One important difference between monasticism in the region before and after the Norman settlement is that monasteries prior to the Viking raids generally had lands which stretched across Francia. In the tenth century and beyond, Norman abbeys, with the notable exception of Mont-Saint-Michel, gained or regained relatively few properties outside the duchy.[12] And after the first

---

into account the fact that a change in rulership is experienced differently at different levels of society.

9   Charters after the Norman settlement frequently measured land by acres, the Anglo-Scandinavian unit of measurement. This was one of the few contributions of the Normans to the agrarian organization of the region. It strengthens the suggestion that a good number of Vikings who came to Normandy had already spent considerable time in England, which casts Dudo's description of Rollo's visit there in a new light. See Renaud, p. 79, and the *index rerum* in Fauroux, p. 455.

10 D'Haenens, pp. 155–60.

11 See the map of monastic property by 1035 on p. xii.

12 For Mont-St-Michel, see below, Chapter Five. Extant edited charters for other Norman abbeys involving lands outside of Normandy before 1066 can be found scattered in Fauroux, Vernier, and Lot, *Etudes critiques*. For English properties in particular, see Cyril Hart, 'The Mersea Charter of Edward the Confessor', *Essex Archaeology and History*, 12 (1980), pp. 94–102; Charles Homer Haskins, 'A Charter of Canute for Fécamp', *EHR*, 33 (1918), pp. 342–44. Unedited charters involving non-Norman property of Norman abbeys before 1066 include ADSM 7H 2141 (this is an original charter for Fécamp regarding lands in Beauvais); ADSM 16H 20, pp. 2056–57, no. 29 and p. 2105, no. 17 = ADSM 16H 14, f. 319r, no. 29 and f. 330r, no. 16 = BN, nouv. acq. lat. 1246, fols. 227r and 229r (this is a charter surviving in several copies regarding St Wandrille's possession of two altars in the diocese of Amiens); Fécamp, Musée de la bénédictine, no. 2 = BN, coll. Moreau, vol. 341, f. 12r (this is an original charter of Robert the Pious in which he gives Villiers St Paul to Fécamp); BN, coll. Moreau, vol. 21, fols. 193r–94r (this is an unedited charter in which Renaud chamberlain of Henry I of France restores Villiers St Paul to Fécamp). In addition, several unedited charters survive in which Norman abbeys were given freedom from tolls by lords outside of Normandy.

third of the eleventh century, several communities deliberately shed what lands they did have outside the duchy.[13] Therefore, while the renewed abbeys recovered property in the Norman period which they had lost previously, they did so primarily within the areas secured by the dukes and within the regional boundaries of the developing duchy.

The most important early Norman ruler from the point of view of monasticism was Rollo's great-grandson Richard II, whose piety was renowned beyond the borders of Norman territory. Not only was Richard II responsible for bringing William of Dijon and Gerard of Crépy to the duchy, but he also endowed churches and monasteries outside of Normandy: Bourgueil, Notre Dame de Chartres, Notre Dame de Noyon, St Père, Chartres, St Riquier and Marmoutier all enjoyed his attention and patronage.[14] Contemporaries agreed that Richard II's reputation as a supporter of monasticism was known as far away as the Holy Land. Envoys from the monastery of Saint Catherine at Mount Sinai travelled to Rouen to receive generous alms from the duke.[15] Richard II's participation in the Peace of God movement, as well as his willingness to assume the expenses of pilgrims like Richard of Saint Vannes, were also widely celebrated.[16] Within Normandy, Richard II donated vast lands and resources from the ducal patrimony to monasteries, establishing a precedent that guided the actions of subsequent dukes.[17] The three charters

---

[13] Musset, 'Consistance géographique', p. 185.

[14] Fauroux no. 14 (Bourgueil); no. 15 (Notre Dame de Chartres); no. 22 (Notre Dame de Noyon); nos. 29, 32, 50 (St Père, Chartres); no. 20 (St Riquier); no. 23 (Marmoutier).

[15] These sources were the Burgundian chronicler Glaber, in *Rodulfus Glaber Opera*, pp. 36–37, and the author of the eleventh-century *Translatio Sanctae Catharinae*. Glaber writes that the duke gave one hundred pounds of gold as well as 'many presents of silver and gold' to monks in the Holy Land. The *Translatio* author simply writes that his gifts comprised 'several horse-loads'. The text of the *Translatio* is published in Albert Poncelet, 'Sanctae Catharinae virginis et martyris translatio et miracula rotomagensia saec. XI', *Analecta Bollandiana*, 22 (1903), pp. 423–38, at pp. 426–31. For a fuller discussion of this text, see Robert Fawtier, 'Les Reliques rouennaises de sainte Catherine d'Alexandrie', *Analecta Bollandiana*, 41 (1923), pp. 357–68.

[16] Jean-François Lemarignier, 'Paix et réforme monastique en Flandre et en Normandie autour de l'année 1023: quelques observations', in *Droit privé et institutions régionales*, pp. 443–68; Henri Prentout, 'Le Règne de Richard II duc de Normandie, 996–1027: Son Importance dans l'histoire', *Academie nationales des sciences arts et belles-lettres de Caen*, 5 (1929), pp. 57–104; Christian Pfister, *Etudes sur le règne de Robert le Pieux (996–1031)* (Paris, 1885, rpt. 1974), pp. 347–49; Hubert Dauphin, *Le Bienheureux Richard: Abbé de Saint-Vanne de Verdun* (Louvain, 1946), pp. 262–63.

[17] Thirty-four charters survive in favor of Norman monasteries issued by Richard II (996–1027): Fauroux nos. 7 (St Wandrille), 9 (Fécamp), 12 (Mont-St-Michel), 13 (St Ouen), 14 (Jumièges), 16 (Mont-St-Michel), 17 (Mont-St-Michel), 19 (St Ouen), 21 (St Ouen), 24 (St Ouen), 25 (Fécamp), 26 (Jumièges), 30 (St Wandrille), 31 (Fécamp), 34 (Fécamp), 35 (Bernay), 36 (Jumièges), 37 (St Ouen), 38 (Fécamp), 39 (St Ouen), 40 (St Ouen), 41 (St Ouen), 42 (St Ouen), 43 (St Ouen), 44 (St Ouen), 45 (St Ouen), 46 (St Wandrille), 47 (Mont-St-Michel), 49 (Mont-St-Michel), 51 (Jumièges), 52 (St Wandrille), 53 (St Ouen), 54 (Fécamp), 55 (St Wandrille).

he issued in August 1025 stand out as examples of his patronage: Fécamp, Bernay and Jumièges received confirmations of all the estates they had received from Richard II's predecessors, his men and himself.[18] Saint Ouen's great confirmation charter, although undated, should also be included in this group.[19] Given his generosity and commitment to monasticism in the duchy, it is understandable that Richard II was known in his own day as 'the father of his country, and especially of the monks'.[20]

In addition to receiving property directly from the ducal demesne, monasteries also occasionally gained lands which had been confiscated by the duke from his enemies or forfeited as a result of legal cases. For example, after the Battle of Val-ès-Dunes in 1047, William the Conqueror seized the property of the rebel Hugh Pasfolet and presented Hugh's church of Saint Marcouf to Robert of Beaumont. Then, at some time during the next six years, the duke donated this church with four others to the abbey of Saint Wandrille, with Robert's consent.[21] A comparable case occurred regarding the lands of Grimoult, who also sided against the duke in 1047. William the Conqueror confiscated his property after the war and handed it over to the bishop of Bayeux, his half-brother Odo. In the twelfth century the abbey of St Etienne du Plessis Grimoult was built there.[22] Another charter shows the abbey of Fécamp receiving the estates of a lord from Daubeuf named Estormit, who had been unwilling to sell his property. Exiled by the duke, he abandoned everything and fled to Spain.[23] And in yet another case dating from after the Conquest, the abbey of Jumièges gained some twelve acres of land through a circuitous route when the duke judged that the heir to an estate was in fact an imposter.[24]

---

18 Fauroux nos. 34 (Fécamp), 35 (Bernay), 36 (Jumièges).

19 Fauroux no. 53; Lemarignier, 'Le monachisme et l'encadrement religieux', p. 386, note 106.

20 *Additamenta ad Historiam Normannorum*, in William of Jumièges, *Gesta Normannorum Ducum*, ed. Jean Marx (Rouen, 1914), p. 339: 'De Ricardo filio primi Ricardi dicitur quod fuerit pater patriae, et maxime monachorum'. The *Additamenta* dates from the first decades of the eleventh century. See Mathieu Arnoux, 'Classe agricole, pouvoir seigneurial et autorité ducale: L'évolution de la Normandie féodale d'après le témoignage des chroniqueurs (Xe–XIIe siècles', *Le Moyen Age*, 98 (1992), pp. 35–60, at pp. 40–41, and note 15.

21 Fauroux no. 128, pp. 300–01: 'Quod ego Willelmus, Nortmannorum gratia Dei princeps . . . concedo et do de meis rebus . . . annuente Roberto, fideli nostro, Hunfredi videlicet filio, ecclesias quas illi dederam . . .'

22 See Lucien Musset, 'L'Abbaye de Saint-Etienne du Plessis-Grimoult', *Art de Basse-Normandie*, 27 (1962), pp. 9–16.

23 Fauroux no. 218, p. 412: 'Comes inde benignus Estormit, cujus vici ipsius servitium erat, ut illud sibi venderet petiit; sed intra petitionis hujus articulum Estormit, universa relinquens, Hispaniam profugus adiit.' See Lucien Musset, 'Autour des modalités juridiques de l'expansion normande au XIe siècle: le droit d'exil', in *Autour du pouvoir*, pp. 45–59, at p. 47.

24 ADSM 9H 1819, edited by Paul le Cacheux, 'Une Charte de Jumièges concernant l'épreuve par le fer chaud (fin du XIe siècle)', *Société de l'histoire de Normandie*,

Private lords also contributed a great deal of property to Norman monasteries. At least two-thirds of the extant ducal charters in favor of ducal monasteries include gifts, sales or other agreements between private individuals and the monks.[25] And the number of non-ducal charters recording transactions of property with private individuals rose sharply during the course of the eleventh century, with the great majority of *acta* dating from the second half of the century. On one hand, this increase reflects a growing tendency to rely more and more on literate forms of evidence. The proliferation of written records was a noticeable trend across western Europe during the eleventh and twelfth centuries.[26] Nevertheless, it is clear that non-ducal benefactions were simply on the rise – if anything, our records underestimate the number. Property donated by the duke was deemed more secure than lands given or sold to a monastery by others, tempting the monks to recast private gifts and sales as ducal donations.[27]

There were obvious reasons why ducal donations were more attractive from the point of view of monasteries than gifts or sales from private individuals. The dukes' gifts were more prestigious, and their acts of patronage were highly public affairs confirmed by many witnesses and frequently recorded in impressive charters, sanctioned by the powerful ecclesiastical lords who surrounded them at court. That point in itself would have deterred would-be predators, since oral and written memory worked to the monks' advantage. The more people present at the time of the benefaction and the more impressive the ceremony, the better. Should anyone dare encroach on lands donated by the duke, the monks' first response would be to report this violation to him. The Norman ruler had a vested interest in seeing that his donations and those of ancestors were respected – his status in both worlds was on the line. And as the most powerful lord in the region, the duke was in the best position to enforce this respect, to punish the wrongdoers and return the property to the monastery. Thus, it is not surprising that charters were occasionally revised in monastic scriptoria to make acquisitions from non-ducal sources appear as ducal donations.

It is only possible to catch them at this when two or more copies of a charter survive and can be compared. For example, according to one docu-

---

mélanges, 11 (1927), pp. 205–16. Jumièges was given the property by Rainald the Chaplain, who had received it from Queen Matilda, whose husband William the Conqueror had given it to her. Duke William had confiscated these lands when he determined that a young child from a different family had been substituted for the heir of an estate when the actual heir had died.

25 Over two-thirds of the ducal charters for ducal abbeys involved individuals outside the duke's immediate family. The charters often explain that the duke was confirming a gift or agreement specifically at the request of another lord.

26 M. T. Clanchy, *From Memory to Written Record: England, 1066–1307* (Cambridge, Ma., 1979).

27 On the dangers of charter evidence in general, see Christopher Brooke, 'Princes and Kings as Patrons of Monasteries: Normandy and England', *Il Monachesimo e la riforma ecclesiastica (1049–1122), Miscellanea del centro di studi medioevali*, 6 (Milan, 1968), pp. 125–52.

ment, Beatrice abbess of Montivilliers bought the nearby village of Cauville for one hundred pounds from Norman de la Bellière in 1049–1053, with the consent of Hugh de la Ferté, Hugh de Gournay and Garnier, Norman's kinsman.[28] A later version, however, claims that Cauville became a possession of Montivilliers when Duke William donated the benefice of his knight Hugh to the abbey.[29] Apparently, donations were preferred to sales even when the monks were honest about the identity of the alienors. For instance, the original charter for the foundation of Fécamp's priory of Saint Martin du Bosc records that William of Columbiers sold several tithes in Langrune to the monks. A thirteenth-century copy of this charter, however, recalls that William of Columbiers gave these tithes in alms to the priory.[30] It is apparent, therefore, that a later scribe decided that it would benefit the abbey if these tithes were perceived to have been given to the monks rather than purchased. It could be that sales were considered more vulnerable than donations because they lacked the abbeys' usual 'first line of defense' against encroachment: the threat to cut the donor and his heirs off from spiritual services.[31] This would at least provide a rationale for recasting sales as gifts.

The kind of property that monasteries acquired from both ducal and non-ducal sources varied widely, from churches and tithes to towns, mills, fisheries, vineyards, cultivated and uncultivated lands, and a vast assortment of rights and privileges. In one charter of Saint Etienne, Caen received a piece of property that was appropriate for building a mill.[32] In two others,

---

28 Bouvris, 'L'Abbaye de Montivilliers', p. 68, no. 2: 'Emit eadem abbatissa Calvelvillam centum libras a Normanno de la Berliere, concedente Hugone de la Ferte et Hugone de Gornay et Varnerio suo consanguineo, sub testimonio Guillelmi comitis de Archis et Hugonis Luxoviensis episcopi aliorumque plurimorum videlicet Osberni, Guillelmi eadem beneficia tenentium.' The earliest copy of this sale survives in a *pancarte* dated June, 1688, copied from a *vidimus* of 1305.

29 Fauroux no. 166, p. 358: 'Wilelmus comes, filius Roberti ducis Normanorum, dedit terram de Calvelvilla, per autoritatem Hugonis militis in cujus beneficio manet. Testes sunt Wilelmus filius Osberti, Wimunt Cusel, Hugo de la Ferte, Nigellus, Willelmus, Rodulphus, Joannes abbas.' The earliest extant copy of this charter was made in November, 1733 (Fauroux's date of 1773 is incorrect). Since it was appended to a copy of Fauroux no. 90, allegedly copied from the original, Fauroux indicates that no. 166 might also have been added the original charter. It made sense for the monastery to destroy the record of the original transaction when it revised the past in this way; thus, it is rare to have both versions survive.

30 Fauroux no. 218, pp. 412–13. A (original): 'Guillelmus de Columbers, filius Goisfridi, vendidit Sancte Trinitati'; B (thirteenth-century copy): 'Guillermus etiam de Columbiers, filius Goiffredi, dedit in elemosinam Sancte Trinitati.'

31 This is Tabuteau's suggestion, *Transfers*, pp. 27–34.

32 A great number of St Etienne charters remain unedited and poorly known, surviving in a nineteenth-century copy which Henri Toustain made of a lost twelfth- and early thirteenth-century cartulary. Toustain's copy is located at the library of the University of Caen, cote 1702 [N. RB II, d³]. I am grateful to Mlle M.-B. Hamel for having helped make this source available to me in Caen. University of Caen, Toustain cartulary, fols. 40rv, no. 130: '. . . unum locum aptum ad molendinum faciendum'.

local lords granted Saint Ouen and Saint Wandrille presses, presumably for squeezing grapes.[33] A common type of property for ducal abbeys to acquire were *villae*. But unfortunately the term *villa* was used very broadly in this period. It could indicate all the various components of a large estate, and thus it essentially masks the specifics of domainal organization.[34] One can only suggest that the monasteries employed a local *familia* supervised by a few monks sent out from the abbey to ensure the cultivation of their lands, as Georges Duby has shown to have been the case for Cluny, and as Marie Fauroux has suggested for Marmoutier.[35]

In numerous charters, ducal abbeys received possession or partial possession of fairs and markets, underlining the role monastic houses played in the economic life of early Normandy. In fact, the earliest *mercatum* mentioned in the sources was associated with the abbey La Croix St Leuffroy in the ninth century.[36] Another indication of the abbeys' commercial interests was how frequently secular lords gave monasteries exemptions from tolls. In fact, the most common concession to Norman abbeys from lords outside the duchy was free passage along the section of a river that they controlled. At Mantes in 1006, for example, both Jumièges and Saint Wandrille received exemption from Walter count of Amiens and the Vexin from tolls collected on their boats as they passed by his castle.[37] And around 1024, Dreux count of Amiens and the Vexin reasserted Saint Wandrille's freedom from tolls at Mantes.[38] Dreux also granted Saint Ouen's boats free passage at Mantes,

---

33 ADSM 14H 314: 'Willelmus filius Rogerii de Amblavilla concessit pressorium de Vilers totum quietum deo et sancto Nigasio sanctoque Audoeno.' BN, coll. Moreau, vol. 27, fols. 46rv: '. . . ego Theobaldus dominus de Marli pro salute anime mee et omnium amicorum meorum concessi in elemosina ecclesie Sancte Guand[regisili] quidquid de pressoragio habebam'.

34 Carabie, *Propriété foncière*, pp. 32–33; 181–90.

35 Georges Duby, 'Economie domaniale et économie monétaire: le budget de l'abbaye de Cluny entre 1080 et 1155', *Annales: économies, sociétés, civilisations*, 7 (1952), pp. 155–71. On Cluny's expansion, see also Guy de Valous, *Le domaine de l'abbaye de Cluny aux X et XI siècles* (Paris, 1923); Simone Berthelier, 'L'Expansion de l'ordre de Cluny et ses rapports avec l'histoire politique et économique du Xe au XIIe siècle', *Revue archéologique*, 11 (1938), pp. 319–26. For Marmoutier, see Marie Fauroux (as Marie Le Roy-Ladurie), 'Rôle des abbayes du Val de Loire dans la colonisation monastique normande (Xe–XIe s.)', *RHDFE*, 31 (1953), pp. 322–23.

36 J. B. Mesnel, *Les Saints du diocèse d'Evreux* (Evreux, 1914), p. 78. For examples of fairs and markets in the charters, see Fauroux nos. 5, 34, 35, 36, 64, 71, 74, 80, 85, 205, 227. An original charter from 1088 shows Robert Curthose granting Fécamp an annual fair that lasts as long as the herring catch (*quamdiu captura haringorum duraverit*): Fécamp, Musée bénédictine, no. 11, ed. Haskins, *Norman Institutions*, pp. 287–89, no. 4. On this subject, see Lucien Musset, 'Foires et marchés en Normandie à l'époque ducale', *AN*, 26 (1976), pp. 3–23.

37 Vernier no. 6. Count Walter made this concession 'on account of an excellent book that [the monks] gave us and especially for the remedy of my soul'.

38 Lot, *Etudes critiques*, no. 8. Lot's edition of this charter, however, omits several attestors recorded in ADSM 16H 14, f. 330v, no. 21.

Pontoise and elsewhere on the Oise River.[39] At Meulan, the monastic houses of Fécamp, Jumièges and Saint Wandrille all enjoyed freedom from various tolls.[40] Concessions from Count Ivo meant that Fécamp and Saint Wandrille also enjoyed free travel through Beaumont sur Oise.[41] And by the late eleventh century, Fécamp had rights of free passage at Pontoise and Creil.[42] Mantes, Meulan, Pontoise, Beaumont sur Oise – these were all lordships on the way from Normandy to Paris. Even though they held few lands outside the duchy, these gifts of free passage underline the commercial activity of Norman monasteries all along the Seine Basin.[43]

Within the duchy, monastic communities which the Normans restored and reformed often received property which was associated with churches or abbeys during the Merovingian and Carolingian periods. For example, Mont-Saint-Michel received the sixth-century abbey of Saint Pair sur Mer from Richard II.[44] And the seventh-century nunnery of Montivilliers also reappeared as a gift from Richard II to Fécamp, only to be later granted its independence by Robert the Magnificent as a separate community.[45] Almenèches had a similar history, known first as a Merovingian nunnery, then as a possession of Fécamp granted from the ducal demesne, then as an inde-

---

[39] ADSM 14H 805. This unedited charter survives in original form. A later copy exists at ADSM 14H 147. As this grant suggests, Count Dreux was on friendly terms with his Norman neighbors; he died on pilgrimage with Duke Robert. Orderic Vitalis even states that he had performed homage to the Norman duke for the Vexin, but that claim was a later invention to justify Norman political ambitions. See Orderic, 4, pp. 76–77 and Chibnall's analysis, pp. xxx–xxiv; Judith A. Green, 'Lords of the Norman Vexin', in War and Government in the Middle Ages: Essays in Honour of J. O. Prestwich, ed. John Gillingham and J. C. Holt (Woodbridge, 1984), pp. 46–63; David Bates, 'Lord Sudeley's Ancestors: The Family of the Counts of Amiens, Valois and the Vexin in France and England during the Eleventh Century', in The Sudeleys: Lords of Toddington (London, 1987), pp. 34–47.

[40] Fauroux no. 25 (1023, Fécamp); Vernier no. 26 (1056, Jumièges); Lot, Etudes critiques, no. 32 (1061, St Wandrille). An unedited charter also survives at BN, ms. lat. 5425, p. 58 in which Galeran's son Robert count of Meulan confirms the free water transport that his predecessors had granted St Wandrille.

[41] Lot, Etudes critiques, nos. 24 (1039, St Wandrille) and 25 (around 1039, St Wandrille); BN, ms. lat. 5425, pp. 55–56 = BN, nouv. acq. fr. 21816, f. 155r (around 1040, St Wandrille); Fécamp, Musée de la bénédictine, no. 12 (1027–1059, Fécamp). The Fécamp charter survives in original form. It is published by J. Depoin in Les Comtes de Beaumont-sur-Oise et le prieuré de Sainte-Honorine de Conflans (Pontoise, 1911), no. 1, pp. 47–48.

[42] BN, coll. Moreau, vol. 40, f. 218 rv = BN, nouv. acq. fr. 21819, f. 155r (Pontoise); BN, coll. Moreau, vol. 40, f. 220r = BN, nouv. acq. fr. 21819, f. 156r (Creil). Both these charters for Fécamp are unedited.

[43] On tolls in Normandy in general, see Lucien Musset, 'Recherches sur le tonlieu en Normandie à l'époque ducale', in Autour du pouvoir, pp. 61–76. Also see Imbart de la Tour, 'Des immunités commerciales accordées aux églises du VIIe au IX siècle', in Etudes d'histoire du moyen âge dédiées à Gabriel Monod (Paris, 1896), pp. 71–87.

[44] Fauroux no. 49.

[45] Fauroux nos. 34, 90.

pendent house around 1060.[46] And Pavilly, another Merovingian nunnery, ended up in the patrimony of Trinité du Mont, Rouen, and became a priory of that community around 1090.[47] The reappearance of these ancient communities as dependants of Norman houses in the eleventh century shows that they were not forgotten. At the very least, the memory of these places as holy remained alive at the local level. By giving them to monasteries which they had reformed and enriched, the Normans associated their authority with the region's oldest religious traditions.

In addition to the sites and properties of former monasteries, Norman abbeys also frequently received secular churches from laymen. In fact, parish churches were among the most common donations to abbeys in Normandy before 1066. The acquisition of churches with their tithes and offerings brought very practical benefits to the monks. And monastic churches often developed into priories, as was the case at the Fécamp dependencies of Argences, Saint Gabriel and Saint Berthe of Blangy, thereby facilitating the administration of distant domains.[48] The monastery would have a handful of monks remain there permanently to oversee the community's nearby interests. Their presence in turn prompted additional acquisitions in the area. Historians frequently link the donation of private churches to monasteries with the Gregorian reform movement and its condemnation of ecclesiastical property in the possession of laymen.[49] Since the charters show Norman

---

[46] On Almenèches and its reconstruction, see below Chapter Six, pp. 120–24.

[47] Musset, 'Problème de la continuité', p. 61.

[48] For Argences and St Gabriel, see Lucien Musset, 'La contribution de Fécamp à la reconquête monastique de la basse-Normandie', in L'Abbaye bénédictine de Fécamp, 1, pp. 57–66, 341–43 at pp. 61–66. The charter recording the donation of Blangy to Fécamp survives in a nineteenth-century copy at BN, nouv. acq. fr. 21819, f. 190r. It is edited by Edmund Martène and Ursin Durand, Thesaurus novus anecdotorum, vol. 1 of 5 vols. (Paris, 1717, rpt. 1968), col. 153. A letter in which John abbot of Fécamp nominates the head of St Berthe survives in original form at Fécamp, Musée de la bénédictine, no. 44. It is also edited in Thesaurus, cols. 153–54, and by Migne, PL, 147, col. 474. The name of the monk elected, interestingly, remains blank in the original. The point that priories facilitated the administration of faraway properties is made by Jacques Dubois, 'Les Moines dans la société du moyen âge (950–1350)', in Jacques Dubois, Histoire monastique en France au XIIe siècle (London, 1982), Chapter 2, pp. 5–37, at pp. 21–22 [originally published in Revue d'histoire de l'église de France, 60 (1974), pp. 5–37]; Also see Jacques Dubois, 'La Vie des moines dans les prieurés du moyen âge', in Dubois, Histoire monastique en France, ch. 3, pp. 10–33 [originally published in Lettre de Ligugé, 133 (1969), pp. 10–33].

[49] A great deal of scholarship has been done on this subject. See in particular Giles Constable, Monastic Tithes from their Origins to the Twelfth Century (Cambridge, 1964), and Giles Constable, 'Monastic Possession of Churches and "Spiritualia" in the Age of Reform', in Il Monachesimo e la riforma ecclesiastica (1049–1122) (Milan, 1971), pp. 304–31; B. R. Kemp, 'Monastic Possession of Parish Churches in England in the Twelfth Century', Journal of Ecclesiastical History, 31 (1980), pp. 133–60; A. Chédeville, 'Les Restitutions d'églises en faveur de l'abbaye de Saint-Vincent du Mans', Cahiers de civilisation médiévale, Xe–XIIe siècles, 3 (1960), pp. 209–17;

monasteries acquiring churches and their *spiritualia* as early as 990, however, their transference from lay to monastic hands clearly preceded the reformers' assault on lay proprietorship.[50]

Monks in Normandy therefore acquired a wide variety of property before 1066. They also entered into a wide variety of arrangements regarding lands and revenues. Abbeys transferred and gained property through gifts, sales, exchanges, mortgages and many other ways. It would be dangerous, however, to insist on clear distinctions between these types of contracts – modern assumptions of property law do not apply. By our standards, arrangements involving land transfers in eleventh-century Normandy were continually in flux.[51] Even to say that Norman monasteries 'owned' lands is in itself problematic, since ownership was a more fluid concept in the central middle ages.[52] As a result, the maps drawn from the charters of Norman ducal abbeys and included in this study do not demonstrate the property of monasteries in the modern sense of clear and definite ownership. But they do show where the monks had active interests and stakes.[53] And while property contracts between monks and laymen in pre-conquest Normandy should not be pigeonholed into neat categories, they do fall generally into two groups: agreements whereby monasteries gained or regained property, and agreements whereby monasteries enriched or protected property already in their possession.

In both cases, reciprocity was the rule. Even gifts made to abbeys as alms anticipated the *quid pro quo* of spiritual benefits.[54] Donations were consistently made to monasteries by laymen 'for the salvation of my soul and the

Christopher Harper-Bill, 'The Struggle for Benefices in Twelfth-Century East Anglia', *Anglo-Norman Studies*, 11 (1989), pp. 113–32.
50 The charter from 990 is printed in Fauroux no. 4. On the subject in general, see Lucien Musset, 'Aperçus sur le dîme ecclésiastique en Normandie au XIe siècle', *RHDFE*, 52 (1974), pp. 544–45. Marjorie Chibnall, 'Ecclesiastical Patronage and the Growth of Feudal Estates at the Time of the Norman Conquest', *AN*, 8 (1958), pp. 102–18, at p. 109, notes that the donation of tithes and churches to monasteries in Normandy 'in time quietly and gradually replaced lay by monastic *Eigenkirchen*'.
51 Emily Zack Tabuteau looks carefully at the legal implications of these transactions in eleventh-century Normandy. She concludes that 'the final impression left by the charters is that any transaction mutually acceptable to the parties involved was legal'. Tabuteau, *Transfers*, pp. 228–29.
52 Barbara Rosenwein came to the same conclusion in her analysis of Cluny's relationship with its lay patrons and neighbors: Rosenwein, *Neighbor*, p. xii, 4: 'A careful examination of the charters of Cluny demonstrates that the transfer of property did not always result in a clear transfer of dominion.'
53 As Rosenwein warns about the maps included in her book, 'They simply plot the places where the monastery and the world outside clearly intersected.' Rosenwein, *Neighbor*, p. 4. White comes to a similar conclusion in *Custom*, pp. 20, 26–28, 158–60.
54 A great deal has been written on this subject. See in particular G. Chevrier, 'Evolution de la notion de donation dans les chartes de Cluny du IXe du XIIe siècle', in *A Cluny, congrès scientifique* (Dijon, 1950), pp. 203–09; Bouchard, *Sword, Miter, and Cloister*, pp. 225–46; White, *Custom*, pp. 25–39; Tabuteau, *Transfers*, pp. 36–43.

souls of my kinsfolk, especially the souls of my mother and father, and my wife and heirs'.[55] Benefactors expected to be included in the prayers of the monks, and they hoped that the monks and the saints of the community would intercede on their behalf in heaven.[56] Secular people thereby enjoyed the *societatem* of the religious community, 'so that they would be participants of the benefits of our church'.[57] Sometimes the promise of hospitality at the abbey was included: for example, Robert of Belfour granted Saint Etienne, Caen various lands in *elemonsinam*, receiving in exchange the *societatem* of the abbey and the right to stay there for one night four times a year – as long as he did not come with a great multitude of people.[58] Modern observers tend to focus on remuneration: if a donor received a boon or privilege in return for a benefaction, our impulse is to view it as a transaction rather than a donation. But this emphasis is misplaced – from the medieval point of view reciprocity was assumed. What mattered most to them was whether the gift itself had strings attached. Thus, a charter of William the Conqueror explains in the conclusion, 'For when the monks said that alms ought to be given freely [Duke William] replied, as a man of wisdom, "Although we are Normans, we know well that it should be so, and this, if it pleases God, we will do." '[59] In other words, the lands which he donated were given freely; as the charter spells out very clearly: they 'retained no secular taxes'.[60]

Donors occasionally asked that specific acts of charity be performed by the monks in their name. For example, when Hugh of Creil and Waleran freed Fécamp's boats from tolls they requested that 'we be included in the benefits and prayers of the above-mentioned church, and also that two poor-

---

55 Fauroux no. 160, p. 349. The speaker in this case was William the Conqueror: '. . . pro remedio animae meae, parentumque meorum, patris maxime et matris meae, necnon etiam uxoris meae, heredumque meorum . . .'

56 For example, Fauroux no. 43, p. 150: '. . . ea scilicet conditione ut tam presentes quam futuri monachi memoriam nostri jugiter habeant in orationibus suis . . . '

57 BN, nouv. acq. lat. 1406, f. 50r (charter of Robert of Grandmesnil in favor of St Etienne, Caen): 'Robertus de Grentonis Maisnilio et Agnes uxor ejus acceperunt societatem suam in ecclesia nostra et concessimus eis ut participes essent totius beneficii ecclesiae nostrae.'

58 University of Caen, Toustain cartulary, fols. 33rv, no. 115: 'Robertus de Belfou concessit sancto Stephano in elemosinam totam terram quam Hugo de Diva tenebat . . . Abbas vero, et monachi ob hoc concesserunt ipsi Roberto et patri et matri ejus et uxori ejus et filiis et filiabus ipsius, societatem suam et beneficium. Convenit etiam ei abbas quod quatuor vicibus per annum, illum hospitio reciperet, unaquaque vice una nocte, si tamen mensurate, id est, non cum multitudine veniret.' This charter is edited by Etienne Deville, 'Notices sur quelques manuscrits normands conservés à la Bibliothèque Sainte-Geneviève', *Revue catholique de Normandie*, 14 (1904), pp. 197–209, 269–324; 15 (1905), pp. 17–42.

59 Fauroux no. 199, p. 387: 'Monachis enim dicentibus helemosinam mundam debere dari, ipse, ut vir prudentissimus, respondit: "Licet Normanni simus, bene tamen novimus quia sic oportet fieri, et ita, si Deo placuerit, faciemus." ' Chibnall, *World*, p. 50 also discusses this passage.

60 Fauroux no. 199, p. 387: '. . . concessa sunt nulla seculari exactione retenta'.

men be fed specifically on our and our successors' behalf'.[61] A similar arrangement was made in 1065 with Fécamp by Hugh count of Dammartin who
exempted the ships of the abbey from tolls on the condition that the monks
maintained and fed one poorman in his name and in the name of his parents.[62] In 1084 Jumièges likewise received from William of Vatteville a
church and tithes *ad victum pauperum*.[63] In some cases, donations were made
to provide the donors themselves with food and clothing. An anchoress
named Rohais, for instance, gave Saint Etienne, Caen, two parts of her house
pro victu et vestitu for the rest of her life. The charter goes on to describe with
great precision the amount of food, drink and clothing Rohais would receive.[64] Monasteries also provided horses for aspiring knights and loaned
money to laypeople who pledged their lands as collateral.[65] A number of
charters from Mont-Saint-Michel show local lords donating lands to the
abbey in exchange for promises to find refuge there should war break out.[66] In
all these cases, the monasteries' social function clearly complemented their
spiritual role.

The timing of benefactions to monasteries in Normandy followed certain
patterns, as historians have noted in studies of monasticism in other regions.[67] Men and women tended to be most generous in periods of personal
crisis when the intercessory function of the monks seemed most urgent. Thus
an individual named Hugh gave the *fiscus* he held of his lord to Saint Taurin
as he was dying, a donation that his lord confirmed.[68] And Anschitillus of
Usseius made a donation to Saint Etienne, Caen, when he was sick and about

---

61 BN, coll. Moreau, vol. 40, f. 220r = BN, nouv. acq. fr. 21819, f. 156r: '. . . eo tenore
    quidam quod prefate ecclesie participemur benefactis et orationibus et etiam duo
    pauperes pascantur ibidem specialiter pro nobis nostrumque successoribus'.
62 BN, coll. Moreau, vol. 28, fols. 192rv = coll. Mathan, vol. 76, p. 193: '. . . si quidem sibi
    unum pauperem domno Iohanne abbate in prefata ecclesia pro se et parentibus suis
    pasturum'.
63 Vernier no. 33
64 University of Caen, Toustain cartulary, f. 30r, no. 106: 'Dedit Rohais nonna Sancto
    Stephano, duas partes domus suae, pro salute animae suae et pro victu et vestitu
    corporis sui, quam diu viveret. Unde unoquoque anno recipiebat ad victum cotidie
    duos panes et duas justas cervisiae, de pisis uno quoque mense quadrantem unum, pro
    carne, per annum, 20 solidos, pro caseo, iiii solidos aut iiii caseos ejusdem pretii. Ad
    vestitum autem, unoquoque anno, super pellicium unum nigrum tinctum, cum uno
    velo similiter nigro . . . Infra tres annos vel duos, cappam unam. Super haec omnia,
    duas carratas lingorum ad focum.' This charter is edited by Deville, 'Notices', 14
    (1904), p. 275.
65 R. Génestal, *Rôle des monastères comme établissements de crédit, étudié en Normandie du
    XIe à la fin du XIIIe siècle* (Paris, 1901), especially pp. 54–77 and appendix 1; Chibnall,
    World, pp. 54–57.
66 See below, Chapter Five, pp. 90, 103–04.
67 See, for example Bouchard, *Sword, Miter, and Cloister*, pp. 238–46; Penelope D.
    Johnson, *Prayer, Patronage, and Power: The Abbey of la Trinité, Vendôme, 1032–1187*
    (New York, 1981), pp. 86–90.
68 ADEure, H 793, f. 72v: 'Agnoscat multitudo fidelium quod ego Osbernus Longeville,

to die so that he could be buried in the cemetery of Saint Etienne.[69] Two other lords who thought they were about to die endowed and hastily entered abbeys, only to overcome their illnesses and resume secular life.[70] And a great many lords decided to join monasteries at the end of their days, such as Gerard Fleitel who became a monk of Saint Wandrille *in ultimo aetatis senio*, giving the abbey five new churches.[71] Monastic writers encouraged these last minute conversions *ad succurrendum*. To Ralph of Canterbury, those who died as monks were like the sun, whereas those who died with the last rites of the church were mere stars.[72]

Other lords prepared for their last days in advance, drawing up agreements with the monks whereby a monastery would receive the bulk of their bene-faction after their deaths. These *post obitum* gifts reflect a natural desire on the part of donors to balance spiritual and secular interests.[73] An individual named Drogo, for example, left his lands and vineyards at Bailleul to Saint Ouen after his and his wife's deaths in order to gain the charity and *societatem* of the monks. Drogo also gave two mills to the abbey on the condition that his sons would be able to rent them from the monks.[74] Another charter of Richard II shows Rotselinus, a canon of the cathedral of Rouen, granting Saint Ouen the tithe of his estates during his life and the lives of his sons; after their deaths the monastery would receive the benefice itself. The same charter records that the nephew of Rotselinus likewise donated the tithe and a third of his benefice to Saint Ouen as long as he and his children lived: after their deaths, the monks would receive his entire benefice.[75] Roger of

Hugonis filius, concedo monachis Sancti Taurini fiscum Picturiceville quem Hugo, filius Hilbaldi, moriens eis largitus est, a me enim ipse tenebat.'

69 University of Caen, Toustain cartulary, f. 41v, no. 134: 'Anschitillus de Usseio concessit sancto Stephano in infirmitate de qua et mortuus est, terra de Locellis quam Grento de illo tenebat, ab hoc scilicet ut frater esset loci, et ut post mortem suam sepeliretur in cimiterio sancti Stephani'. This charter is edited by Deville, 'Notices', 14 (1904), p. 320.

70 Orderic, 2, p. 46, tells the story of one of these lords, a priest named Adelard. The other, Tréhan of St Broladre, is known through charters in Bibl. Avranches, ms. 210, fols. 44rv; 74rv; Bibl. Avranches, ms. 210, fols. 44rv; BN, ms. lat. 5430A, p. 288; BN, nouv. acq. fr. 21815, f. 226v; Caen, Musée des Beaux Arts, coll. Mancel, ms. 300, fols. 148rv. Tréhan is also discussed by A. Guillotin de Corson, *Pouillé historique de l'archevêché de Rennes*, vol. 2 of 6 vols. (Rennes, 1880–86), pp. 527–30; Jacques Dubois, 'Les Dépendances de l'abbaye du Mont Saint-Michel et la vie monastique dans les prieurés', in *Millénaire*, 1, pp. 619–76, at pp. 643–44.

71 Fauroux no. 108. Other examples include Richard II's brothers-in-law, Osbern and Ansfred, who also entered St Wandrille *in ultimo aetatis senio*: Fauroux no. 46bis.

72 As cited in Christopher Harper-Bill, 'The Piety of the Anglo-Norman Knightly Class', *Anglo-Norman Studies*, 2 (1980), pp. 63–77, 173–76, at p. 69.

73 Barbara H. Rosenwein, *Rhinoceros Bound*, pp. 33–34, indicates that over half the charters from Cluny before 980 describe *post obitum* gifts of this type.

74 Fauroux no. 19. This charter survives in original form at ADSM 14H 279.

75 Fauroux no. 21. This charter survives in original form at ADSM 14H 915.

Montgomery made a similar agreement with Saint Etienne, Caen,[76] and several other cases are known in which lords sought spiritual benefits from gifts not actually made until after their or their children's deaths.[77] In cases like these we see laypeople making arrangements whereby they could gain the spiritual benefits of being benefactors of monasteries without paying the immediate price.

Besides sickness and death, another frequent occasion for granting lands to monasteries was the admission of a new member to the community. In theory, entrance gifts were made freely to help compensate the community for the expenses of having a new member.[78] The reciprocal element of this arrangement is clear. Parents often presented their children to the abbey as oblates offering entrance gifts from their own lands, but the size and value of these gifts varied greatly. Thus Ralph Havot brought his son to Jumièges around 1040 to become a monk, granting the abbey ninety acres of land and all the tithes he possessed at Boschyons.[79] In another case, a lord sent his son to Mont-Saint-Michel, granting just one-third of a church as an entrance gift. After the boy learned how to read, he was ordained a priest and received custody of the same property.[80] In this case, the entrance gift became the boy's legacy, despite the monastery's possession. In a third example, an individual named Wigrin and his wife offered one of their sons to Fécamp, donating half their land at Boissy on the condition that Wigrin would be able to hold there one arpent, the house and the garden as a tenant of the abbot. Wigrin therefore appears to have transformed part of his freehold into a benefice in order to place his son at Fécamp.[81] This could be compared to taking out a second mortgage to send the children to college. Later, when Wigrin decided to join the community himself, he granted Fécamp another church, an arpent of land and a fruit orchard.

---

[76] Fauroux no. 223. This charter survives in original form at ADOrne, H 421, no. 1 (Fauroux mistakenly identifies this charter as H 421, no. 2).

[77] For example, University of Caen, Toustain cartulary fols. 28rv, no. 101, and fols. 31v–32r, no. 111; BN, nouv. acq. fr. 21816, f. 193r = BN, nouv. acq. lat. 1246, f. 238r = ADSM 16H 20, pp. 2077–78, no. 52 = ADSM 16H 14, f. 324r, no. 6.

[78] The most recent scholarship on this subject indicates that entrance gifts were not set at a fixed fee or amount. See Joseph H. Lynch, 'Monastic Recruitment in the Eleventh and Twelfth Centuries: Some Social and Economic Considerations', *American Benedictine Review*, 26 (1975), pp. 425–47, at p. 432.

[79] Vernier no. 21. Vernier considered this charter an original, but in fact it appears to have been a contemporary copy: ADSM 9H 1747.

[80] ADCalva, coll. Beausse, F 5276.

[81] BN, coll. Moreau, vol. 21, fols. 20r–21r = BN, nouv. acq. fr. 21819, f. 167r: 'Notum sit omnibus vobis quod quidam homo nomine Wigrinus cum uxore sua nomine Adeliza, tacti respectu divino, venerunt ad Fiscannum et obtulerunt unum filium suum super altare sancte Trinitatis et medietatem terre que dicitur Bussi, tali scilicet tenore ut unum arpentum et hortum et domum suam in beneficio de Fiscannensi abbate teneant.' This agreement took place during the abbacy of John of Ravenna, 1028–1079.

Adults who decided to enter monastic houses generally presented entrance gifts with the consent of their lords and their families. For instance, Richard II confirmed the charters of Achardus for Fécamp and Imma for Saint Wandrille, approving the gifts these people brought their respective monasteries.[82] William the Conqueror did the same for Osbern d'Ectot before 1066, and Bernard de Neufmarché after the Conquest.[83] When an individual named Richard accepted the habit at Jumièges, he offered his possessions at Verneuil to the monks with the consent of his three sons.[84] And a knight named Odard returning from Jerusalem in 1097 granted various lands to Jumièges with the consent of his brother when Odard retired there.[85] Sometimes the lords themselves made the gift at the request of their men who entered monastic life. Thus, Hugh bishop of Bayeux granted Jumièges the land of his knight Ralph at Ralph's request when he became a monk.[86] Jumièges also received from Roger of Montgomery the fief that his *fidelis* Goisfredus had held of him before Goisfredus joined the abbey.[87] Likewise, William Talbot granted Fécamp the land of Septimanville that Robert had held of him before he became a monk.[88]

In addition to gaining property through donations and entrance gifts, monks also increased their lands through sales, exchanges and mortgages. As explained above, however, the line between donations and sales is often blurred. For example, between 1047 and 1063 Ralph Dancel gave the abbey of Saint Wandrille his estates at Esclavelles; in exchange, he received a certain amount of money from the abbey.[89] It cannot be said whether this sum represented the price of the lands or merely a countergift which the monks made to Ralph.[90] But the reason it is unclear to us is that the categories of gift and sale were not strictly defined in the eleventh century. In a society based upon mutual obligations and responsibilities, it was common to offer a counter-gift when a donation was made. The act of exchange sealed the agreement between the monks and their lay benefactor, establishing a

---

82 Fauroux nos. 38, 55.
83 Osbern d'Ectot: Fauroux no. 210 (St Ouen, 1055–1066); Bernard de Neufmarché: BN, coll. Moreau, vol. 29, fols. 90rv = coll. Mathan, vol. 76, pp. 177–203 = BN, nouv. acq. fr. 21819, f. 98r = BN, nouv. acq. lat. 1243, f. 174r, no. 124 (Fécamp, 1066–1087).
84 Vernier no. 43 (11th century).
85 Vernier no. 39.
86 Vernier no. 8 (1020–1030).
87 Fauroux no. 113 (1043–1048).
88 BN, coll. Moreau, vol. 341, f. 28r.
89 Fauroux no. 154: 'Quod, ego Rodulfus cognomento Dancel, prudenter advertens et sollicite agere contendens, omne quod tenebam in villam que vulgo eloquio dicitur Sclaveles, in terris, in silvis, in pratis, in aquis, perpetualiter ex toto, apostolorum principi beato Petro sanctoque Wandregisilo ac sancto Wlfranno, accepta ab abbate Rodberto non modica peccunia, et pro redemptione anime ... trado in alodo, quam donationem manu et ore confirmo ...'
90 On countergifts, see White, *Custom*, pp. 26–29; Tabuteau, *Transfers*, pp. 21–23.

mutual bond. The counter-gift, however, would not necessarily be commensurate to the donation. In fact, since there is no evidence that a distinction between a countergift and a payment was even made at the time, attempting to separate the two is inherently anachronistic.

Exchanges took place in eleventh-century Normandy between monasteries and laymen as well as between monasteries and other ecclesiastical institutions. One lay lord even acknowledged in his charter that he would consent if the monastery to which he had made a donation wished to exchange the land he had given for a closer piece of property.[91] In another case, John of Ravenna ceded Fontaine-Bellenger, given to Fécamp by Richard II in 1025, to a woman named Emma *pro commutatione alterius terrae*.[92] In another, the abbeys of Jumièges and Bourgueil made an exchange whereby each house traded a distant property for a closer one: Jumièges received Longueville which was in Normandy and close to Jumièges; in return Bourgueil gained Tourtenay which was in Aquitaine and located near Bourgueil.[93] In this instance the trade was fairly well-balanced, but exchanges, like sales, sometimes assume the appearance of gifts when the interchange occurred between properties of disparate value.[94]

Historians have generally considered mortgage agreements rare in eleventh-century Normandy since they appear infrequently in the documents.[95] It could well be, however, that more mortgages took place than the records indicate. Ecclesiastical institutions were more likely to keep records of mortgages when they acquired the property pledged, and indeed, a high proportion of the mortgage agreements that survive from eleventh-century Normandy resulted in the transfer of title to the creditors.[96] If, on the other hand, the mortgagors successfully redeemed their property, the church or

---

91 Tabuteau, *Transfers*, pp. 35–36. The monastery in question was Marmoutier, c. 1048.

92 Eure, canton Gaillon. This act is known only through extracts in Gilles-André de la Roque, *Histoire généalogique de la maison de Harcourt*, vol. 4 of 4 (Paris, 1662), p. 1310, from a copy by A. Mareste.

93 Fauroux no. 14: Longueville, canton Vernon, commune St Pierre d'Autils; Tourtenay, canton Thouars.

94 Tabuteau, *Transfers*, pp. 36 and 292, note 224.

95 An important work on mortgages in medieval Normandy is Génestal, *Rôle des monastères comme établissements de crédit*. Also, see Tabuteau, *Transfers*, pp. 80–87; Lucien Musset, 'A-t-il existé en Normandie au XIe siècle une aristocratie d'argent?' *AN*, 9 (1959), pp. 285–99, at pp. 287–88.

96 This point is made in Tabuteau, *Transfers*, p. 317, note 285: 'Presumably, when a *scriptorium* decided to draw up a retrospective charter or to compile a pancart or a cartulary from the charters in its charge, it relatively infrequently bothered to include out-of-date agreements which had resulted in no permanent acquisitions.' This view is reinforced by evidence from other regions. For instance, see Patricia A. Lewis, 'Mortgages in the Bordelais and Bazadais', *Viator*, 10 (1979), pp. 23–38. Lewis notes (p. 25) that 'only unredeemed loans were retained in the cartularies, since a monastery had no need to keep a contract after the loan had been repaid. Thus the number of mortgages actually contracted may have been much larger than the records reveal.'

monastery would have little reason to preserve the charter. This argument finds indirect support in the relatively large amount of money in circulation in Normandy and in the number of Normans who left the duchy for periods of time to travel to Spain, Italy and the Holy Land.[97] In most parts of Francia the First Crusade marked the turning point in the use of mortgages, as more and more laymen pledged their lands for cash, expecting to return with fortunes to redeem them.[98] In Normandy, however, men were lured to adventures in distant lands long before the First Crusade. It could well be that Norman monasteries extended more of the credit which financed these ventures than the number of extant mortgage agreements at first glance suggests.

Monks entered into agreements with laymen not only to gain property, but also to enrich and protect property already in their possession. A fairly common agreement was the life estate, whereby the monks would grant property to certain individuals for the rest of their lives, and then reclaim that land after their deaths with improvements made to it, as well as additional property or money formerly in the individual's possession.[99] Several charters show John of Ravenna extending life estates for Fécamp property in upper and lower Normandy.[100] For example, toward the end of the reign of Robert the Magnificent, Goscelin, the *vicomte* of Rouen, received from John of Ravenna estates that the previous *vicomte* of Arques had given to the abbey.[101] The terms of this agreement were very explicit: Goscelin would hold three pieces of property near Dieppe, about fifty kilometers north-east of Fécamp, which 'he would build on, increase and fill with plows and pigs and cattle'. Then, after Goscelin and his wife died, these lands would return to Fécamp 'clothed' in the improvements Goscelin had made, along with three

---

97   On the quantity of cash circulating in eleventh-century Normandy, see Musset, 'Aristocrate d'argent'.

98   Bouchard, *Sword, Miter, and Cloister*, pp. 222–23; Constance Berman, 'Land Acquisition and the Use of the Mortgage Contract by the Cistercians of Berdoues', *Speculum*, 57 (1982), pp. 250–66. The clearest description of a mortgage agreement in eleventh-century Normandy surviving in an original charter nevertheless dates from the First Crusade: ADSM 7H 43.

99   In at least one case, an individual rather than a piece of property was the subject of a life estate. Between 1028–1079, an agreement occurred between John abbot of Fécamp and Rannulf son of Conan, regarding a man named Stabilis and land at Amblie. Rannulf appealed to Fécamp that the abbey should give him the man Stabilis until he died. Stabilis would then return back to the abbey after Rannulf's death. The charter is preserved in a twelfth-century copy at BN, ms. lat. 1939, f.171v = BN, nouv. acq. fr. 21819, f. 166r: 'Noticia facta ab abbate Iohanno et sua congregatione de Fiscanno cum quodam milite nomine Rannulfo filio condam (*sic*) Conani, posteris recitanda. Adiit igitur presentiam nostram predictus Rannulfus de precando quatinus concederemus ei quendam hominem nomine Stabilem donec adviveret in villa qua dicitur Amblida, post decessum vero eius reveniret predictus Stabilis in dominicatura abbatis et fratrum'.

100   According to Tabuteau, *Transfers*, p. 79, 'it is possible that, for Normandy, John [of Ravenna] invented the life-estate'.

101   Fauroux nos. 54, 72.

additional plowlands in the vicinity.[102] The monastery looked forward to clear advantages from this agreement: at Goscelin's death, Fécamp would not only regain its former lands enriched by the *vicomte*'s attention, but also receive more property in the bargain.[103]

In a similar case between 1035 and 1040, 'at the request, indeed the insistence' of Duke William, Abbot John conferred to Hugh son of the *vicomte* Hugh the land of Trungy, south of Bayeux, on the condition that Fécamp would continue to receive the tithes of all the churches, and that Trungy would return to the monastery without any dispute after Hugh's death.[104] In another example, a cleric named Renaud received from Fécamp the tithes, church and property at Anneville sur Seine at the request of the duke's wife Matilda and on the condition that during his life 'he would endeavor to increase and multiply the tithes and the land as much as he could'.[105] Renaud gave the abbot of Fécamp four pounds of *denarii* at the time the agreement was made, and he pledged that thirty additional *solidi* would be added to the estate when Fécamp regained it all after his death. William the Conqueror's instigation of the former agreement and Matilda's of the latter suggest that they saw life estates of monastic lands as a means to reward certain lords. By encouraging and overseeing these agreements, the Norman rulers could use their relationship with Fécamp to enrich friends and *fideles*, especially since monastic burgs like Argences often received special privileges from the dukes, making them very attractive pieces of real estate.[106]

---

[102] Fauroux no. 72: '. . . ego Johannes indignus abbas Fiscannensis monasterii quandam convenientiam feci cum Gozelino filio Heddonis, . . . dedi ei, cum consensu fratrum nostrorum . . . tali modo ut in vita sua habeat, edificet, amplificet et carrucis, porcariis, pecudibus repleat, post decessum autem ejus et uxoris sue, predictis et aliis bonis vestita . . . adjuncta de sua terra quantum pertinet ad tres carrucas in loco qui Catta-villa vocatur'.

[103] To the monks' disappointment, Goscelin did not abide by the terms they set. He seized more lands than agreed, and he distributed this property among his men. An original charter dated 1047 shows John of Ravenna persuading Goscelin's successor to restore the abbey's lands which the previous *vicomte* had seized. Fécamp, Musée bénédictine, no. 8 = BN, coll. Moreau, vol. 341, ff. 17r–v, edited in *Thesaurus*, cols. 166–67: 'Porro jam dictus Gozelinus parvipendens convenientiam cum abbate et fratribus habitam, beneficium acceptum non solum, non auxit, sed etiam ad nihilum redegit, atque suis hominibus contra statutam pactionem distribuit, insuper namque ipsam partem quam sepefatus abbas sibi retinuerat, absque ulla justitia Deique timore . . .' This was the danger with life estates. As Tabuteau notes, *Transfers*, p. 79, 'The suspicion arises . . . that the person against whom protection was most necessary was the one to whom the life estate was given.'

[104] Fauroux no. 93, p. 244: 'Nunc autem de ipso alodo, ego Johannes abbas, deprecatione, immo compulsione Willelmi Northmannorum comitis . . .'

[105] BN, coll. Moreau, vol. 21, fols. 24rv = BN, nouv. acq. fr. 21819, f. 165r; Musset, 'La vie économique', pp. 75 and 347, note 52, identifies *Anslecvilla* as Anneville sur Seine, canton Duclair.

[106] Fauroux no. 85: 'Donavi apud Argentias, leuvam juxta morem patriae nostrae, propter mercatum ipsius villae.' The *banleuca* was a special zone of protection promising

Later in William's reign, John of Ravenna granted to Hugh, bishop of Avranches, the tithes and lands of Ryes, just north of Bayeux, for the rest of his life, again stressing that the property would automatically return to the abbey after Hugh's death.[107] Since Hugh was not only the bishop of Avranches but also the bishop who had consecrated John as abbot of Fécamp, this agreement implies that the abbot himself considered the allocation of monastic lands a means to strengthen personal as well as ecclesiastical ties. For Fécamp, these life estate contracts helped develop and augment the abbey's lands, an arrangement especially convenient for distant or scattered possessions. Thus, a local man named John received a fishery and woods at Pont Audemer from John of Ravenna that would return to Fécamp after his death, along with additional lands from his own estates.[108] And between 1028 and 1040, the abbot granted to a certain Ralph and his wife Fécamp's lands at Beaunay, south of Dieppe. At their deaths, this property would return to Fécamp, along with all of Ralph's inheritance.[109] Like distant priories, life estates were clearly a catalyst for acquiring additional property in areas where monasteries already had an interest.

A local man, moreover, would be better suited than monks to protect the properties he held of the abbey from violence or depredation, and he would have a vested interest in their welfare. An original charter of Jumièges in which Robert, abbot from 1059 to 1078, struck a deal with Hugh of Montfort reinforces this point.[110] Abbot Robert granted Hugh land at Lilletot, roughly twenty kilometers west of the abbey, and he included in the package an individual named Adhemar who held this land of Jumièges. In return, Hugh agreed to free the land from all disturbance, and to guard and defend (*custodiat et defendat*) the estates of the abbey which were in the vicinity. The charter also stresses that this property would return to Jumièges after Hugh's death. This agreement between Jumièges and Hugh of Montfort occurred during the relatively secure times following the battle of Mortemer in 1054. How much more willing ducal abbeys must have been to negotiate protective alliances with local lords during the more dangerous days following Robert the Magnificent's accession and his son's minority.

Although the professed goal of monasticism was withdrawal from secular

immunity from local lords. See M. D. Lobel, 'The Ecclesiastical *Banleuca* in England', in *Oxford Essays in Medieval History Presented to Herbert Edward Salter* (Oxford, 1934, rpt. 1968), pp. 122–40.

107 Fauroux no. 145.

108 BN, coll. Moreau, vol. 21, fols. 30rv = coll. Mathan, vol. 76, p. 197.

109 BN, coll. Moreau, vol. 21, fols. 25rv = coll. Mathan, vol. 76, p. 123. Musset, 'La vie économique', pp. 75 and 347, note 50, identifies *Belniacus* as Beaunay, canton Tôtes, which had been given to Fécamp by Ansgottus, and confirmed by Richard II in 1025: Fauroux no. 34, p. 130.

110 ADSM 9H 31, edited by Vernier, no. 42, and noted in *Gallia*, 11, c. 959. Tabuteau, *Transfers*, p. 79, suspects that Hugh de Montfort was the one against whom the abbey most needed protection.

life, it is clear that Norman abbeys in the tenth and eleventh centuries were not isolated from lay society. Transactions between monks and laymen involved many reciprocal obligations and commitments, and the charters attest that relationships between monks and lay communities ran very deep and operated on many levels: economic, legal, and of course religious. The economic significance of monasteries in local Norman society has already been suggested by their possession of fairs and markets, and their freedom from commercial tolls. Throughout Europe, monasteries traditionally were centers of economic growth and exchange.[111] In Normandy specifically, the monks' sophistication in economic matters is attested by a charter that makes precise allusion to possible fluctuations in the value of certain currencies.[112] Since they were sources of ready cash, monasteries often served as banks, making loans to finance pilgrimages, to pay ransoms and later in the century to cover the costs of joining the crusaders.[113] And since they were concerned with the transport of goods, monks helped maintain the network of roads that unified the duchy. For instance, one charter describes the abbey of Fécamp coming to an agreement with the abbey of Troarn regarding a road that needed to be repaved in stone. It was important to both communities that the road be sufficient 'not only for travellers and asses, but for wagons and other vehicles'.[114]

The role that Norman monasteries played in legal affairs at the local level is not well documented, but it is evident that the duke granted ducal abbeys jurisdiction over those who lived on their lands. One unpublished charter records that when John of Ravenna granted Beaunay to Ralph and his wife as a life estate in 1028–1040, he reserved the right of public justice for Fécamp.[115] The monastery not only enjoyed rights of justice, it apparently avoided relinquishing them. Precisely what this jurisdiction comprised is not

---

[111] Indeed, J. A. Raftis describes the monasteries of western Europe as 'repositories of the "economic wisdom" of the age. With this wisdom came economic success.' J. A. Raftis, 'Western Monasticism and Economic Organization', *Comparative Studies in Society and History: An International Quarterly*, 3 (1961), pp. 452–69, at p. 455. Also see Dubois, 'Les Moines dans la société', pp. 22–24; J. Lestocquoy, 'Abbayes et origines des villes', *Revue d'histoire de l'église de France*, 33 (1947), pp. 108–12.

[112] BN, ms. lat. 5650, fols. 33r–40r: '. . . si vero moneta mutanda fuerit'. Also see Musset, 'Aristocratie d'argent', p. 294, note 51.

[113] For example, one charter records that between 1087–1095 Hugh of Pesnel made a generous donation to St Etienne, Caen: 'pro hac nostra donatione, quarter viginti (*LXXX* in nouv. acq. fr.) libras Cenomannensis monetae, de quibus redemi me de captione in qua diu cum multa anxietate et ingenti damno meo nostrarumque rerum detentus fueram'. This charter is found in the Toustain cartulary, fols. 49r–50v, no. 153 = BN, nouv. acq. fr. 21813, fols. 800r–801r = BN, nouv. acq. lat. 1406, fols. 86r–87r. It is summarized by Deville, 'Notices', 14 (1904), p. 323.

[114] This charter is edited by R. N. Sauvage, *L'Abbaye de Saint-Martin de Troarn* (Caen, 1911), no. 6, p. 365: '. . . et talem etiam viam quae sufficiat non solum viatoribus et asinis, sed carris et caeteris vehiculis'.

[115] See above, note 109; '. . . retenta publica iusticia in consilio nostro'.

clear, but a charter of Jumièges shows Robert abbot of Jumièges presiding over a duel held between vassals of the monastery.[116] Thus, Robert of Jumièges exercised *haute justice* in his court, a jurisdiction that must have been conceded the abbey by the duke.[117] It would not be surprising if Fécamp and the other ducal abbeys enjoyed this privilege as well. Several charters describe fines or punishments that abbeys inflicted on men who had usurped or destroyed monastic property. One individual named Robert burned four houses and a wine press along with all the wine containers during the wine harvest at Moult one year. For these deeds he was excommunicated by the monks of Saint Etienne, Caen, to whom these properties had belonged. When he approached the abbot seeking forgiveness, Robert had to pay four hundred *solidi* from Maine to be absolved.[118] There is every indication that the monastery enjoyed a free hand in this affair and that other ducal abbeys likewise exercised similar rights of justice.

While the charters provide information indirectly concerning the economic and legal importance of Norman abbeys to their neighbors, they speak much more openly about the monks' religious role in the lay community. As intercessors for the rest of society, Benedictine monks were the focus of spiritual hope for lay people. For this reason above all others, men and women who lived in the world visited monasteries, bringing gifts and even their children to offer to the saints whom the monks served, sometimes travelling long distances on pilgrimage.[119] Indeed, if judged by standards of worldly gain alone, the generosity of the Norman dukes toward their monasteries makes little sense, economically or politically. In the Middle Ages, however, piety and pragmaticism could go hand in hand, and practical considerations often guided the pattern of patronage. In tracing that pattern in Normandy, it should be emphasized that the rulers of Normandy who restored and enriched the monasteries in their realm looked forward to rewards their support merited both in this world and in the one hereafter.

The possession of secular churches and their tithes by monasteries meant that the monks were to a large extent responsible for the quality and content of religious life at the local level. Richard II appears to have been the first ruler to appreciate the potential advantages of granting rural churches to a select group of ducal abbeys. The charters of 1025 for the communities of Fécamp, Jumièges and Saint Ouen suggest a conscious policy to link ducal houses with local centers of worship.[120] The privileges of exemption that the

---

116 Vernier no. 24: 'Ipse abbas duellum in castello tenuit.'

117 Haskins, *Norman Institutions*, pp. 27–30.

118 This event occurred during the Robert's abbacy at St Etienne, Caen, 1101–1107. It is recorded in a charter included in the Toustain cartulary, fols. 53v–54r, no. 159, and is summarized by Deville, 'Notices', 15 (1905), p. 20.

119 Lucien Musset, 'Recherches sur les pèlerins et les pèlerinages en Normandie jusqu'à la Première Croisade', AN, 12 (1962), pp. 127–50.

120 Lemarignier, 'Le Monachisme et l'encadrement religieux', pp. 384–91 and Map 1.

dukes granted to these abbeys meant that they were free from outside authorities, whether ecclesiastical or secular – except, of course, for the duke himself.
The monks, rather than the diocesan bishop, consequently chose and over-
saw the priests who served in their churches.[121] Ninth-century councils determined that parish priests should deliver sermons in everyday speech on
Sundays and special feast days.[122] Since hagiography provided the main
themes for sermons in this period, it is reasonable to conclude that the new
versions of *vitae* and translation accounts which included the Norman rulers
would have spread from the cloisters to these local churches.[123] In this
period, saints' lives also circulated as popular songs in Normandy: the
eleventh-century *Inventio* even mentions a canon whose practice it was to
translate saints' lives, especially Saint Wandrille's, from Latin into the vernacular to compose songs.[124] Acceptance of the Normans and identification
with their regime would have been facilitated at the local level by hearing
sermons, songs and stories which linked the new rulers with the traditional
saints of the region.

The charters indicate that monasteries kept close watch over the secular
churches in their care. Through most of the eleventh century, however,
Norman abbots showed no compunction against allowing married priests to
hold churches. One charter shows John of Ravenna accepting the priest of

---

[121] Lemarignier, 'Le Monachisme et l'encadrement religieux', pp. 389; Bates, 1066, pp.
193–94.

[122] Rosamond McKitterick, The Frankish Church and the Carolingian Reforms, 789–895
(London, 1977), pp. 80–85; Pierre Riché, Education and Culture in the Barbarian West,
Sixth through Eighth Centuries, trans. John J. Contreni (Columbia, South Carolina,
1976), pp. 483–85.

[123] The classic article on the relationship between hagiography and the religious instruc-
tion of the people is: Baudouin de Gaiffier d'Hestroy, 'L'Hagiographe et son public au
XIe siècle', in Miscellanea Historica in honorem Leonis van der Essen, vol. 1 (Brussels
and Paris, 1947), pp. 135–66. Also see Riché, Education and Culture, pp. 486–89;
McKitterick, Frankish Church, p. 108; Katrien Heene, 'Merovingian and Carolingian Hagiography: Continuity or Change in Public and Aims?' Analecta Bollandiana, 107 (1989), pp. 415–28. The argument summarized above is developed more
fully, especially with respect to liturgical celebration, in Potts, 'When the Saints', pp.
25–31.

[124] Inventio, p. 70: 'Hic quippe est ille Tetbaldus Vernonensis qui multorum gesta sanctorum sed et sancti Vuandregisili a sua latinitate transtulit atque in communis linguae
usu satis facunde refudit, ac sic ad quandam tinnuli rithmi similitudinem urbanas ex
illis cantilenas edidit.' Additional proof that hagiography circulated in lay circles is
found in the rhymed vernacular vita of Saint Alexis which was composed in Normandy around the middle of the eleventh century. Gaston Paris, La Vie de Saint Alexis:
poème du XIe siècle (Paris, 1933). Yet another example of a vernacular poem from the
mid-eleventh century describing a saint's life and miracles is La Chanson de Sainte Foi
d'Agen, ed. Antoine Thomas (Paris, 1925). Also see Orderic's description of a clerk
who told stories of the saints in the court of Hugh of Avranches. Orderic, 3, pp.
216–17.

the church of St Leger and his wife into the *societatem* of Fécamp.[125] In another charter, John of Ravenna granted the sons of a priest 'whatever their father on this day rightly held of the abbey' including all the offerings of the altar of the church and a third of the tithe of the burial place.[126] A letter from Pope Urban to Fécamp around 1088–1099 provides the first indication that incontinent priests were seen as an abuse: Urban specifically complained against the abbey's practice of condoning hereditary priesthood in their churches.[127] Similar practices took place at other monasteries. For instance, Saint Wandrille presented a piece of land to a certain clerk between 1031 and 1047; the clerk in turn gave it to his wife *in dotem*.[128] The abbot clearly did not object that this *clericus* was married.

The tolerance of Norman monks toward married secular clergy and church property in the hands of laymen, however, should not be judged by later reform ideals. Like Cluny, eleventh-century Norman monasteries followed the tradition of the Carolingian age in their attitude toward these practices which were only later deemed abuses.[129] Norman ducal abbeys also followed tradition in their close alliance with the most powerful secular authorities in the province, the dukes who restored and reformed them. And they were repaid with benefactions and protection. Already noted is the exile of Estormit who refused to sell his property to Fécamp.[130] On another occasion, the abbot of Mont-Saint-Michel complained to William the Conqueror about a man who had killed a swineherd of the monastery: the duke again exiled the man.[131] This protection was not limited to ducal houses: in the confirmation charter for the monastery of Saint Evroul, for instance, William warned that any potential predators of the community would be disinherited.[132] The exemption of ducal monasteries from secular and ecclesiastical authority

---

125 BN, coll. Moreau, vol. 21, fols. 22r–23r.

126 BN, coll. Moreau, vol. 21, fols. 27rv = BN, nouv. acq. fr. 21819, f. 164: '. . . quod pater eorum ipso die per rectum tenebat de abbate . . . altarium totum oblatiunum . . . et tertium denarium de sepultura'.

127 ADSM 7H 2030: '. . . indignum quod in quibusdam ecclesiis monasterio vestro utroque iure subjectis nonulli sicut accepimus suis parentibus successerunt easque contra disciplinam canonicam detinent in scandalum plurimorum'.

128 BN, nouv. acq. lat. 1246, f. 216r = ADSM 16H 14, f. 317r, no. 3 = ADSM 16H 20, p. 2041, no. 4: 'Abbas G[radulfe] concessit terram Angotisilvan cuidam clerico Iohanni de Alouvilla quam ipse silvanus uxori suae Emmae in dotem dederat.'

129 Bouchard, *Sword, Miter, and Cloister*, pp. 100–01.

130 See above, note 23.

131 Fauroux no. 232, p. 447: 'Abbas autem, accepta terra in dominio ad opus ecclesiae, fecit de illa medietariam; post multum vero temporis isdem Rogerius instigante diabolo quadam die in nemore Bivie porcos Sancti Michaelis inveniens fraudulenter et nequiter subulcum interfecit. Quod audiens abbas Ranulfus incunctanter comiti Normanniae patrati sceleris clamorem ostendit. Comes autem continuo ipsum Rogerium ut suae majestatis reum a totius Normanniae patria eliminavit.'

132 Fauroux no. 122, p. 289: '. . . ut si quis ex adverso veniens ad dampnum prefati cenobii grande aut parvum aliquid machinari temptaverit, et nostri hujus privilegii cartulam

meant that they were beholden only to the dukes. And the integral role they played within society helped form the ties that bound the duchy. Indeed, it was through their monasteries and the lands they controlled that dukes established their earliest link to lay as well as religious communities, encouraging even those without Viking blood in their veins to consider themselves a part of Normandy.

violare temptaverit, noscat se nostre reum esse majestatis et omne patrimonium suum nostris rebus dominicis asscribi debere.' Also see Chibnall, *World*, p. 48.

4

Wider Horizons:
Monasticism Beyond Upper Normandy

The whole of the province subject to their might lived as one clan or
family united in unbroken faith.[1]
— Ralph Glaber, early eleventh century

While monastic communities operated at the local level helping the Norman
rulers reach across social distances, they also contributed to the evolution of
the duchy by spanning distances geographically. In doing so, they advanced
the development of Normandy as a region, strengthening the associations
between the two areas known later as upper and lower Normandy. In the
early eleventh century, Dudo of Saint Quentin claimed that in 911 Rollo had
received all the lands of the later duchy, as well as rights over Brittany, from
Charles the Simple.[2] This statement should be dismissed as an expression of
the political ambitions of Dudo's duke, Richard II. The limits of Rollo's
authority were described much more narrowly by his contemporary Flodoard,
to whom he was no more than the chief of the *northmanni* in the neighborhood of Rouen.[3]

---

1 Glaber, pp. 36–37: 'Nam omnis provintia quae illorum ditioni subici contingebat ac si
   unius consanguinitatis domus vel familia inviolatae fidei concors degebat.'
2 Dudo, p. 169: 'Dedit itaque rex filiam suam, Gislam nomine, uxorem illi duci, terramque determinatam in alodo et in fundo, a flumine Eptae usque ad mare, totamque
   Britanniam de qua posset vivere.' It could perhaps be interpreted that the land 'from
   the Epte River to the sea' signified only upper Normandy north of the Epte, but this
   interpretation would conflict with Dudo's later claim that the churches of Evreux and
   Bayeux and the abbey of Mont-St-Michel lay within Rollo's realm. On this point, see
   Douglas, 'Rollo', p. 430, note 1.
3 Flodoard, *Les Annales de Flodoard*, ed. Philippe Lauer (Paris, 1906), pp. 30–31. On the
   boundaries of medieval Normandy, see most recently Lucien Musset, 'Considerations
   sur la genèse et le trace des frontières de la Normandie', in *Media in Francia . . . Recueil
   de mélanges offert à Karl Ferdinand Werner à l'occasion de son 65 anniversaire par ses amis
   et collègues français* (Maulévrier, 1989), pp. 309–18. Musset emphasizes that Norman
   expansion followed the lines of the ancient *pagi*. On this subject, also see Prentout,
   Etude critique, pp. 1–32; Bates, *1066*, pp. 8–11, and Map 2, p. 265; Le Patourel, *Empire*,
   pp. 3–15; Werner, 'Quelques observations'. For a recent and insightful examination of
   the Norman frontier, see D. J. Power, 'What did the Frontier of Angevin Normandy

The Viking rulers of Rouen only gradually asserted their rule beyond upper Normandy and the Seine basin. Although the king granted them the Bessin and the Hiémois in 924, and the Cotentin and the Avranchin in 933, Rollo and his heirs throughout the tenth century held no more than a tenuous grasp over these western territories.[4] And despite his grandiose claims, Dudo himself knew this was the case: in his account of a rebellion during William Longsword's reign, Dudo has Rollo's son admit that he could not meet the rebels' demands for the territory between the Seine to the Risle because he did not control it.[5] Thus, even Dudo knew that Longsword effectively held only upper Normandy, Rouen and the area north-east of the Seine. A century after Rollo, Duke Richard II still summoned much less support in the west than in the east. Less than ten per cent of the vassals who appear in Richard II's charters held any lands beyond upper Normandy.[6]

The actual stages of this expansion of Norman authority remain a subject of controversy and dispute,[7] but the configuration of monastic holdings delineates the spread of Rouen's influence. The map of Norman monastic property before 1035 shows some, albeit limited, monastic endowment and expansion in lower Normandy. Although significant pockets remained outside the sphere of ducal houses, this pattern continued during the reign of the Conqueror and was supplemented by the rise of new monasteries in the west. A closer look at the lands these abbeys acquired and the agreements they entered beyond upper Normandy both demonstrates the development of monastic ties across the province and helps to trace the growth of Rouen's sovereignty before the Conquest of England.

The proposition that monastic settlement accompanied and reinforced political expansion is certainly not new.[8] Monasteries in Champagne, for

---

Comprise?' *Anglo-Norman Studies*, 17 (1995), pp. 181–201. Although Power focuses on the twelfth century, the issues he raises are pertinent to the earlier period under discussion here. Most significantly, he raises the question of 'how far the frontier of Normandy existed in the minds of the inhabitants of the frontier regions themselves' (p. 193). Since boundaries depend largely on perception and consensus, this question is important to keep in mind as we consider the evolution of the Norman frontier in the tenth and eleventh centuries. Power explores this subject in greater length in his doctoral thesis, 'The Norman Frontier in the Twelfth and early Thirteenth Centuries', University of Cambridge, 1994. I would like to thank Dr Power for providing me with a copy of his thesis in advance of its publication.

4 Flodoard, pp. 24, 55. It is important to realize that these grants involved lands which were only nominally under royal control. Their purpose was primarily to direct Norse aggression away from the Ile de France.

5 Dudo, p. 187: 'Terram quam a me requiritis non possum largiri vobis'. This point is made and discussed in greater length in Searle, *Predatory Kinship*, pp. 73–77.

6 Bates, 1066, p. 170.

7 Compare Bates, 1066, p. xiv, to Searle, *Predatory Kinship*, pp. 69–70.

8 For example, Marjorie Chibnall writes, '. . . the use of monastic patronage to initiate or consolidate political control in disputed territory was a long-established practice all over western Europe'. Marjorie Chibnall, 'The Empress Matilda and Church Reform',

example, have been described as points of anchorage of comital authority, and since Champagne, like Normandy, was not an earlier political unit, it provides an especially good comparison with the duchy.[9] David Bates has suggested that Richard II 'tried to supplement the deficiencies of ducal government' by transferring lands in upper Normandy to monasteries.[10] And in a brief article Lucien Musset has discussed Fécamp's role in the monastic reconquest of lower Normandy.[11] Musset, however, admits, 'This first expansion of monasticism in the west of ducal Normandy remains rather poorly known.'[12] A survey of the possessions that ducal abbeys acquired beyond the Seine is therefore useful, making clearer the stages of assimilation between upper and lower Normandy, and showing that Bates' suggestion that monasticism supplemented ducal government in upper Normandy held true across the duchy.

One of the first areas outside the Seine basin and Upper Normandy to witness a concentration of monastic patronage was the district of Evreux.

TRHS, 38 (1988), pp. 107–30, at p. 109. For other regions, see: Julia M. H. Smith, *Province and Empire: Brittany and the Carolingians* (Cambridge, 1992), pp. 56–59; Theodor Mayer, 'The State of the Dukes of Zähringen', in *Medieval Germany, 911–1250: Essays by German Historians*, ed. and trans. Geoffrey Barraclough, 2 (Oxford, 1948), pp. 175–202, especially pp. 182–83; Francis X. Hartigan, 'Reform of the Collegiate Clergy in the Eleventh Century: The Case of Saint-Nicholas at Poitiers', *Studies in Medieval Culture*, 6 and 7 (1976), pp. 55–62. For Anglo-Norman England specifically, see Emma Mason, 'Pro statu et incolumnitate regni mei: Royal Monastic Patronage, 1066–1154', *Studies in Church History*, 18 (1982), pp. 99–117; Victoria Chandler, 'Politics and Piety: Influences on Charitable Donations during the Anglo-Norman Period', *Revue Bénédictine*, 90 (1980), pp. 63–71; Le Patourel, *Norman Empire*, pp. 279–318. Constance Bouchard presents an opposing view, challenging the assumption that monastic endowment and reform enhanced a noble's control over a given area: Bouchard, *Sword, Miter, and Cloister*, pp. 229–38. It seems reasonable, however, that investment in both worlds could coincide when spiritual and worldly interests went hand in hand.

9 Michel Bur, *La Formation du comté de Champagne, v. 950–1150* (Nancy, 1977), pp. 316–19. Bur also maps the counts' donations to monasteries and churches in order to learn more about their domain in the eleventh and twelfth centuries (map 10). Jean-François Lemarignier took a similar approach of mapping monastic benefactions to discuss the range of effective royal power in eleventh-century France. And Nicholas Banton traces the parallel progress of monastic reform and political development in tenth-century England. Jean-François Lemarignier, 'Aspects politiques des fondations de collégiales dans le royaume de France au XIe siècle', in *La Vita comune del clero nei secoli XI e XII* (Milan, 1962), pp. 19–40: Nicholas Banton, 'Monastic Reform and the Unification of Tenth-Century England', *Studies in Church History*, 18 (1982), pp. 71–85.

10 Bates, *1066*, pp. 194–95.

11 Musset, 'Contribution de Fécamp'.

12 Lucien Musset, 'Actes inédits du XIe siècle: I, Les plus anciennes chartes du prieuré de Saint-Gabriel (Calvados)', *BSAN*, 52 (1955), pp. 117–41, at p. 117. For a similar approach to Normandy's south-east border, see Lucien Musset, 'Actes inédits du XIe siècle: III, Les plus anciennes chartes normandes de l'abbaye de Bourgueil', *BSAN*, 54 (1959), pp. 15–54.

The earliest reference to a Norman abbey gaining property in this region appears in a charter issued by Richard II in which he confirms to Saint Ouen a *villa* west of the Eure River which his grandfather William Longsword allegedly donated, as well as benefactions from his great-grandfather Rollo.[13] While these early benefactions might have happened, since the relics of Saint Ouen returned to Rouen during Rollo's reign, it is more probable that the eleventh-century monks found it in their interests to give their claim the stamp of long-standing authority by projecting it back a century. A more definite step toward reasserting monasticism in the Evrecin was taken with Richard I's refoundation of the monastery of Saint Taurin during the second half of the tenth century.[14] The restoration of Saint Taurin must be seen against the background of a desperate war between the 940s and 966 involving the Norman ruler, the Carolingian king Lothar and the counts of Blois-Chartres, Flanders and Anjou.[15]

According to Dudo, the treachery of Theobald the Trickster count of Blois-Chartres was responsible for turning the king against his loyal vassal.[16] The terse but more reliable Flodoard, on the other hand, considered Richard the aggressor.[17] Whoever was to blame, the united forces of the counts and the king presented a formidable threat, and Richard appealed for aid from a Viking chieftain named Harold who had established a powerbase in Bayeux.[18] Under siege, Evreux fell to Theobald toward the end of 961, but Richard managed with Harold's help to recapture the city and stop Theobald outside Rouen in 962. Harold's Danes proceeded to pillage the lands bordering Normandy until 965, when Richard and Lothar finally made a peace settlement at Gisors.

It is difficult to say whether Richard had gained anything in this war against King Lothar and Theobald; in fact, a Norman charter for the Poitevin abbey of Bourgueil suggests instead that he lost lands dangerously close to Rouen to the count of Blois-Chartres. In 1001 Theobald's daughter Emma, the founder of Bourgueil, gave to this community the towns of Coudres in the Evrecin and Saint Pierre d'Autils just south of Les Andelys on the Seine.[19]

---

13 Fauroux no. 53. This charter survives as a copy from the second half of the eleventh century. The property in question is Tourneville, canton Gaillon.

14 Fauroux no. 5. The charter says that Richard I *instituit* this abbey, but Robert of Torigny and the editors of *Neustria* wrote that Richard restored it. Torigny, *De immutatione*, pp. 194–95; *Neustria*, p. 360. Debidour suggests that in the tenth century before Richard I's endowment, St Taurin was merely a chapel rather than an abbey. Debidour, pp. 18–31.

15 The fullest account of this war remains Ferdinand Lot, *Les Derniers Carolingiens: Lothaire, Louis V, Charles de Lorraine 954–991* (Paris, 1891, rpt. 1975), pp. 346–57.

16 Dudo, pp. 265–72.

17 Flodoard, pp. 149–50.

18 Richer, *Histoire de France, 888–995*, ed. and trans. Robert Latouche, 1 (Paris, 1930, rpt. 1967), pp. 202–03; Dudo, pp. 238–40; Flodoard, p. 98; Lot, *Derniers*, pp. 350–57. On this Harold (or Hagrold), see below, note 69.

19 The charter is edited in Musset, 'Bourgueil', pp. 48–49. Coudres, canton of St André; St Pierre d'Autils is today Longueville, canton Vernon.

Presumably, her father had wrenched these lands from Richard I during the war in the preceding century. Moreover, when Richard I's daughter Matilda married Theobald's son Odo II around 1005, Richard II handed over to his neighbor half the castle of Dreux, as well as adjacent lands along the Avre.[20] This concession underlines the weakness of the duke's hold over these territories. By granting them in dowry to Odo, Richard suggests that his grasp was already tenuous.

Within the next decade, however, the tables turned. A charter of 1012 in which Richard II and William of Aquitaine approve an exchange of lands between Bourgueil and Jumièges signals the shift.[21] Jumièges agreed to give Bourgueil the domain of Tourtenay, near Bourgueil, in exchange for Saint Pierre d'Autils. This arrangement attests that Richard II encouraged consolidation of monastic lands as he gradually gained the hold his father had sought over the south-east frontier. When Matilda died some years later without heirs, her brother reclaimed the lands he had alienated as her dowry.[22] A second war broke out between the Norman duke and the count of Blois-Chartres from 1013 to 1014. William of Jumièges records the peace settlement at Coudres: Odo kept the castle at Dreux, but in return Richard II received 'the land he had seized with the stronghold of Tillières remaining permanently, as it was then, in the power of the duke and his heirs'.[23] After this settlement, tensions eased between the two neighbors, and the Norman dukes concentrated on consolidating their hold on lands north of the Avre.

Military force was the first step in asserting ducal authority in the Evrecin following Richard I's struggle against King Lothar and Count Theobald. The town of Evreux was fortified with defensive walls and received as its count Duke Richard I's son Robert sometime around the year 1000.[24] As archbishop of Rouen as well as count of Evreux, Robert was clearly one of the most powerful Norman lords in the first third of the eleventh century, and an analysis of the charters of Richard II shows Robert as his brother's closest advisor, attesting twenty-nine of Richard's forty-nine surviving acts.[25] The

---

20 Jumièges, GND, 2, pp. 22–23. On this point, also see Musset, 'Bourgueil', especially pp. 43–45.

21 Fauroux no. 14.

22 Jumièges, GND, 2, pp. 22–23.

23 Jumièges, GND, 2, pp. 26–27: 'Ubi, dum causas dissensionum uterque in parte audisset, sopitis eorum animis, protinus illos concordes reddidit, eo quidem tenore, ut Odo Dorcasinum castrum teneret et dux prereptam terram reciperet reciproce. Tegulensi castro in suo statu perpetualiter persistente in eius scilicet suorumque heredum potestate.'

24 Jean Yver, 'Les Châteaux forts en Normandie jusqu'au milieu du XIIe siècle', BSAN, 53 (1957), pp. 28–115, at p. 33.

25 Fauroux nos. 13, 14b, 15a, 16, 17, 18, 19, 20, 21, 24, 25, 26, 29, 31, 32, 33, 35, 36, 37, 38, 39, 43, 45, 47, 49, 50, 52b, 54, 55.

appointment of such an important kinsman to the position of count of Evreux underlines the duke's commitment to pacify and secure this area.

Richard I's decision to restore the abbey of Saint Taurin in Evreux following the treaty of Gisors also reflects his determination to strengthen his hold on the Evrecin.[26] By extending the circle of ducal monasteries south from upper Normandy to the Evrecin, he thereby placed the lands he gave to the abbey in hands over which he had some control. Richard I generously endowed the house, passing to it many churches and estates including property in the Cotentin and Lieuvin, which gave the new community province-wide interests.[27] The presence of *hospites* on the lands which Saint Taurin received near Evreux suggests that much of this territory was farmland, but among the donations granted the new abbey also appears the first mention of a burg in Norman charters.[28] When it was given to Saint Taurin, this market adjoined the church, having most likely grown to serve its community. The duke also provided the monastery with the revenues generated by the annual fair on the feast day of Saint Taurin.[29] The association of this fair and the first visible Norman bourg with Saint Taurin underlines the monastery's role in the economic development of the area.

In 1034 Robert the Magnificent brought the community of Saint Taurin more firmly into the circle of upper Norman abbeys by placing it directly under the authority of Fécamp.[30] In exchange, Fécamp gave the duke the ancient house of Montivilliers to restore.[31] Since this trade occurred during a quarrel between Robert the Magnificent and his uncle, Robert archbishop of Rouen, it implies that the duke considered Saint Taurin too powerful or too valuable to leave in the hands of his angry uncle.[32] By giving it to Fécamp,

---

[26] The date of the refoundation of St Taurin is in dispute, and estimates have ranged from 945 to 990. Compare Debidour, p. 35 and L. H. Cottineau, *Répertoire topobibliographique des abbayes et prieurés*, vol. 1 of 2 vols. (Mâcon, 1939), pp. 1088–89. I agree with Fauroux, p. 75 that the act probably followed the recapture of Evreux in 962.

[27] Fauroux no 5.

[28] *Hospites* are equated with rural peasants in contemporary charters. For example, Fauroux no. 9, p. 80, refers to 'partem hospitum, quos colonos vocant', and Fauroux no. 38, p. 143, refers to 'hospites, quos agricolas nuncupamus'. For a fuller discussion of this term, see Léopold Delisle, *Etudes sur la condition de la classe agricole et l'état de l'agriculture en Normandie au moyen âge* (Evreux, 1851), pp. 8–14. The reference to the burg appears at Fauroux no. 5, p. 75: '. . . et burgum eidem ecclesie propinquum soli ecclesie serviens . . .'. Its significance is discussed in Lucien Musset, 'Peuplement en bourgage et bourgs ruraux en Normandie du Xe au XIIIe siècle', *Cahiers de civilisation médiévale, Xe–XIIe siècles*, 9 (1966), pp. 177–205, in particular pp. 179–80.

[29] Fauroux no. 5: 'Et in festivitate sancti Taurini nundinas totius civitatis et omnes illius diei consuetudines.' On the subject of fairs and markets in Normandy, see Musset, 'Foires et marchés en Normandie'.

[30] Fauroux no. 87.

[31] The most recent studies of Montivilliers are found in *L'Abbaye de Montivilliers à travers les ages*.

[32] This point has been argued by Jean-François Lemarignier, Evelyne Lamon, and

which was then ruled by William of Dijon's talented successor John of Ravenna, Robert the Magnificent ensured Saint Taurin's loyalty and support. That he took the trouble to do so, again, emphasizes the strategic importance of this abbey. The monks of Saint Taurin resisted this change and struggled unsuccessfully through the rest of the century to regain their independent status from Fécamp. In 1106 Saint Taurin finally lost the case for its independence from Fécamp when the abbot of Fécamp, William of Ros, produced Robert the Magnificent's charter before the court of King Henry I.[33] Saint Taurin was thereafter ruled by an unbroken series of abbots from Fécamp until 1240.[34]

Ducal charters show Saint Taurin gaining no further property after its initial foundation. In fact, the only known acquisitions by Saint Taurin in the century or so between its establishment and 1066 were from Archbishop Robert's son Richard, count of Evreux, and a vassal of his named Roger Harenc. Count Richard donated the tithe of a town near the mouth of the Seine, and Roger gave to the monks the tithe of the mills in a town near Evreux.[35] Richard of Evreux also abandoned the customary rights that he held as count over the men of Saint Taurin and anyone staying at the abbey overnight.[36] These were not substantial endowments; compared to other ducal abbeys, Saint Taurin fared poorly during the eleventh century as a reluctant daughter of Fécamp.

John Le Patourel has argued that a monastery-bourg-castle complex was

Véronique Gazeau, 'Monachisme et aristocratie autour de Saint-Taurin d'Evreux et du Bec (Xe–XIIe siècles)', in Aspects du monachisme, pp. 91–108.

[33] Fauroux no. 87; Gallia, 11, Instr. cols. 127–28.

[34] Gallia, 11, c. 626.

[35] ADEure preserves in a thirteenth-century cartulary (Petite Cartulaire de Saint Taurin, H793) and a fourteenth-century cartulary (Grande Cartulaire de Saint Taurin, H794) a pancarte issued by King Richard the Lion Hearted on January 15, 1195. This pancarte, which summarizes some thirty-seven individual acta, is the most important source for the patrimony of St Taurin during the eleventh and twelfth centuries. ADEure, H793, f. 58v: Richard count of Evreux with consent of his son William gives St Taurin the tithe of Buieville, today St Thurien, canton Quillebeuf sur Seine; ADEure, H793, f. 59r: Roger Harenc gives St Taurin the tithe of the mills of Glisoles, today Glisolles, canton Conches. This pancarte is edited in Gallia, 11, Instr. cols. 138–41. Since the town of Evreux was devastated during the Hundred Years War and the French Revolution, St Taurin's archives possibly contained charters now lost and not included in the 1195 pancarte.

[36] ADEure, H793, f. 72v: 'Richardus comes Ebroicensis . . . dedit deo et sancto Taurino tres consuetudines quas habebat in terra sancti Taurini, videlicet sanguinem, septenagium et theoloneum de eo qui remansurus in terra sancti vel unam noctem hospitatus fuit'. This charter is not included in the pancarte of 1195. The significance of these three customs has been discussed by Debidour, pp. 40–41, and Haskins, Norman Institutions, pp. 28–29, and note 112. The meaning of septenagium, however, continues to evade historians. I am grateful to David Bates and Lucien Musset for their comments on this charter.

the key to Norman expansion in post-Conquest England.[37] This pattern is suggested a century before the Conquest of England in the area around Evreux, where monastic and economic expansion accompanied military consolidation after the peace of Gisors. But after the initial ducal investment, Saint Taurin was subordinated to Fécamp and, it appears from the extant charters, ignored by the dukes. The early history of the abbey of Bernay, which Richard II established on the river Charentonne, discloses a similar pattern of foundation and endowment, delegation to Fécamp, and then no further attention. But unlike Saint Taurin, Bernay was placed under Fécamp's authority from the time of its foundation in order to assist the duke in settling and developing territory beyond the Seine valley.

Bernay was founded in 1025 on the lands which Richard II had given his wife Judith of Brittany when they married. On Judith's death, the duke recalled that she had dedicated her dower for the construction of an abbey and he wished to continue her work, entrusting the new community of Bernay directly to William of Dijon abbot of Fécamp, and his successors.[38] It was during the same period of time that Richard II entrusted the fortress of Brionne just up river from Bernay to his brother Geoffrey. Since this fortress was located on the right bank of the Risle River, it was established to defend the east against the west.[39] This suggests that as late as the 1020s, the Risle was still considered a frontier and the land beyond it to the west was not yet secured as part of the Norman polity. The location of the new community of Bernay therefore, just below the fortress of Brionne, suggests that its establishment and immediate commitment to Fécamp was part of a two-pronged effort by Richard II to strengthen ducal authority in the Lieuvin.

The foundation charter of Bernay provides a glimpse at the material assets of this new house: more than twenty *villae* with their churches, mills, meadows, tilled and untilled lands and fisheries – all located in a compact cluster south-west of the fortress of Brionne. The duke also added a weekly market and annual fairs to Bernay's domain.[40] Thus, as in the foundation charter of Saint Taurin, the economic significance of the new community was highlighted. The commitment of Bernay and its holdings to Fécamp no doubt contributed richly to the already considerable wealth of this ducal abbey. But again, as at Saint Taurin, extant sources show the abbey of Bernay receiving no further benefactions from the Norman dukes before 1066. Once the new house was in Fécamp's hands, the dukes left it up to the monks of Fécamp to develop and discipline their new daughter.

The dukes' parsimony toward Bernay appears to have been shared by their aristocrats. Only one charter shows Bernay acquiring any further lands before

---

[37] Le Patourel, *Norman Empire*, pp. 279–318.
[38] Fauroux no. 35; The *villa* of Bernay had belonged to Jumièges before the Viking raids: Vernier, no. 3.
[39] Yver, 'Les Châteaux forts', pp. 37–38.
[40] Fauroux no. 35.

the Conquest of England, and the date of this document raises some difficulties. The property in question was the church of Saint Michel of Bolbec, about twenty-five kilometers south of Fécamp, which was a priory of Bernay by the second half of the eleventh century. The charter, which survives as a late eleventh or early twelfth-century cyrograph, shows Walter Giffard approving the gifts of several men who donated portions of this church and various tithes to Bernay.[41] Since the charter is confirmed by William 'serenissimus rex' at Lillebonne in concilio, historians generally date the acquisition of the church of Saint Michel by Bernay to 1080, by which time William was king of England and in which year he held the well-known council at Lillebonne.[42] The charter itself, however, claims that it was read and approved by William in 1061, five years before he could have assumed the royal title.[43] Since the document was clearly a later copy of the original agreement, it would not have been surprising for the scribe responsible for this copy to refer to William by his more exalted post-Conquest title, even though he was recounting events which had occurred before the Battle of Hastings.[44] But the appearance on the charter of attestors who were present at the 1080 Council of Lillebonne and who were less likely to be at the ducal court in 1061 further complicates the dating of this act.[45] One possible conclusion to draw from this charter is that Bernay received Saint Michel of Bolbec sometime in 1061, but that the grant was not confirmed until 1080 in Lillebonne. A scribe writing some years later might have confused the dates of the initial endowment and the confirmation in the extant copy.

The examples of Saint Taurin in the Evrecin and Bernay in the Lieuvin suggest that the dukes were interested in establishing these abbeys as outposts in areas where Rouen's authority was expanding. In both cases, economic and military development accompanied the rise of monastic establishments. And in both cases, it took only one act to place these communities more firmly under Rouen's control by subordinating them to Fécamp. The association between monasteries in upper Normandy and the central region of the prov-

---

41 ADEure H123. It is edited in Neustria, pp. 401–02, and in Mémoires et notes de M. Auguste le Prévost pour servir à l'histoire du département de l'Eure, ed. Léopold Delisle and Louis Passy, vol. 1 of 3 (Evreux, 1862–1869), pp. 286–87.

42 Fauroux p. 32, note 67. Also see John Horace Round, Calendar of Documents Preserved in France Illustrative of the History of Great Britain and Ireland (London, 1899, rpt. 1967), p. 137, no. 412, and his preface, pp. xxvi–xxvii, where he argues for the 1080 date.

43 ADEure H 123: 'Acta et recitata atque concessa ante serenissimum regem Willelmum, anno ab Incarnatione Domini millesimo sexagesimo primo, apud Illebonam, in concilio, tercia feria sollemnitatis Pentecostes.'

44 The crosses were not fashioned to appear as autographs and the attestation list is not separate from the text. The charter was clearly not intended to pass as the original. Bénet, Diplomatique, vol. 7, p. 1369, and the copyist of BN, nouv. acq. fr. 21807, fols. 427rv, agree that this charter should be seen as a later copy rather than discounted as a forgery.

45 Among the attestors appear William archbishop of Rouen (1079–1110) and Michael archbishop of Avranches (1068–1096).

ince, however, developed much more gradually. Instead of founding new communities and then delegating them to Fécamp, the dukes simply gave ducal monasteries in upper Normandy properties in the Bessin and the Hiémois. In doing so, the early dukes helped to integrate distant territories into a wider framework, creating a network of monastic holdings centered on a circle of loyal communities.

Perhaps the first observation to be made from the configuration of holdings, however, is how limited monastic development was in the central, and especially in the southern region of lower Normandy in 1035. Although the area around Caen and Bayeux witnessed fairly heavy monastic colonization, upper Norman monasteries held very little indeed in the western portion of the Evrecin, the Hiémois and the southern half of the Bessin. The insecurity of the southern border goes far in explaining the paucity of monastic holdings in this area. During much of the eleventh century, the counts of Rouen vied with the lords of Bellême along the frontier between Normandy and Maine.[46]

At the end of his reign, Richard II allotted the Hiémois to his son Robert, the future duke of Normandy, to help secure the border.[47] But the Bellêmes nevertheless built castles at Domfront and Alençon and established a powerful, independent lordship which straddled Normandy's frontier, from the Avranchin to the county of Chartres.[48] In this period the bishopric of Sées swung between Bellême and bishops – between 1017 and 1023 the bishop was a member of the Bellême clan, but after him Richard II appointed a Norman bishop to Sées.[49] In 1027 to check Bellême expansion, Duke Robert established Roger I of Montgomery as *vicomte* of Exmes. After the duke's departure for Jerusalem in 1035, however, the appearance of Ivo III lord of

---

[46] For a detailed analysis of the Bellême lordship, see the recent study by Gérard Louise, *La Seigneurie de Bellême Xe–XIIe siècles: dévolution des pouvoirs territoriaux et construction d'une seigneurie de frontière aux confins de la Normandie et du Maine à la charnière de l'an mil*, 2 vols. (Flers, 1992–1993). The following works are also useful in understanding the uneasy relationship between the Bellême lordship and the Norman realm: Lemarignier, *Hommage*, pp. 60–72; Jacques Boussard, 'La seigneurie de Bellême aux Xe et XIe siècles', in *Mélanges d'histoire du moyen âge dédiés à la mémoire de Louis Halphen* (Paris, 1951), pp. 43–54; Geoffrey H. White, 'The First House of Bellême', TRHS, 22 (1940), pp. 67–95; Kathleen Thompson, 'Family and Influence to the South of Normandy in the Eleventh Century: the Lordship of Bellême', *Journal of Medieval History*, 11 (1985), pp. 215–26. Compare these studies with the lively, but dated and hopelessly partisan Henry Renault du Motey, *Origines de la Normandie et du duché d'Alençon* (Paris, 1920).

[47] Jumièges, GND, 2, pp. 40–41.

[48] See Louise, *Bellême*, 1, chapter 3, pp. 269–352.

[49] The bishops of Sées were Sigefridus (1017–1023), Radbod (1023–c. 1035), and Ivo (c. 1035–1070). Sigefridus and Ivo were both Bellêmes; Radbod, on the other hand, was a prominent member of the Norman aristocracy and the father of William Bona Anima, abbot of Caen (1070–1079) and archbishop of Rouen (1079–1110). Orderic, 4, pp. 254–55, and appendix 1, pp. 362–65; Louise, *Bellême*, 1, pp. 151, 157–61; Thompson, 'Family', p. 216. While Sigefridus was bishop, William of Bellême apologized and made restitution for the many injustices which he and his predecessors had inflicted upon the church of Sées: Fauroux no. 33

Bellême as bishop at Sées indicates that the southern family's ambitions were not contained.[50]

Of Norman houses, only Saint Taurin held any property in this area before the 1020s, and this was a *villa* given by Duke Richard I which appears on the map of monastic property before 1035 in the north-easternmost corner of the group around Vimoutiers, closest to Bernay.[51] Most of the lands in the Hiémois passed to Norman abbeys during the third decade of the eleventh century. In 1025, Fécamp and Jumièges received the sites of former monasteries at Almenèches and Vimoutiers with some adjacent lands and churches.[52] And between 1024 and 1026, Richard II gave Saint Wandrille the church of Argentan with four dependent chapels.[53] Richard II also confirmed the donation that Stigand the Old made to Saint Ouen of Les Autils, just north-east of Vimoutiers.[54] Thus, upper Norman abbeys gained a foothold in this area during Richard II's reign.

But properties in this region were difficult to maintain, and both Robert the Magnificent and Roger of Montgomery helped themselves to lands which Richard II and his men had given to upper Norman abbeys.[55] Duke Robert was guilty of usurping the domain of Ticheville from Saint Wandrille.[56] And Roger of Montgomery later confessed that, 'seduced by the evil example of the duke', he had destroyed the market at Vimoutiers which belonged to Jumièges, in order to establish one on his own lands.[57] Almenèches, which Roger of Montgomery also gained from Fécamp sometime between 1025 and 1060, was in an especially vulnerable location, less than ten kilometers from lands which the Bellêmes had seized.[58] Usurpation of monastic lands by the

---

[50] Orderic Vitalis portrays the conflicts between the Bellême family and the Norman lords as vassals rebelling against their overlords, but Boussard, 'Seigneurie', pp. 43–45, has shown this view to be incorrect. As Jean-François Lemarignier concludes, the Norman dukes were never able to incorporate this 'bastion avancé' definitively into their state. Lemarignier, *Hommage*, p. 65; Lucien Musset, 'Observations sur l'histoire et la signification de la frontière normande (Xe–XIIe siècles)', *RHDFE*, 41 (1963), pp. 545–46.

[51] Meulles, canton Orbec: Fauroux no. 5.

[52] Almenèches, canton Mortrée; Vimoutiers, canton Vimoutiers: Fauroux nos. 34, 36.

[53] Argentan, with the chapels of Chiffreville, Coulandon, Mauvaisville and Sarceaux, are all in the canton of Argentan: Fauroux no. 52.

[54] Les Autels St Bazile, canton Livarot: Fauroux no. 158. This grant is recalled in a charter of 1063.

[55] See Lucien Musset, 'Actes inédits du XIe siècle: II, Une nouvelle charte de Robert le Magnifique pour Fécamp', *BSAN*, 52 (1955), pp. 142–53. One is reminded of Geoffrey of Anjou dipping into the possessions of la Trinité, Vendôme, when in conflict with his neighbors. See Johnson, *Prayer, Patronage, and Power*, pp. 69–73.

[56] Fauroux no. 95.

[57] Fauroux no. 74: '. . . ego Rodgerus cernens et omnium malefactorum malitiam excedens contra Deum instigante diabolo memetipsum, erex [. . . Sanct]i Petri Gemmeticensis innumera mala ingerere cepi, vi illius bona auferendo'.

[58] Roger's acquisition of this property is discussed below in Chapter Six, p. 120. The

two earliest *vicomtes* of the Hiémois, whether a product of gratuitous predation or military emergency, underlines the adverse conditions in this *pagus* for
monastic expansion.

During the reign of William the Conqueror, the area around Argentan and
Vimoutiers experienced more, albeit modest, monastic development. In
1046–1047 Duke William confirmed a charter in which Gerard Fleitel, becoming a monk in his old age, gave three churches just north of Exmes to
Saint Wandrille.[59] This is particularly interesting since Gerard was related,
by blood or marriage, to Radbod the bishop of Sées (1023–c. 1035).[60] Had his
kinsman still held the episcopal seat, one imagines that Gerard would have
been inclined to retire closer to his home near Exmes. Instead, with a
Bellême on the episcopal seat, Gerard spent his last days in upper Normandy,
granting Saint Wandrille a vested interest in this disputed territory through
his entrance gift.

In addition to Gerard's donation, an individual named Hadvis gave half of
the land of O to Montivilliers, with the church and its tithe, sometime before
1050.[61] This was the southernmost property that an upper Norman ducal
abbey held in the duchy before 1066. But the recently founded lower Norman abbeys of La Trinité, Caen, Saint Etienne, Caen, and Cerisy also received claims in this area during William's reign. La Trinité had the largest
stake, receiving in 1066 the churches, mills and dependences of Villebarge
and Chauffour next to Exmes, as well as the tithes of Gacé and Ecouché to
the east and west.[62] Saint Etienne, Caen, was given the bourg of Trun with its
dependencies by Roger of Montgomery between 1063 and 1066, although
this gift would only take effect after Roger's and Duke William's deaths.[63]
And the abbey of Cerisy received from Turstin Haldup all his possessions at
Marcei, just north of Montivillier's property at O.[64]

Despite these acquisitions, however, the presence of ducal monasteries in
the Hiémois remained limited before 1066. The swath of properties from

---

Bellême family had seized land of Chailloué, canton Seés, from the cathedral of Sées.
Their crime is known through an act of William of Bellême who around 1025 returned
to the cathedral properties that his predecessors had usurped: Fauroux no. 33.

[59] Chambois, canton Trun; Omméel, canton Exmes; Avenelles, canton Exmes: Fauroux
108.

[60] Orderic, 2, pp. 254–55. Louise, *Bellême*, pp. 158–59 assumes that Orderic's term,
consobrinus, meant that William *Bona Anima* and William bishop of Evreux were first
cousins, and therefore their fathers, Radbod bishop of Sées and Gerard Fleitel, respectively, must have been brothers-in-law. While I would hesitate to translate *consobrinus*
so precisely, Orderic's information nevertheless indicates that Radbod and Gerard were
linked in some degree of kinship.

[61] O, former parish, canton of Mortrée: Bouvris, 'L'Abbaye de Montivilliers', p. 70, no. 5.

[62] Villebarge, canton Exmes; Chauffour, canton Exmes; Gacé, canton Gacé; Ecouché,
canton Ecouché: Fauroux no. 231

[63] Trun, canton Trun: Fauroux no. 223.

[64] Marcei, canton Mortrée: Fauroux no. 167.

Vimoutiers to Argentan which Saint Wandrille, Jumièges, Saint Ouen, Fécamp, Montivilliers, Cerisy and the Caen abbeys all held only reached tentatively toward the eventual southern border of the duchy. Nevertheless, monastic development followed a pattern there similar to that established in the Evrecin and Lieuvin. With the political climate so volatile, lands which abbeys held were centered again around a stronghold, the fortified city of Exmes which was in effect the capital of the Hiémois.[65] And the abbeys encouraged economic growth in the area. Indeed, sometime between 1029 and 1035, Saint Wandrille received from Duke Robert the tithe of the fairs and markets in all the Hiémois.[66] Thus, even though no new communities were established in this southern region by the dukes, it is once again possible to see monastic interests coinciding with political and economic development.

Farther to the north in the Bessin, ducal abbeys developed a stronger presence. The region of the Bessin according to Flodoard had been granted by the king to Rollo in 924, but the following year saw the *Baiocenses*, the people of Bayeux, ravaging lands only nominally Rouen's all the way to the Seine.[67] By the middle of the tenth century, however, the Bessin was controlled by a new group of Vikings who chose to ally with the Normans of Rouen. Dudo's account, for what it is worth, describes young Richard I being sent to Bayeux to learn Scandinavian as a child.[68] More reliably, Flodoard identifies as chieftain of Bayeux Harold, the Scandinavian who foiled King Louis' attempt to reconquer the province in 945 and who came to Richard I's rescue again in the 960s when Normandy was invaded by the king and the counts of Blois-Chartres, Flanders and Anjou.[69] In this region where the Rouen lords had gained friends, upper Norman abbeys were able to make significant progress.

Fécamp once again played the leading role in monastic expansion from the east. As early as 990 this abbey received Mondeville and Argences from Richard I, and subsequent *acta* attest that these *villae* proved to be valuable

---

[65] Yver, 'Les Châteaux forts', p. 35.

[66] Fauroux no. 80: '. . . decimam insuper nundinarum totiusque comitatus Oximensis et omnium mercationum . . .'

[67] Flodoard, p. 30: 'Baiocenses interim terram Nordmannorum, ultra Sequanam, depraedantur.' Prentout suggests that the Hiémois and the Bessin had been dominated by Bretons in the ninth century, along with the Cotentin and Avranchin, which had been formally ceded to Salomon. See Prentout, *Etudes critiques*, pp. 279–88.

[68] Dudo, pp. 221–22.

[69] Flodoard, p. 98 speaks of 'Hagroldus Nordmannus, qui Baiocis preerat'. Compare with Richer, pp. 202–05. In Jumièges, *GND*, 1, p. 88, he receives the exalted but erroneous identity of 'Heroldus Danorum rex'. For further discussion of this chieftain, see note 3 by Van Houts, Jumièges, *GND*, 1, pp. 89–90; Prentout, *Etude critique*, pp. 359–63; Henri Prentout, *Essai sur les origines et la fondation du duché de Normandie* (Paris 1911), pp. 241–45; Bates, *1066*, pp. 13, 34; Searle, *Predatory Kinship*, pp. 84–85, 286, note 13; Philippe Lauer, *Le Règne de Louis IV d'Outremer* (Paris 1900, rpt. 1977), pp. 287–89.

domains.[70] Richard II confirmed his father's donation of Mondeville and Argences in 1025, including in his description of their appurtenances: churches, mills, vineyards, meadows, forests, and lands cultivated and uncultivated.[71] As in other areas of the duchy, monastic settlement and economic development proceeded side by side. With its abundance of rivers the Bessin was well suited for trade, and Bayeux was the only town besides Rouen to possess a mint in the tenth century.[72] Between 1031 and 1035 Argences received from the duke a special zone of protection and exemption 'on account of its market', the first example of this franchise in Normandy.[73] And these lands also served as points of departure for further acquisitions in lower Normandy by Fécamp, including, among the several lands and *villae*, Troarn, the site of the future Montgomery abbey.[74]

Fécamp's infiltration of the Bessin initiated a gradual movement into the area by three other upper Norman abbeys, Saint Wandrille, Jumièges and Saint Ouen, all of which had gained significant interests in the area by the 1020s. In 1032, Robert the Magnificent restored the abbey of Cerisy in the Bessin.[75] And Cerisy in turn commenced restoring as priories ancient monasteries in the region which had suffered disruption during the invasion period, thus creating its own network of houses. Deux Jumeaux, Saint Fromond, Saint Marcouf and Saint Martin were all Carolingian abbeys in the Bessin which had disappeared during the Viking incursions and which reappeared as priories of Cerisy in the eleventh century.[76] More than a century after the Bessin had allegedly been granted to them, Cerisy's foundation was the first attempt by the dukes to establish an independent community in the west. And except for the ambivalent Mont-Saint-Michel, it remained the only functioning monastery in lower Normandy until William the Conqueror and his wife founded their two monasteries at Caen sometime between 1059 and 1066.

[70] Mondeville, canton Caen-Est; Argences, canton Troarn: Fauroux no. 4.

[71] Fauroux no. 34.

[72] On the tenth-century mint at Bayeux, see Dumas-Dubourg, *Le Trésor de Fécamp*, pp. 104–05.

[73] Fauroux no. 85: 'Donavi apud Argentias, leuvam juxta morem patriae nostrae, propter mercatum ipsius villae.' Also see Musset, 'Peuplement en bourgage', p. 185. For a valuable description of the importance of an abbey's *leuga* or 'banlieu' in an area of economic and demographic growth, see Eleanor Searle, *Lordship and Community: Battle Abbey and its Banlieu, 1066–1538* (Toronto, 1974), pp. 21–35. Further evidence of the economic vitality of this region is provided by the confirmation charter of St Etienne, Caen, dated 1066–1077, in which William the Conqueror makes reference to the 'foreign merchants' (*extranei mercatores*) who came to Caen: Musset, *Abbayes caennaises*, no. 4, p. 61.

[74] Musset, 'Contribution de Fécamp', p. 61; Fauroux no. 34; For the first charter of donation for the monastery of Troarn, see Sauvage, *Troarn*, no. 1. On Troarn and its relations with Fécamp, see below Chapter Six.

[75] Fauroux no. 64.

[76] Lucien Musset, 'Notes sur l'ancienne abbaye de Deux-Jumeaux', BSAN, 53 (1957), pp. 405–21; Lucien Musset, 'Les Origines du prieuré de Saint-Fromond: un acte négligé de Richard II', BSAN, 53 (1957), pp. 475–89.

The earliest charters of the priory of Saint Gabriel indicate the level of commitment that Fécamp was willing to assume by 1058–1060 in order to establish a priory in the Bessin.[77] To provide Saint Gabriel with enough resources to thrive so far away from Fécamp, the monks invested approximately 312 pounds of *denarii* into lands, churches, tithes and mills for the community.[78] In at least one case, the monks gained property for Saint Gabriel in a vill where another Fécamp priory, Saint Martin du Bosc, also acquired lands at roughly the same time.[79] The monks probably found this a convenient arrangement for administration of their estates. And the establishment of upper Norman monks in lower Norman *cellae* and priories encouraged greater religious and economic ties between the two areas.

When a monastery gained a foothold in one area, it tended to collect more property nearby.[80] The abbey of Cerisy provides the most striking example of this. When the map of monastic holdings by 1035 is compared to the map which shows the acquisitions of ducal abbeys from 1035 to 1066, it is readily apparent that Cerisy was intent on collecting property in the region west of Bayeux and the abbey. Upper Norman monasteries similarly began to concentrate their holdings in particular regions. For example, between 996 and 1006, an individual named Albert gave Saint Wandrille the site of the former Carolingian abbey of Livry in the Bessin, with churches and appurtenances. Richard II, subscribing the gift, added a quarter of the town and church of Juvigny, about twelve kilometers away, to the donation.[81] Some twenty years later, Richard II confirmed these properties of Saint Wandrille, noting also that a certain Odo had given a church in the commune adjacent to Livry to the monks.[82] Similarly, when a different Odo, son of Gosfrid, donated half the *villa* of Ryes to Fécamp, the monks struck a deal with the duke and gained the other half of Ryes in exchange for property in upper Normandy.[83] This Odo *filius Gosfredi* is the first ducal vassal known by name in lower Normandy.[84] That he is known through his patronage to an upper Norman abbey underlines the connection between political and monastic interests.

The most significant change in the monastic map of the Bessin from 1035

---

[77] Lucien Musset, 'Saint-Gabriel'. Musset's edition of the charter confirming the foundation of St Gabriel omits the copy surviving at ADCalva, H 5229, 'copy from original'. The earliest *pancarte* of the priory of St Gabriel has been discovered at Hull University Library, DDC 37/46 (f). See David Bates, 'Four Recently Rediscovered Norman Charters', AN, 45 (1995), pp. 35–48.

[78] Musset, 'Saint Gabriel', p. 120. This was, as Musset notes, 'a veritable fortune'.

[79] The vill in question was Langrune, canton Douvre. For St Martin du Bosc, canton Honfleur, commune St Gatien des Bois, see Fauroux no. 218.

[80] This was a common pattern for monasteries outside of Normandy as well. For example, see Bouchard, *Sword, Miter, and Cloister*, pp. 201–02; Johnson, *Prayer, Patronage, and Power*, p. 53.

[81] Livry, canton Caumont; Juvigny, canton Tilly sur Seulle: Fauroux no. 7.

[82] The church was in Caumont, canton Caumont l'Eventé: Fauroux no. 52.

[83] Ryes, canton Ryes: Fauroux no. 34.

[84] Musset, 'Notules fécampoises', p. 588.

to 1066 was due to the double foundation of Saint Etienne and La Trinité at Caen by William the Conqueror and his wife Matilda in the early 1060s. As the map of monastic properties by 1066 illustrates, La Trinité received a wealth of lands in the area around Caen, in particular north-east of the town. Saint Etienne no doubt also enjoyed a substantial initial endowment, but unfortunately its confirmation charter dates from 1066 to 1077, and does not indicate which properties the monastery received before 1066.[85] The choice of Caen as the site of these new monasteries resulted from William the Conqueror's decision to establish there his base for the governance of lower Normandy. Around 1060, the duke also constructed a castle on a rise and enclosed the town with walls.[86] By building a new castle and establishing their two new abbeys at Caen, William and Matilda signaled their determination to make this town their second capital in the duchy.

The final areas of Normandy in which to consider the growth of estates of ducal abbeys are the Cotentin and the Avranchin. In both of these *pagi*, the distribution of upper Norman monastic holdings is quite thin. Mont-Saint-Michel, located at the south-western corner of the duchy, remained unrivalled as the foremost monastery in the Avranchin in 1066.[87] And Cerisy clearly held more lands in the Cotentin than any other ducal abbey during the Conqueror's reign. Of upper Norman monasteries, only the abbey of Saint Taurin possessed any property in the Cotentin before the Conqueror's reign. It received these lands at the time of its foundation between the 960s and 996.[88] This group of holdings, a total of three *villae* near the former pre-Norman abbey of *Malduinum*, perhaps came into the duke's possession through his wife Gunnor, who came to Rouen from the Cotentin and whose brother Herfast is known to have held lands a bit further north, inland from St-Sauveur.[89] Unfortunately, the witness list to the foundation charter of Saint Taurin has been lost, so it cannot be known if Gunnor was even present.[90] It is difficult to discern how useful these far-away lands would have been to the abbey in Evreux, but perhaps the monks simply sent out agents periodically to collect revenues. Thirteenth-century sources show no further lands acquired in the Cotentin by Saint Taurin, although the monks did collect rents and tithes from nearby properties through the eleventh and twelfth centuries.[91]

---

85 Musset, *Abbayes caennaises*, no. 4.
86 Michel de Boüard, *Le Château de Caen* (Caen, 1979), pp. 10–11.
87 For Mont-St-Michel's possession of these lands and relations with Rouen, see Chapter Five.
88 Fauroux nos. 5, 87.
89 Searle, *Predatory Kinship*, p. 94. Herfast gave to St Père de Chartres the *villa* of Le Ham and a mill at Barneville-Carteret, as well as a third of Teurteville-Hague (canton Octeville) in the 1020s: *Cartulaire de l'abbaye de Saint-Père de Chartres*, ed. M. Guérard, 1 (Paris, 1840), pp. 108–15; Searle, 'Fact and Pattern', p. 85, note 86.
90 Fauroux no. 5.
91 Chapron and Vecile, p. 37.

Apart from these few exceptions, the Cotentin remained beyond the sphere of upper Norman monasteries in 1035. Richard I's marriage to Gunnor had forged an alliance with the rival Vikings in the Cotentin, but for half a century after Richard I's death the dukes chose to grant lands in this region to Mont-Saint-Michel and Cerisy rather than to monasteries closer to home. During Duke William's reign, however, two upper Norman abbeys gained significant interests there. Around 1047–1053, Saint Wandrille received a cluster of five churches and various tithes at the western foot of the Cherbourg peninsula which William the Conqueror had given to Robert of Beaumont, son of Humphrey of Vieilles.[92] And between 1051 and 1066, Robert Bertram gave Saint Ouen four churches with assorted holdings on the other side of the peninsula.[93]

The charter that records Saint Wandrille's acquisition of five churches in the Cotentin indicates that the duke had confiscated these properties from Hugh Pasfolet, one of the lords who had participated in the rebellion of 1046.[94] This revolt had been based in lower Normandy and led by William's cousin Guy of Burgundy, who held the fortress of Brionne after 1040 and who was suspected of wishing to become duke himself.[95] Among the rebels were several important western lords, including Neil I *vicomte* of the Cotentin, Rannulf I *vicomte* of the Bessin, Grimoald of Plessis and Haimo of Creully. The threat to young William's rule was considerable, and although the rebel forces were quashed in 1047 at the battle of Val-ès-Dunes, the support which Guy had been able to muster in the west against the duke attests to the limited reach of Rouen into lower Normandy in the middle of the century. It also shows clearly why William later sought to establish a stronghold at Caen, with a new castle and two abbeys.

In conclusion, *Normannia*, 'the land of the Northmen', did not exist before the Viking settlement. An outsider writing in the first decades of the eleventh century explained to his readers that *Normannia* before the Normans was just the border lands of Francia and Brittany.[96] Over the course of

---

92 St Marcouf, canton Montebourg; St Germain and St Martin de Varreville, canton St Mère Eglise; Ste Honorine d'Audouville, canton Audouville la Hubert; Notre Dame de Poupeville, canton St Marie du Mont: Fauroux no. 128; St Wandrille also possessed the tithe of the fish caught off St Marcouf and the tithe of the sheep and the pigs in Varreville, canton St Mère Eglise, plus one *hospes*. ADSM 16H 20, pp. 2088–89, no. 74; BN, nouv. acq. fr. 21816, f. 149r; BN, nouv. acq. lat. 1246, f. 223r. Lot, *Etudes critiques*, no. 18, has edited this charter, but his version, based on ADSM 16H 14, f. 325v, no. 26, departs from these other manuscripts at several points.

93 Notre Dame de Magneville, canton Bricquebec; Notre-Dame du Vrétot, canton Bricquebec; St Pierre de Surtainville, canton Les Pieux; Notre-Dame de Bricquebec, canton Bricquebec: Fauroux no. 205.

94 Fauroux no. 128.

95 On this rebellion, see Douglas, *William the Conqueror*, pp. 47–50 and Searle, *Predatory Kinship*, pp. 199–204.

96 Adémar de Chabannes, *Chronique*, ed. Jules Chavanon (Paris, 1897), p. 148: '. . . Normannia, quae antea vocabatur marcha Franciae et Britanniae'.

the tenth and early eleventh centuries, the name Normandy assumed meaning as the region evolved geographically and politically, and it changed meaning in response to this evolution. Rollo's successors succeeded in expanding their horizons from the 'neighborhood of Rouen' to extend across most of the archdiocese, from the Bresle and Epte Rivers to the Cotentin. As the area grew in size, the sense of this name shifted as well. No longer simply 'the lands where the Vikings settled', Normandy by the middle of the eleventh century had come to designate a region not only much greater in area than in the time of Rollo, but also a state of political permanence. Indeed, the cohesion of this new duchy prompted Ralph Glaber to exclaim in the early eleventh century, 'The whole of the province subject to their might have lived as one clan or family united in unbroken faith.'[97]

This process of state-building, however, progressed unevenly. Despite the royal grants in the first half of the tenth century, the limits of the duchy were defined only by the extent to which ducal authority and control were recognized there. In this gradual process of regional expansion, upper Norman monasteries played an important role, and the lands they administered in lower Normandy represented enclaves of Norman support. Through their patronage and support of monasticism, the Norman rulers placed extensive and valuable lands in the hands of trustworthy landlords. And by giving abbeys in upper Normandy properties in the west, the dukes gradually integrated distant territories into a wider framework, creating a network of monastic holdings centered on a circle of ducal houses and tied closely to the authority of Rouen.

Since the dukes' authority was limited in the west, however, monastic endowment did not follow uniformly. In the Evrecin and Lieuvin, generosity dropped off after the initial foundation and delegation of new abbeys to Fécamp. Along the southern border, the dukes' rivalry with the lords of Bellême restricted both political and monastic expansion, so that the properties which abbeys acquired were limited to the districts around Argentan, Exmes and Vimoutiers. In the Avranchin, ducal patronage aimed primarily at winning the allegiance of Mont-Saint-Michel rather than endowing upper Norman abbeys before 1066. And in the Cotentin, the lower Norman abbey of Cerisy held the lead, although Saint Wandrille and Saint Ouen gained interests there in the decades before the Conquest. The greatest presence of upper Norman abbeys appeared in the Bessin, where the donation of properties to monasteries in upper Normandy provided a peaceful means to tie these lands to the leadership at Rouen.

In England after 1066, Emma Mason writes that 'William [the Conqueror] established a prudent tradition of granting the monks land which had only

---

[97] Glaber, pp. 36–37: 'Nam omnis provintia quae illorum ditioni subici contingebat ac si unius consanguinitatis domus vel familia inviolatae fidei concors degebat'.

recently come into the king's possession.'[98] In Normandy before 1066, a similar pattern appears as monasteries became instruments of consolidation for the ducal house. In Normandy as in Norman England, monastic expansion tended to proceed side by side with military and economic development. The practical advantages of ducal patronage did not, however, detract from the gratitude it won. From Dudo to Orderic Vitalis, Norman chroniclers lavish praise on their rulers, and only in Normandy did monks add a special acclamation for the duke in their *Laudes regiae*.[99] By 1066, a firm partnership had been built between the Norman dukes and their abbeys, an alliance of interests that strengthened the coherence of the realm. In the years immediately following, that partnership would be taken across the channel.

[98] Emma Mason, 'Pro statu', p. 102.
[99] H. E. J. Cowdrey, 'The Anglo-Norman *Laudes regiae*', *Viator*, 12 (1981), pp. 37–78.

5

Resisting the Tide at Mont-Saint-Michel

In the circle of Norman ducal monasteries of the tenth and eleventh centuries, Mont-Saint-Michel was in many ways unique. While other houses reformed and endowed by the dukes were clearly allied to Rouen, Mont-Saint-Michel stood apart, with interests and commitments tying the community to areas outside the eventual boundaries of Normandy.[1] Unlike other abbeys owing their reform to the Norman rulers, Mont-Saint-Michel resisted the centralizing authority of the dukes and their reformers throughout the eleventh century and into the twelfth century. André Dufief has already brought the later stages of this resistance to the attention of scholars, describing the years from 1085 to 1154 as a troubled time during which the abbey endeavored to gain its independence from William the Conqueror and his successors.[2] A closer look at the early history of Mont-Saint-Michel reveals that the tensions which surfaced in the last quarter of the century in fact had deep roots stretching back through the abbey's earliest records. The Mont encapsulates and illuminates exactly those issues that are integral to the process of regional identification.

On 7 February 966, King Lothar issued a charter on behalf of Mont-Saint-Michel which has traditionally been seen to mark the beginning of Norman dominance over the reformed Benedictine community.[3] The document,

---

[1] On the history of the revival and reform of Mont-St-Michel in general, see collected articles in *Millénaire*, in particular Michel Le Pesant, 'Les Relations du Mont Saint-Michel avec les autres abbayes normandes', in *Millénaire*, 1, pp. 743–50, and Jean Laporte, 'L'Abbaye du Mont Saint-Michel aux Xe et XIe siècles', 1, pp. 53–80. The following works also provide brief surveys of the abbey's history: René Herval, 'L'Abbaye du Mont-Saint-Michel', in *Normandie Bénédictine*, pp. 117–36; J. J. G. Alexander, *Norman Illumination at Mont St Michel, 966–1100* (Oxford, 1970), pp. 1–21.

[2] André Dufief, 'La Vie monastique au Mont Saint-Michel pendant le XIIe siècle (1085–1186)', in *Millénaire*, 1, pp. 81–126, especially pp. 82–101.

[3] *Recueil des actes de Lothaire et de Louis V, rois de France (954–987)*, ed. Louis Halphen and Ferdinand Lot (Paris, 1908), no. 24, pp. 53–57. Ferdinand Lot argued in *Derniers*, pp. 346–57 (1891) that the refoundation of Mont-St-Michel should be seen in the context of the peace of Gisors, which he dated to 966 rather than 965. He consequently redated Lothar's charter to 967 in order to have it follow the settlement of peace. When Lot and Halphen published the Lothar's charter seventeen years later in

which survives as an interpolated pseudo-original from the mid-eleventh century, states that Richard I of Normandy restored (*restauravit in melius*) the place called Mont-Saint-Michel, and that he, Pope John XIII and the archbishop of Rouen all requested that King Lothar confirm its reformation, a petition which the king willingly granted. Although the editors of the charter accept the essential content of Lothar's confirmation, John XIII's role in the reform of the abbey should be discounted since the scribe's purpose in redrafting the charter a century later was to include a forged bull from this pope promising free abbatial elections.[4]

Lothar's confirmation, if it can be trusted, represents the earliest surviving evidence of Norman involvement in the revival and reform of Mont-Saint-Michel. It does not indicate, however, that Duke Richard I or his archbishop approached Lothar directly; it merely says that their request 'came to our ears'.[5] No attestation list reveals who was present at the time of the confirmation, and the only signator of the document was the king himself. It is possible that Mainard I, the Flemish reformer of Saint Wandrille, should receive credit for gaining Lothar's consent rather than Richard I or the archbishop. But regardless of who brought this monastery to the king's attention, the case was very unusual: Mont-Saint-Michel was the only monastery in the tenth century within the later boundaries of Normandy to receive a royal confirmation of its refoundation.[6] And the first time that Mont-Saint-Michel appears in Norman charters was in 1009.[7] For over forty years after the traditional date of the revival and reform of Mont-Saint-Michel, therefore, the records are conspicuously silent regarding Norman involvement in the community's welfare.

No contemporary narrative sources help to fill in the picture, although Dudo of Saint Quentin writing during the first decades of the eleventh century briefly describes Richard I's construction of monastic buildings and the gathering of monks at the Mont.[8] The fullest description of the community's reformation is found in the *Introductio monachorum*, composed several

---

Recueil, however, Lot apparently had changed his mind, since they chose 966 as the date of the act.

4   The editors suggest that the monks destroyed a genuine tenth-century document when they concocted the extant act a century later. Two charters actually survive from the eleventh century, one which is interpolated, and another, which Lot and Halphen consider the first attempt at falsification, in which the papal bull follows the act, rather than being interpolated. On this charter, also see Lemarignier, *Etude sur les privilèges*, p. 29, note 10.

5   Halphen, *Recueil*, p. 56: 'Pro cujus perpetuo roboramine atque stabilitate, domni prefati papae necnon et memorati marchisi atque Hugonis, sanctae Rotomagensis aeclesiae archiepiscopi, ad cujus diocesim pertinet jamdictus locus, nostras devenit ad aures petitio id ipsum nostro perpetuo manendum roborare fulcimine.'

6   Lemarignier, *Hommage*, p. 68, note 165.

7   Fauroux no. 12.

8   Dudo, p. 290: 'In Monte namque maritimo, refluae lunari dispositione inundationis gurgite undique secus circumdato, delubrum mirae amplitudinis, spatiosaque mon-

generations thereafter, during the second half of the eleventh century.[9] Thoroughly Norman in its outlook and its bias, the *Introductio* dwells on the corruption and decadence of the canons whom the Benedictines allegedly replaced and extols the generosity of Richard I who is said – in this source and this source alone – to have made frequent gifts and visits to the community. While historians have tended to accept the *Introductio*'s account of the refoundation of Mont-Saint-Michel at face value, no subsequent evidence supports its claims. Moreover, the importance which the *Introductio* places on the spurious bull of Pope John XIII and the freedom of elections which it purports to guarantee further undermines confidence in its account.[10]

Although written a century after the event, the *Introductio monachorum* has led historians to see the refoundation of Mont-Saint-Michel primarily in the context of the Norman realm. Thus, Jean Laporte ascribes the revival of the abbey to the Norman dukes' desire to have a base for the reconquest of Brittany; and Jean-François Lemarignier describes the monks at the Mont as being 'at the front rank of Norman pioneers at the border of Brittany'.[11] T. D. Wilson Smith states furthermore that after the 960s, 'the Mount became a typical Norman monastery'.[12] The view of Brittany as a land for the Norman dukes to reconquer, however, did not even exist before Dudo wove his tale of the Norman past. And it was by no means a foregone conclusion that the Norman duchy would even include Mont-Saint-Michel. The fact that it did has led historians to minimize the difficulty of the monks' position and the complexity of their response in a society disrupted by Viking raids and Frankish wars.

The refoundation and subsequent early history of the monastery of Mont-Saint-Michel, therefore, needs re-evaluation – first, with respect to the abbey itself as a community of monks with urgent, immediate responsibilities to

achilis habitationis moenia construxit: ibique monachos, sub aerumnosa theoricae vitae palaestra, normalibus celebris itineris decretis astrictos, Christo coegit famulari.' For a description and analysis of the earliest written sources on Mont-St-Michel, see Jacques Hourlier, 'Les Sources écrites de l'histoire montoise antérieure à 966', in *Millénaire*, 2, pp. 121–32.

9 *Introductio monachorum et miracula insigniora* in Thomas Le Roy, *Livre des curieuses recherches du Mont-Sainct-Michel*, ed. Eugène de Robillard de Beaurepaire, *Mémoires de la société des antiquaires de Normandie*, 29 (Caen, 1876), Appendix III, pp. 864–92.

10 M. Lelegard, 'Saint Aubert', in *Millénaire*, 1, pp. 29–52, suggests that the *Introductio* might have been composed by Renouf of Bayeux, abbot of the Mont from around 1055 to 1085. His suggestion is strengthened by the correspondence in dates between Renouf's abbacy and the fabrication of Pope John XIII's bull. Also see Jacques Hourlier, 'Le Mont Saint-Michel avant 966', in *Millénaire* 1, pp. 13–28; Hourlier, 'Sources écrites', pp. 128–29.

11 Jean Laporte, 'Gérard de Brogne', p. 164; Lemarignier, *Hommage*, p. 68: 'La Puissante Abbaye du Mont-Saint-Michel est également au premier rang des pionniers normands aux confins de la Bretagne.'

12 T. D. Wilson Smith, 'The Millenium of the Mont-Saint-Michel', *Downside Review*, 84 (1966), pp. 408–22, at p. 412.

neighboring communities and lordships; and second, with respect to the Rouen Normans, by no means destined to control the Mont and hardly in a position to do so at the time of the abbey's official refoundation. These two lines of inquiry, the local ties of the monks and the political range of Rouen, converge in the early 1030s when the Mont found itself in the middle of a quarrel between two cousins, Robert the Magnificent of Normandy and Alan III of Rennes. At the center of this dispute and caught between conflicting loyalties, the Mont demonstrates the predicament of an abbey whose patrimony cut across frontiers and alliances still forming in the wake of the disruptions of the ninth and tenth centuries.

Those frontiers, it must be emphasized, were by no means fixed and certain. Although evident to the editors of *Neustria Pia* and *Gallia Christiana* that Mont-Saint-Michel stood *in confinio Britonum ac Normannorum*, it would not have been clear to the inhabitants of the monastery in the tenth and eleventh centuries just where the boundaries between these two realms might lie.[13] The *Annals of Saint-Bertin* reports that Charles the Bald had ceded the Avranchin and Cotentin in 867 to his *fidelis* the Breton ruler Salomon.[14] Then in 933 according to Flodoard, King Ralph granted Rollo's son William Longsword 'the land of the Bretons situated on the seacoast', presumably those same *pagi* that Salomon had received some sixty years earlier.[15] Thus the Mont, along with the Avranchin and the Cotentin, officially passed from the Bretons to the Normans of the Seine in 933. These grants, however, were vague and ill-defined, involving lands no longer under royal control; their purpose was primarily to direct Breton and Norse aggression away from the Ile de France.[16]

Royal concessions as limited as the royal resources were of less concern to the Mont than the immediate conditions within the territory where the monks lived and held property. Unfortunately, no Mont-Saint-Michel *acta* survive from the pre-Viking period and only one charter exists in which lands explicitly described as having been lost during the Viking raids were regained.[17] It is not possible, therefore, to reconstruct the patrimony of the monastery before the invasion period. Indeed, very little is known about the early community at Mont-Saint-Michel. The primary source of information is the *Revelatio ecclesiae Sancti Michaelis*, dating perhaps from the ninth cen-

---

13 *Neustria*, p. 371; *Gallia*, 11, c. 510.
14 *Annals of St-Bertin*, p. 140; On these grants, see Smith, *Province and Empire*, pp. 86–87; Wendy Davies, *Small Worlds: The Village Community in Early Medieval Brittany* (Berkeley, 1988), pp. 19–20.
15 *Flodoard*, p. 55: 'Willelmus, princeps Nordmannorum, eidem regi se committit; cui etiam rex dat terram Brittonum in ora maritima sitam.'
16 Searle, 'Frankish Rivalries', pp. 208–09, has aptly described the king's grant to William Longsword in 933 as being as 'idle' as the grant of Brittany and Nantes to the Vikings of the Loire in the 920s.
17 *Cartulaire de Saint-Michel de l'Abbayette, prieuré de l'Abbaye du Mont-Saint-Michel*, ed. Bertrand de Broussillon (Paris, 1894), pp. 9–12, no. 1.

tury, which describes the environs of the Mont, the visions which the archangel Michael sent Autbert bishop of Avranches, the subsequent construction of a sanctuary around 708, and Autbert's acquisition of relics from Mont Gargano.[18] A final section states that Autbert also established twelve clerks to serve the church and gave the villages of Genêts and Huisnes to them from his diocese.[19]

Since the *Revelatio* calls the men whom Autbert established at Mont-Saint-Michel *clerici* rather than *monachi* or *canonici*, it seems likely that the Mont was inhabited before 966 by non-Benedictine monks practising a Breton form of asceticism rather than the decadent canons portrayed by the later *Introductio monachorum*.[20] The *Revelatio* author, following the reforms of Benedict of Aniane and Louis the Pious, would have hesitated to call non-Benedictines 'monks'. The single known head of the Mont between Autbert in the early eighth century and Mainard I in the second half of the tenth century was *abbas* Phinimontius *brito*, c. 865. This fact strengthens the case that monastic observance, albeit non-Benedictine, was practised there.[21] By depicting Mont-Saint-Michel's previous inhabitants as resisting reform, intent only on feasting, hunting and other pleasures, the author followed a convention which Benedictines often employed to justify their reform.[22] We have already seen it used to denigrate the community which William of Dijon's monks supplanted at Fécamp. Indeed, in the case of Mont-Saint-Michel, the author may have had a double axe to grind, since in his eyes the virtuous Benedictines had come from upper Normandy.

The first three centuries of religious life at the Mont, however, must remain largely shrouded in mystery. For the ninth and tenth centuries, it can only be said with some assurance that the territory in the vicinity of Mont-Saint-Michel sustained many hardships from conflicts between Bretons, Franks and Vikings; and that the community at the Mont would have suffered from the prolonged disruption. In the ninth century, Breton leaders

[18] *Revelatio ecclesiae Sancti Michaelis* in Le Roy, Appendix II, pp. 856–63. The earliest copy of the *Revelatio* that exists (Bibl. Avranches, ms. 211, fols 156r–210v) was transcribed by the monk Hervardus between 990 and 1015. For a description of ms. 211 and other work by Hervardus, see Alexander, pp. 224–27; François Avril, 'La Décoration des manuscrits au Mont Saint-Michel (XIe–XIIe siècles)', in *Millénaire*, 2, pp. 203–38, at pp. 204–05.

[19] Hourlier, 'Sources écrites', pp. 125–28, considers this last section an appendix added to the ninth-century text in the mid-tenth century. It seems possible, however, that the gifts attributed to Aubert in the *Revelatio* were indeed among the community's earliest possessions.

[20] Hourlier, 'Le Mont', pp. 22–28.

[21] *Descriptiones Terrae Sanctae ex saeculo VIII, IX, XII, et XV*, ed. Titus Tobler (Leipzig, 1874), pp. 97–98.

[22] *Introductio*, p. 868. For a comparable example of canons with lands along a sensitive frontier charged with decadence to justify a Benedictine take-over, see Hartigan, 'Reform'. On this subject more generally, see Lucien Musset, 'Recherches sur les communautés de clercs séculiers en Normandie au XIe siècle', *BSAN*, 55 (1961), pp. 5–38.

alternated between alliance and enmity toward the Franks as it suited their interests and intrigues.[23] In the early tenth century, the ravages of the Vikings forced many Bretons to flee into Francia or across the channel. When they returned in the 930s, rallied by Alan Twistedbeard and backed by King Athelstan of Wessex, they took their vengeance in blood.[24] But even after Alan had 'driven the Vikings out of all the Breton region' – undoubtedly an overstatement coming from the *Chronicle of Nantes* – peace did not follow the Breton homecoming.[25] Before Alan's death in mid-century, internal rivalry between houses, in particular between the counts of Nantes and Rennes, undermined hope for security in this region.[26] Outside intervention further exacerbated tensions as the counts of Anjou and Blois-Chartres attempted to profit from Brittany's disunity, and Vikings, especially those who had settled on the Loire, continued to make raids on Breton lands.[27]

If they knew that the king had given the Cotentin and Avranchin to the Vikings of Rouen in 933, territories which had been formerly ceded to Salomon, it is doubtful that Breton lords would have much cared. The reality of the situation in the early tenth century was a free-for-all in which Bretons, Franks and rival bands of Vikings all participated. Toponymic evidence shows that Bretons and Scandinavians both settled in the Cotentin and Avranchin.[28] Fighting between these groups stretched as far east as Caen during the

---

[23] Smith, *Province and Empire*, especially chapters 3 and 4; Davies, *Small Worlds*, pp. 7–28.

[24] Flodoard, p. 63: *La Chronique de Nantes*, ed. René Merlet (Paris, 1896), pp. 87–91. For a brief account, see Smith, *Province and Empire*, pp. 196–98.

[25] *Nantes*, p. 88: '. . . donec Alanus Barbatorta, Alani Magni nepos, surrexit et hos Normannos ab omni regione Britannica et a fluvio Ligeris, qui illis erat nutrimentum magnum, omnino depulsos dejecit'. Since Flodoard, p. 94, reports that Northmen attacked Brittany and captured Dol in 944, the *Chronicle of Nantes* must have overestimated Alan's success.

[26] Flodoard, p. 94, discusses discord between Berenger, count of Rennes, and Alan Twistedbeard. Also see Lemarignier, *Hommage*, p. 116; Arthur de la Borderie, *Essai sur la géographie féodale de la Bretagne* (Rennes, 1889), pp. 1–5; Guy Devailly, 'Les Dépendances bretonnes des abbayes normandes (Xe–XIIIe siècles)', in *Aspects du monachism*, pp. 115–24.

[27] *Nantes*, pp. 111–20; Richer, 2, pp. 278–97; Guillot, *Le Comte d'Anjou*, 1, pp. 8–12. Most recently on Anjou, see Bernard S. Bachrach, *Fulk Nerra, the Neo-Roman Consul*, 987–1040 (Berkeley, 1993).

[28] François de Beaurepaire, *Les Noms des communes et anciennes paroisses de la Manche* (Paris, 1986), especially pp. 42–48; Prentout, *Etude critique*, pp. 284–91. François de Beaurepaire notes that Anglo-Saxon elements in Norman placenames suggest the immigration of Vikings who had spent time in England. This conclusion is reinforced by Maylis Baylé's analysis of Norman romanesque sculpture which finds significant Anglo-Scandinavian elements in Norman capitals in the Cotentin. François de Beaurepaire, 'Les Noms d'Anglo-Saxons contenus dans la toponymie normande', *AN*, 10 (1960), pp. 307–16; François de Beaurepaire, 'Quelques Finales anglo-saxonnes dans la toponymie normande', *AN*, 13 (1963), pp. 219–36; Maylis Baylé, 'Interlace Patterns in Norman Romanesque Sculpture: Regional Groups and their Historical Background', *Anglo-Norman Studies*, 5 (1983), pp. 1–20.

first half of the tenth century, and by mid-century the Viking leader Harold of Bayeux had gained power in the Bessin.[29] Excavations at La Hague Dike likewise point to an entrenched Viking camp at the western tip of the Cherbourg peninsula.[30] Those Scandinavians who settled in the Cotentin in the ninth and tenth centuries, as well as those in the Bessin, would have had scant reason to consider the Vikings of Rouen as their overlords; the royal grants that declared these areas for the house of Rollo would have carried as little meaning for rival Vikings as for Bretons. It was up to Rollo's successors to collect.

The monks who accompanied Mainard I to Mont-Saint-Michel in 966 or thereabouts would have therefore encountered a challenging situation. Far from their protector in Rouen, in a contested area, they were located like the monks of Redon to their south on a border area lacking stability.[31] Their situation was also analogous to that of la Trinité, Vendôme, whose ties reached beyond Vendôme into Blois, Anjou and Beaugency.[32] It is possible that the house suffered at least initially from internal dissension as well, divided between the newcomers, perhaps around thirty monks, and the previous inhabitants of the Mont.[33] The *Introductio* certainly expects its readers to believe that the pre-existing community on the Mont had been hostile to Benedictine reform, but evidence indicates that the two groups co-existed.[34] Moreover, since Bretons continued to enter the monastery in the eleventh century, the community apparently reconciled Breton and Norman elements.

Mont-Saint-Michel's charters indicate that the ecclesiastical hierarchy of Rouen played little role in the abbey's affairs before the second decade of the eleventh century. The first charter which the archbishop or any bishop

---

[29] Flodoard, p. 50, note 5; Prentout, *Etude critique*, pp. 284–91. Lauer and Prentout both discuss the account Pierre le Baud composed at the beginning of the sixteenth century of the Battle of Caen in 931 (*Histoire de Bretagne*, Paris 1638). On Harold the Viking, see above, Chapter Four, note 69.

[30] Boüard, 'Camp retranché?'; Michel de Boüard, 'Le Hague-Dike', *Cahiers Archéologiques: fin de l'antiquité et moyen âge*, 8 (1956), pp. 117–45; Michel de Boüard, 'A Propos de la Datation du Hague-Dike', AN, 14 (1964), pp. 270–71.

[31] Davies, *Small Worlds*, pp. 27–28.

[32] Johnson, *Prayer, Patronage, and Power*, pp. 97–98.

[33] Le Roy, pp. 281–82, who cites the lost cartulary known as the *Livre Blanc* as one of his sources, numbers the group sent from Rouen to the Mont at thirty monks, including Maynard. On Le Roy, and his history of Mont-St-Michel, see F. Vandenbroucke, 'Dom Jean Huynes et Dom Thomas Le Roy, historiens Mauristes du Mont Saint-Michel', in *Millénaire*, 2, pp. 155–67. A list of monks, alive and dead, dated 996 to 1008, indicates that about fifty monks belonged to the community under the second abbot. Denis Grémont and Lin Donnat, 'Fleury, le Mont Saint-Michel et l'Angleterre à la fin du Xe et au début du XIe siècle à propos du manuscrit d'Orléans no. 127 (105)', in *Millénaire*, 1, pp. 751–93. Grémont and Donnat present the list on p. 783. On this list, also see Claude Simonnet, 'L'Enluminure dans les manuscrits normands', in *Trésors des abbayes*, pp. 103–62, at pp. 104–05.

[34] Lelegard, pp. 51–52; Dubois, 'Les Moines dans la société', p. 17.

within Rouen's archdiocese attested dates from c. 1015.[35] The bishops of Brittany and Maine, meanwhile, had witnessed and confirmed several of the Mont's *acta* by this time.[36] The monastic map of Normandy also accentuates Mont-Saint-Michel's distance from Rouen during the first decades of the eleventh century. Of the eight monasteries founded or refounded by 1025 in the lands by then considered Norman, only Mont-Saint-Michel stood west of the Touques River. This contrast cannot be seen as a legacy of pre-Viking conditions, since over twenty monasteries had existed beyond the Touques before the invasions.[37] The distribution of monastic property during the first three decades of the eleventh century reinforces the Mont's isolation, since the majority of lands which other houses held were located in upper Normandy or along the Seine.[38] All of Mont-Saint-Michel's Norman property, on the other hand, as late as the accession of William the Conqueror, fell west of Caen.

The map of Mont-Saint-Michel's possessions in 1035 illustrates that the community gained as much or more property in Brittany and Maine as in Normandy during the early years between its refoundation and the reign of William the Conqueror. Since the rich *fonds* of Mont-Saint-Michel were gutted during the Second World War, any study of Mont-Saint-Michel's patrimony during the tenth and early eleventh centuries must rely on the community's twelfth-century cartulary now at Avranches, and on copies of charters which survive at other archives and various *acta* which were edited before the war.[39] The cartulary was compiled under the authority of Robert of Torigny (1154–1186), an abbot from Bec who would not have been inclined to overlook the generosity of Normans when he had recorded the grants and agreements of Breton and Manceaux lords.[40] Indeed, the Norman bias of the cartulary is apparent in its organization, which places charters of Richard II, Gunnor, Robert the Magnificent, and William the Conqueror all before benefactions from other sources, several of which predate the Norman acts.[41]

---

35 Fauroux no. 16.
36 BN, nouv. acq. fr. 21821, f. 138rv; Bibl Avranches, ms. 210, fols. 47r–48r; Broussillon, *Abbayette*, nos. 1, 2; Bertrand de Broussillon, *Cartulaire de Saint-Victeur au Mans* (Paris, 1895), no. 4.
37 Laporte, 'Origines', pp. 25–41.
38 See the map of the property of ducal abbeys by 1035, and above Chapter Four.
39 I will limit citations to printed editions, except when published versions are difficult to find or differ significantly from the cartulary or from archive copies. For a description of the cartulary, see François Burckard, 'Chartes, cartulaires et archives des abbayes', in *Trésors des abbayes*, p. 75; Michel Bourgeois-Lechartier, 'A la Recherche du scriptorium de l'abbaye du Mont Saint-Michel', in *Millénaire*, 2, pp. 171–202.
40 On Robert of Torigny, see Dufief, pp. 101–26; Raymonde Foreville, 'Robert de Torigni et "Clio" ', in *Millénaire*, 2, pp. 141–53; Marjorie Chibnall, 'Orderic Vitalis and Robert of Torigni', in *Millénaire*, 2, pp. 133–39.
41 The cartulary begins with a copy of the *Revelatio* (fols. 5r–10r), followed by a copy of the *Introductio monachorum* (fols. 10r–17r), which is followed by a copy of Pope John

This arrangement, nevertheless, cannot hide the fact that over forty years elapsed between Mont-Saint-Michel's refoundation and its endowment by the counts of Rouen. In the meantime, the monks developed ties elsewhere.

Thirteen years after King Lothar's confirmation of the monastery's reformation, Conan count of Rennes presented the next extant charter in favor of the Mont, dated 990. Issued from Rennes, the act explains that Abbot Mainard I had sent two members of the community as *legatores* to Conan in Dol to approve his donation of four *villae* southeast of the Mont: Villamée, Lillèle, Passillé and Villeperdue.[42] This was only the first of many gifts from the counts of Rennes. In addition to his father's gifts, Conan's son Geoffrey granted several important properties to the Mont along the western side of the bay: the vill of Cancale with its adjacent port, the church of Saint Méloir des Ondes and the vill of Saint Benoît des Ondes, with all its pertaining lands.[43] Geoffrey's son Alan III was also a generous benefactor of the Mont, coming to the monastery to confirm his father's gifts and add his own, which included the vill of Roz sur Couesnon with the surrounding marsh, and Montrouault with half a mill. When one of his men entered the community as a monk, Alan granted the land of *Lavas* with its mill, property which the

XII's forged bull (fols. 17r–18r), and a copy of King Lothar's charter of 966 (fols. 18v–19r). A picture of Richard II appears on f. 19v, which is followed by: Fauroux no. 49 (fols. 20r–22v); Fauroux no. 47 (fols. 22v–23r); a picture of Gunnor (f. 23v); Fauroux no. 17 (fols. 24r–25r); a picture of Robert the Magnificent (f. 25v); Fauroux no. 73 (fols. 26r–27v); Fauroux 148 (fols. 27v–29r); Fauroux no. 111 (fols. 29v–30r); Fauroux 110 (fols 30r–31r); Fauroux no. 133 (fols. 30r–31r); Fauroux no. 76 (f. 32v); *Regesta* no. 208 (fols. 33r–34v). The charters which follow f. 34v are arranged fairly haphazardly, although the *acta* of certain priories tend to be grouped together. These charters range in date from the tenth century to the twelfth, and describe possessions throughout France, Italy, and England. Given Robert of Torigny's loyalties, the placement of Norman ducal charters foremost is understandable, but it nevertheless obscures the monastery's debt to non-Norman patrons during the early years after its refoundation.

42 Although this charter survives in several modern copies, it does not appear in Bibl. Avranches, ms. 210. Copies exist at: BN, nouv. acq. fr. 21821, f. 138rv = BN, nouv. acq. fr. 21821, f. 139rv = BN, ms. lat. 5430A, pp. 48–49 = BN, ms. lat. 10072, f. 3r = BN, coll. Moreau, 14, fols. 141r–143r. These copies differ in several respects from the version edited by Hyacinthe Morice, *Mémoires pour servir de preuves à l'histoire ecclésiastique et civile de Bretagne*, vol. 1 of 3 vols. (Paris, 1742–1746, rpt. 1974), cols. 350–51. I am following Dubois, 'Les Dépendances', p. 643, on the identification of these placenames.

43 Geoffrey's gifts are known only through a charter of his son: Bibl. Avranches, ms. 210, fols. 40r–42r. This charter also appears in BN, nouv. acq. fr. 21815, fols. 225rv = BN, coll. Moreau, 21, fols. 70r–74v = BN, coll. Moreau, 21, fols. 76r–79v. It is edited by Morice, cols. 379–81, but his version departs from the cartulary and the BN texts, especially with regard to placenames. Dubois, 'Les Dépendances', identifies *Cancavena* and *Semmeler* as Cancale and St Méloir des Ondes. François de Beaurepaire, 'Toponymie et évolution du peuplement sur le pourtour de la baie du Mont Saint-Michel', in *Millénaire*, 2, pp. 49–72, at p. 58, identifies *Landeguethoi* as St Benoît des Ondes.

new monk had held.[44] Both Conan and Geoffrey, moreover, are traditionally said to have been buried at the Mont, which suggests that the counts of Rennes intended Mont-Saint-Michel to become their family monastery and mausoleum.[45]

For three generations, therefore, the counts of Rennes acted as benefactors of Mont-Saint-Michel. And the lands which they gave gained in importance, so that by 1200, Villamée, Montrouault and Saint Méloir had developed into priories.[46] Other Breton lords followed the lead of the counts of Rennes, endowing and entering into transactions with the Mont. An individual named Grallon, for example, mortgaged his church at Poilley to Mont-Saint-Michel for four pounds of *denarii* sometime before 1009.[47] Later, probably because he could not clear the mortgage, Grallon gave up the church to the abbey and his wife offered the monks a cloak of very high quality. In exchange, the Mont was to provide them with refuge in the event of war and, should Grallon and his sons go into battle, they were to receive two horses, which they were to return intact. The monks, so a later agreement reveals, did not live up to their end of the bargain regarding the horses, so Grallon's sons resumed possession of the church. They returned it in the late 1020s, however, in exchange for eight pounds of *denarii* and a confirmation that they could still find refuge at the monastery should war break out.[48] This example of Mont-Saint-Michel's relations with Grallon and his sons affirms that lay involvement with the monks went far beyond pious gifts *ad succurrendum*. It would be difficult to ask for a better illustration of Mont-Saint-Michel's role in local Breton society over two generations.

Guy Devailly, however, attaches long-range political goals to Breton patronage, arguing that the Breton counts endowed the Mont because they sought the support of the Norman dukes against their rivals, the counts of

[44] Bibl. Avranches, ms. 210, fols. 40r–42r. Guillotin de Corson, *Pouillé historique*, 2, p. 524, identifies *villa Bohel* as Roz sur Couesnon; Dubois, 'Les Dépendances', p. 644, identifies *Mons Rohalt* as Montrouault; *Lavas* is unidentified, but it was located in the commune of Pleine-Fougères.

[45] *Gallia*, 11, c. 514; Le Roy, p. 288. Gui Alexis Lobineau, *Histoire de Bretagne*, vol. 1 of 2 vols. (Paris, 1707), pp. 85–86, discusses the possibility of Conan having been carried from the battlefield of Conquéreuil and taken to Mont-St-Michel to be buried 'as he had ordered before his death'. Le Roy cites his source as Bertran of Argentré, whom Lobineau praises as a reliable historian. Since Bertran followed and was guided by Pierre le Baud, he must have composed his history between c. 1550 and 1647, the date of Le Roy's entry. On the battle of Conquereuil in 982, see Bachrach, *Fulk Nerra*, pp. 41–45.

[46] Dubois, 'Les Dépendances', p. 660.

[47] Bibl. Avranches, ms. 210, fols. 47r–48r = BN, ms. lat. 5430A, pp. 49–50 and 170–71 = BN, coll. Moreau, 40, fols. 196r–197v and 231r–232v. The contents of this charter are summarised by Laporte, 'Abbaye', p. 73; Tabuteau, *Transfers*, p. 51.

[48] Bibl. Avranches, ms. 210, fols. 47r–48r: '. . . et si necessitas WERRE nobis evenerit, habeamus refugium ad sanctam Michaelem'.

[49] Devailly, pp. 118–22.

Nantes.[49] The evidence that Conan sought an alliance with Richard I, however, is very slim.[50] It is unlikely that Norse allies supported Rennes during the first battle of Conquéreuil against the counts of Nantes and Anjou in 982.[51] And Richer makes it clear that the Vikings supporting Conan in the second battle of Conquéreuil ten years later came from the Loire rather than the Seine.[52] As for Geoffrey, who did ally with the Rouen Normans, if he had sought to win their lord's favor through monastic patronage, a gift to Fécamp or Saint Ouen in upper Normandy would have been more persuasive.

In fact, the Breton counts' generosity to Mont-Saint-Michel needs no elaborate explanations. To the counts of Rennes and to their men, the Mont was a nearby community in an area where, as Devailly himself explains, monasteries were few and poor.[53] It is not surprising that they turned their favor toward this house; to ascribe Breton patronage to political incentive introduces unnecessary complexity into the situation. Was Rolland, a monk of Mont-Saint-Michel, chosen to be bishop of Dol at the beginning of the eleventh century in order to please Duke Richard II?[54] It seems unlikely. Moreover, Bretons continued to visit the community, endow it and seek its prayers and protection, regardless of the state of affairs between Rennes and Rouen. To the counts of Rennes as well as to other Bretons in the vicinity, the community represented a major landlord and a religious center – not a Norman outpost or a means to curry Rouen's support.

Brittany was not the only area outside of the boundaries of later Normandy in which the Mont acquired property. As the map of its possessions in 1035 indicates, the monks also gained interests south-east of the abbey. One of the earliest extant charters to the Mont after its refoundation is a grant from Mayeul abbot of Cluny in which he presents to the monks lands in the *villa* of Le Mortier, just outside of Tours.[55] A condition was written into the agreement that they would hold this property only 'as long as the monks live according to the rule of Saint Benedict'.[56] This extra clause was perhaps

---

[50] Lot, *Derniers*, pp. 110, 346–57. Lot argued that Richard I's war in the 960s against Theobald of Blois-Chartres concerned affairs in Brittany, but the story in *Nantes*, pp. 111–12, of the 'palus magnus, in ore Ligeris fixus, metum Normannis faciens', only makes sense if the Vikings who attacked Nantes in 960 were based on the Loire (*Ligeris*) rather than the Seine. Richard I did not launch any major expeditions against Brittany. See P. Chesnel, *Le Cotentin et l'Avranchin sous les ducs de Normandie (911–1204)* (Caen, 1912), pp. 82–83.

[51] *Nantes*, pp. 118–19.

[52] Richer, 2, pp. 280–83: 'Ad alterum vero per Ligerim classes Piratarum adhibet', and note 1, p. 282.

[53] Devailly, p. 116.

[54] *Gallia*, 14, col. 1044.

[55] Bibl. Avranches, ms. 210, f. 55rv. The date of this act poses some difficulty since it claims to be written in the forty-first year of King Lothar's reign, which would be 994, yet Mayeul, who appears as abbot in the text, was no longer active after 991. Dubois, 'Les dépendances', pp. 640–41, discusses this problem.

[56] Bibl. Avranches, ms. 210, f. 55rv: '. . . ut quam diu ipsi monachi secundum regulam

deemed critical in the case of the Mont, supporting the view that the original community had been non-Benedictine. As Mayeul's refusal to send monks to Fécamp indicates, his confidence in monastic reforms in the lands of former Neustria was not high.

Le Mortier was the abbey's most distant holding before 1066. The remainder of its lands to the south-east lay in the county of Maine, a principality that had emerged in the tenth century. It was in this area that Abbot Mainard I's successor Mainard II (991–1009) requested that former lands lost during the Viking incursions be restored, namely eight *villae* which became the core foundation for the priory of l'Abbayette.[57] The concession was made by a certain Ivo, whose references to his parents, Fulk and Rothaïs, and his uncles, Bishop Sigefridus and William, have caused a great deal of consternation among genealogists of the Bellême clan. The most recent study of the Bellêmes argues convincingly that Ivo of l'Abbayette was the nephew of Ivo I of Bellême.[58] Placing the question of Ivo's identity aside, however, this charter underlines Mainard II's willingness to travel some distance to recover the monastery's properties, since the act, issued from Fresnay and dated by Broussillon to 997, describes him approaching Ivo with this request, and it bears the abbot's cross.[59]

Mainard II's efforts were well-rewarded. The priory of l'Abbayette, some forty-two kilometers from Mont-Saint-Michel, became an important overnight stop for pilgrims on their way to the Mont, and it attracted many gifts from its neighbors.[60] On occasion, the same piece of property could be the subject of a series of transactions. For example, a short time after he had sought out Ivo, Mainard II approached an individual named Guy, requesting that he sell Mont-Saint-Michel two-thirds of the church of Saint Berthevin, southeast of l'Abbayette, which his parents had mortgaged to the abbey.[61] Guy admitted that he had taken the property, along with various other

---

sancti Benedicti regulariter uixerint, teneant, et possideant'. Since this charter is entitled 'De vineis Turonis' in the cartulary, it can be concluded that the monks had planted vineyards on these lands near Tours by the mid-twelfth century.

57 Broussillon, *Abbayette*, pp. 9–12, no. 1.

58 Du Motey, *Origines*, pp. 119–20, 301, assumes that Ivo the benefactor of Mont-St-Michel was the same man as Ivo I of Bellême. This view is shared by Laporte, 'Séries', p. 271. Broussillon, however, in his introduction to *Abbayette*, dissociates Ivo of l'Abbayette from the Bellême family. White, 'First House', Appendix B, pp. 91–95, concurs, 'It is necessary to abandon the attempt to make the founder of l'Abbayette a member of the House of Bellême.' On the other hand, Boussard, 'Seigneurie', pp. 45–46, note 2, suggests that Ivo the benefactor of Mont-St-Michel might have been the nephew of Ivo of Bellême, and this is the suggestion that Louise, *Bellême*, 1, pp. 231–35, has confirmed in his recent work.

59 Broussillon, *Abbeyette*, no. 1, has also published a facsimile of the original charter.

60 Broussillon, *Abbayette*, p. 5; Broussillon also edits the subsequent gifts to this priory in *Abbayette*.

61 Broussillon, *Abbayette*, no. 2. Dubois, 'Les dépendances', p. 642, identifies the church of *Centrannis* as St Berthevin.

beneficia, after the death of his parents, and he agreed to sell them back to the monks.[62] Then, about fifteen years later, Guy's son-in-law made the same agreement, to sell two-thirds of the church of Saint Berthevin to Mont-Saint-Michel, thereby demonstrating that it had again been appropriated by the family.[63] The son-in-law settled for an annual fee of eight *denarii*, to be received at the feast of Saint Denis, and the monks proceeded to acquire several other churches in the vicinity in the course of the eleventh and twelfth centuries.[64]

The advantage of a compromise settlement, such as Guy's son-in-law's, meant that neither party was left empty-handed. Relations between monks and specific families could be very tricky over generations since the sons and heirs would often contest a gift of their ancestors. And yet, those same sons were the ones most likely to endow the monastery themselves further down the line, since patronage to a certain abbey tended to run in the family.[65] The monks would not wish to alienate the family members of a benefactor, instead preferring mutual concession to confrontation. Barbara Rosenwein has discussed how land, given and taken over generations, forged a continuing chain of relationships between the monks and a lay family; appropriation should not simply be seen in the context of lay rapacity.[66] The church of Saint Berthevin was the focus of an ongoing relationship between the monks of Mont-Saint-Michel and one family, an association initiated by Guy's parents which set the stage for later acquisitions and relations in this area during the eleventh and twelfth centuries.[67]

Mont-Saint-Michel also acquired considerable interests in the area around Le Mans, especially during the reign of Hugh III, count of Maine from 992 to 1015.[68] Thus Ralph, *vicomte* of Maine, gave a close of vineyards outside Le Mans to the monks around 994,[69] and Count Hugh added four more vineyards[70]

---

[62] Unfortunately, the charter does not quote the price.

[63] Broussillon, *Abbayette*, no. 3.

[64] Dubois, 'Les Dépendances', p. 643.

[65] For a discussion of this problem in Burgundy, see Bouchard, *Sword, Miter, and Cloister*, pp. 150–52; 209–17. Stephen White's work on Marmoutier's settlement of disputes with laymen in eleventh-century western France also underlines the importance of compromise and reciprocity in assuring the security of agreements. Stephen D. White, 'Pactum . . . *Legem Vincit et Amor Judicium*: The Settlement of Disputes by Compromise in Eleventh-Century Western France', *The American Journal of Legal History*, 22 (1978), pp. 281–308. This subject is placed in a broader context by Frederic L. Cheyette, '*Suum cuique tribuere*', *French Historical Studies*, 6 (1970), pp. 287–99.

[66] Rosenwein, *Neighbor*, pp. 49–77.

[67] Dubois, 'Les Dépendances', pp. 642–43, describes later possessions in the neighborhood of St Berthevin.

[68] Robert Latouche, *Histoire du comté du Maine pendant le Xe et le XIe siècle* (Paris, 1910), pp. 14–21. Latouche also presents a catalogue of acts of the counts of Maine, which summarises their gifts to Mont-St-Michel, pp. 140–42.

[69] Broussillon, *Saint-Victeur au Mans*, no. 1.

[70] Broussillon, *Saint-Victeur au Mans*, no. 2.

and three mills[71] to their possessions in the area between 995 and 1015. Ralph's charter makes it clear that he had journeyed to the abbey himself with his wife and son to make his offering on the altar of Saint Michael. On his return, he secured Hugh's consent and ordered that the charter be written. Count Hugh's grant of three mills took place at the request of Hugh son of Hebrannus who held them of the count, on the condition that this Hugh son of Hebrannus would be paid by the monks three *solidi* each year at the festival of Saint John the Baptist. It is difficult to gauge the value of coin at this time, but scholars have estimated three *solidi* as the value of an ox in ninth-century Brittany, and horses in early eleventh-century Normandy valued from two or three pounds up to ten – ten pounds for a 'cheval de luxe'.[72] Three *solidi* would therefore seem a low price for three mills, which suggests that the money, delivered each year by the monks to Hugh son of Hebrannus, had symbolic value as well.

A similar conclusion should be derived regarding the eight *denarii* which Guy's son-in-law received annually for giving up his claim to the church of Saint Berthevin. Eight *denarii* was worth about the price of a pig, and Grallon's charter indicates that a church could be worth a great deal more.[73] The money these men received from the monks, no doubt publicly, on a certain feast day would have reaffirmed each year their relationship with the monastery. It assured the recipient that he was still associated with the original transaction and thereby included in the spiritual benefits enjoyed by patrons of the Mont. And it reminded the lay community of these facts as well, enhancing his prestige and perhaps prompting more gifts from his neighbors.

These examples make it clear that it would be a mistake to view the monks at Mont-Saint-Michel as passive recipients of non-Norman patronage. They sought out patrons beyond the duchy and were persistent in keeping the property they acquired and maintaining relationships with patrons and their families. Once they established a foothold in one area, the monks endeavored to accumulate more lands nearby. For instance, in 1014 Abbot Hildebert (1009–1023) approached the generous Hugh III of Maine, expressly asking that he donate or sell at a just price some land in the vicinity of property which they had already received.[74] The count agreed to give the monks the land of Voivres, a bit south-west of Le Mans, and he came personally to the Mont to place this gift on the altar. The monastery's holdings around Le Mans continued to grow. Sometime between 1033 and 1040,

---

71 Broussillon, *Saint-Victeur au Mans*, no. 3.
72 Davies, *Small Worlds*, p. 57; Musset, 'La vie économique', p. 71.
73 Davies, *Small Worlds*, p. 57.
74 Broussillon, *Saint-Victeur au Mans*, no. 4: 'Adiit sepe nostram presentiam Heldebertus abbas . . . et aliqui sub eo degentes monachi, petentes ut in vicino earum rerum quas in pago Cenomannico tam a nobis quam etiam ab aliis possident, aliquam bene utilem terram vel precio quanto dignum esset eis venderem, vel . . . donarem'.

Mont-Saint-Michel received more vineyards in the area,[75] and in 1040, the monks gained a former monastery, Saint Victeur, which then flourished as a priory of the Mont.[76]

The accumulation of lands in a given area, followed by the establishment of a nearby priory, was a pattern common among monasteries. Upper Norman abbeys, as noted in the previous chapter, pursued this policy in lower Normandy. Obviously, there were administrative advantages in having a priory in the midst of their lands to watch over the tenants and collect revenues.[77] It is important to note, however, that in the case of Mont-Saint-Michel, the first priories, indeed the first seeds of its patrimony, were planted outside of Normandy. The view from the Mont, therefore, would have naturally been oriented more toward its holdings and its commitments in Brittany and Maine than toward Rouen, at least through the first decades of the eleventh century.

This was especially the case because Mont-Saint-Michel's ecclesiastical ties with Rouen were very weak during this period. Although the *Revelatio* acknowledged Autbert bishop of Avranches as the monastery's original founder, and although the Mont stood technically within the boundaries of the archdiocese of Rouen, the Viking invasions had weakened the ecclesiastical chain of command and the west was slowest to recover. Episcopal lists in the *Gallia Christiana* for the diocese of Avranches show a gap for over a century, from 862 to 990,[78] and the cathedral church of Avranches did not regain its lands until Duke Richard II's reign.[79] The diocese of Coutances, we are told, was 'devoid of Christians' in the ninth and tenth centuries, the church 'crushed by pagan thieves and the pollution of idolatry'.[80] Although later writers no doubt indulged in hyperbole, the residence of five bishops of

---

[75] Broussillon, *Saint-Victeur au Mans*, no. 5; Broussillon, *Abbayette*, no. 4.

[76] Broussillon, *Saint-Victeur au Mans*, nos. 6 and 7; *Gallia*, 11, *Instr.* cols. 106–07. Dubois, 'Les Moines dans la société', pp. 32–33, discusses the three different versions of this charter.

[77] Dubois, 'Les Dépendances', pp. 659–60.

[78] *Gallia*, 11, c. 474. Between Bishops Waltbertus and Norgotus, the *Gallia Christiana* editors write: 'Aliquot adhuc praesulum Abrincensium nomenclatura seculo toto deficit.'

[79] Fauroux, p. 24, note 24, from a *pancarte*, c. 1060–1066.

[80] *De statu hujus (Constantiensis) ecclesiae ab anno 836 ad 1093*, in *Gallia*, 11, *Instr.* cols. 217–24, at c. 217. On this source, see John Le Patourel, 'Geoffrey of Montbray, Bishop of Coutances, 1049–1093', *EHR*, 59 (1944), pp. 129–61, specifically pp. 130–39. The traditional story of the sufferings of the church of Coutances during the Viking invasions is one of gloom and doom. According to Toustain de Billy, for example, 'Coutances et tout le Cotentin étant désoleés, de sorte qu'il n'y avait ni ville, ni église, ni maison, ni habitants autres que des païens.' René Toustain de Billy, *Histoire ecclésiastique du diocèse de Coutances* (Rouen, 1874), 1, p. 94. A similar vision of desolation is found in E. A. Pigeon, *Histoire de la cathédrale de Coutances* (Coutances, 1876), pp. 16–34. Some revision of this extreme view is in order. Musset, 'Monachisme d'époque franque', pp. 67–71, has shown that even in the Cotentin the memory of ruined abbeys remained active.

Coutances in a row at Rouen, from Rollo's time until 1025, attests to the disruption of ecclesiastical life in the west.[81]

No charters recall any gifts to Mont-Saint-Michel by Richard I; even Dudo does not elaborate beyond the initial restoration in 966. The first indication that the Norman duke intended to assert his authority over the community appeared in 1009, when Richard II relieved Mainard II of his position as abbot and replaced him with Hildebert, taking the unusual precaution of having a charter drawn up to confirm the appointment.[82] Laporte argues that the formality of the 1009 charter 'leads readily to the conclusion that its goal was to impose on the monks an abbot whom they did not want'.[83] After almost half a century, it would not be surprising for the monks to resist Richard II's intervention; and their desire to elect an abbot freely remained a point of contention between the monks of Mont-Saint-Michel and the counts of Rouen into the twelfth century.[84]

Richard II's decision to assume an active role at Mont-Saint-Michel occurred subsequent to his alliance with Geoffrey count of Rennes, a pact of friendship and aid sealed by their double marriage to each other's sister. According to William of Jumièges, the weddings appropriately enough took place at Mont-Saint-Michel.[85] In 1008, Count Geoffrey left on a pilgrimage during which he died and his two sons were raised in the court of their uncle, Richard II. It was therefore in the absence of the count of Rennes – indeed, just one year after Geoffrey's departure that Richard II decided it was time to take a hand in the affairs of the monks at Mont-Saint-Michel. Richard's charter justifies Mainard II's replacement on the grounds that he was too old to perform his duties any longer, but it could be that Mainard II no longer enjoyed the favor of the Norman duke.[86] The timing of the abbot's deposition suggests that Richard chose to act in 1009 precisely because the count of Rennes was out of the picture.

It was also in this context, during the years while Count Geoffrey's heirs remained under the guardianship of the Norman duke, that Dudo composed his work. Brittany, according to Dudo, had been under Norman authority from the origins of the duchy, and the chronicler describes William Longsword invading the Breton territory to suppress a rebellion.[87] Thus the

81 De statu, cols. 217–18.
82 Fauroux no. 12.
83 Laporte, 'Abbaye', p. 67.
84 Laporte, 'Abbaye', pp. 76–80; Dufief, pp. 81–101.
85 Jumièges, GND, 2, pp. 14–15, 28–29. Lemarignier, Hommage, pp. 116–17, following Arthur de La Borderie and Jacques Flach, dates the alliance between the counts of Rennes and Rouen to 996. David Douglas, 'Some Problems of Early Norman Chronology', EHR, 65 (1950), pp. 289–303, discusses the dates of the two sets of marriages.
86 Fauroux no. 12, p. 86: '. . . pastoralis et enim curam sollicitudinis quam idem memorabilis senex proficere nequit viribus propriis, subrogati sibi laudabiliter exposcit complere adjutorio fratris'. Laporte, 'Abbaye', p. 69.
87 Dudo, pp. 183–85.

view of Brittany as a land to reconquer was conceived, and Dudo has the Bretons crushed under Longsword's righteous fury and begging the Norman leader to regard them as 'a conscientious lord regards his wayward servants'.[88] But as we have seen, Dudo tailored his account of the Norman past to please his audience; his description of Brittany's subjugation to Rouen reflected the political ambitions of Richard II rather than an accurate appraisal of any raids William Longsword might have launched against the Bretons. There is no reason to deny the possibility of Rollo or William Longsword attacking the Breton coast. The *Chronicle of Nantes* very clearly identifies the diabolical Vikings who arrived from Rouen by boat and 'devastated all Brittany' in 919, joining their brothers from the Loire in the rampage.[89] The Rouen Normans would have come to Brittany, however, not on a campaign of reconquest as Dudo paints it, but with the same ruthless opportunism as they struck the Beauvaisis and the Amiénois.[90]

The *Introductio monachorum* borrows Dudo's account of unfaithful Bretons rebelling against their proper Norman lords, and it also accepts his assertion that Rollo endowed Mont-Saint-Michel immediately after his conversion to Christianity.[91] Historians have generally rejected Dudo's description of Rollo's patronage to the Mont, especially given the limits of the Viking lord's authority.[92] However, the contention that William Longsword gave the monastery lands which a charter of Richard II purports to return is usually accepted.[93] Perhaps Longsword did make a donation or confirm the community's lands, but the scenario seems improbable. One imagines that the inhabitants of the Mont, most likely Bretons themselves, would have been more inclined to flee from William Longsword and his band raiding the Breton shores than ask him for favors. Moreover, the charter itself does not

---

88 Dudo, p. 185: 'Videntes autem Berengerus et Alannus caeterique Britones, quod non sufficerent nec praevalerent adversus Willelmum, miserunt ad eum verbis deprecativis legatum: "Patri tuo obedienter servivimus, tibique incumbentes famulari cupimus. Ne despicias nos, quaesumus, neque abomineris servitium nostrum ullatenus; sed respice nos, ut servos offensos pius dominus".'

89 *Nantes*, pp. 81–82, note 1: 'Tunc ipsi Normanni, viri diabolici crudelissimique et perversi homines, primum Franciam aggredientes, totam provinciam Rothomagensium in dominicatu suo retinuerunt et Karolo stulto abstulerunt. Deinde, cum ingenti navium classe per mare Oceanum navigantes, totam Britanniam devastarunt.' Also see Searle, *Predatory Kinship*, p. 71.

90 Flodoard, pp. 29–30. The medallion or coin found at Mont-St-Michel, with the legend that reads + VVILIEM DU + IRB, is too ambiguous to accept as corroboration of Dudo's version. Michael Dolley and Jacques Yvon, 'A Group of Tenth-Century Coins Found at Mont-Saint-Michel', *The British Numismatic Journal*, 40 (1971), pp. 1–16; Searle, 'Frankish Rivalries', p. 209.

91 *Introductio*, pp. 866–67; Dudo, pp. 170–71.

92 Prentout, *Etude critique*, pp. 198–200; Douglas, 'Rollo', p. 433. Laporte, 'Abbaye', p. 55, suggests that it might be more than just a legend.

93 Fauroux no. 49; Bates, *1066*, p. 12; Laporte, 'Abbaye', p. 56. Hourlier, 'Le Mont', pp. 26–27, bases his argument for the redating of the last section of the *Revelatio* on this reference to William Longsword's gifts.

inspire confidence, existing only as a twelfth-century copy with Longsword's alleged gifts immediately followed by a reference to Pope John XIII's forged bull.[94]

The earliest Norman benefactor of Mont-Saint-Michel of whom we can be certain was not a son of Rollo's line at all, but rather his grandson's wife.[95] In 1015 Richard II made it known that the Duchess Gunnor had decided to give the monks at Mont-Saint-Michel two pieces of property southwest of Caen which she had received in dower from her husband, Richard I.[96] Gunnor's role in the restoration of the church of Coutances attests to her commitment to the recovery of ecclesiastical life in the west.[97] And Gunnor, coming from a rival Viking clan of the Cotentin, would have been more likely than her husband to be familiar with the Mont, its history as a place of religion and its spectacular location. Richard I's union with Gunnor was an opportunity for the Norman leader from Rouen to unite his family in kinship with Gunnor's.[98] His refoundation of Mont-Saint-Michel should be seen in a similar light. By sending Benedictine monks from upper Normandy to the Mont, perhaps even at Gunnor's prompting, Richard I laid a cornerstone for his realm. It was a tentative step, neither inevitable nor definitive. Like his alliance with Gunnor's people, there was no assurance of success. It would therefore be more accurate to view Richard I's implantation of Benedictine monks at Mont-Saint-Michel as a signal of his aspirations for, rather than his dominance over, this monastery.

Mont-Saint-Michel's only other Norman patron around 1015 was a Robert *comes*, the first count of Mortain, who granted the monastery his property of Tissy, just north of the Mont.[99] This Robert was an illegitimate

94 This charter is discussed in greater detail by Lemarignier, *Etude sur les privilèges*, pp. 264–66.

95 Fauroux no. 17.

96 Bretteville sur Odon and Domjean. Searle, *Predatory Kinship*, p. 295, note 7, suggests that the charter, the earliest copy of which dates from the twelfth century, might have confused dower and dowry. It is also possible that Richard I gave Gunnor lands in the Bessin over which he had a theoretical claim, but in an area where her family in fact had practical control – thus, the marriage portion would represent an amicable solution. This is no more than speculation, but the subsequent gift of these lands to Mont-St-Michel in that case would have been most appropriate. In any event, as Searle notes, the grant of these properties indicates that the Normans from Rouen toward the end of the tenth century claimed possession over lands in central Normandy. Henri Navel, 'Les Vavassories du Mont-Saint-Michel à Bretteville-sur-Odon et Verson (Calvados)', BSAN, 45 (1937), pp. 137–65, and Carabie, *Propriété foncière*, 1, pp. 25–146, have subjected the properties of Bretteville and Verson (given to Mont-St-Michel by Richard II, Fauroux no. 47) to careful analysis; they argue that these possessions attest to the continuity of manorial institutions, under different masters, from the Carolingian to the Norman ducal period.

97 *De statu*, c. 218; Fauroux, no. 214, p. 406.

98 Searle, *Predatory Kinship*, pp. 61–67; 87–90; 25.

99 Fauroux no. 16.

son of Richard I; the latter probably hoped that his son's presence at Mortain would help secure this corner of the province.[100] But the earliest counts of Mortain proved unreliable at best. Robert seized several properties from the Mont, those same *villulae* which the monks claimed to have received from William Longsword, and his son Richard fled to England after having become embroiled in a conspiracy against Richard II.[101] William Werlenc, the next count of Mortain, was summarily deprived of the county by William the Conqueror and replaced by the duke's half-brother circa 1055.[102] If Richard I had intended the count of Mortain to bolster his authority in the west, the brace proved unsteady for over half a century.

In the years following his confirmation of Robert of Mortain's donation of Tissy, Richard II added a nearby *villa* to Mont-Saint-Michel's holdings in the Bessin and gave the community several lands along the west coast; he also reconfirmed Gunnor's gifts.[103] If Richard I had granted Mont-Saint-Michel any property in the past, one would expect Richard II to have sanctioned his father's benefactions, at the very least when he confirmed his mother's gifts to the Mont. But no mention is made of Richard I providing any lands to this community he is said to have refounded. Richard I's want of patronage toward Mont-Saint-Michel suggests that whatever theoretical rights he claimed as count, his effective power circa 966 had not stretched so far from Rouen. For Richard II, on the other hand, thanks to the increased stability of his rule, his mother's connections, his alliance with the count of Rennes and the latter's convenient departure on pilgrimage, the monastery on the Mont appeared within range of more active intervention, as attested by his appointment of Hildebert and his subsequent benefactions.

The sequence of abbots, however, becomes muddled after Hildebert's reign. The *Annals* of Mont-Saint-Michel contradict each other regarding the order and even the existence of certain abbots.[104] The most likely chain of events is that when Hildebert died in 1023, the monks elected a successor whom the duke rejected. Instead, Richard II placed Thierry, a disciple of William of Dijon and abbot of Jumièges, in charge of the community, perhaps as *custos*. And the monks in reaction chose Almod from Maine as their head. The community of Mont-Saint-Michel therefore rejected Richard II's first clear attempt to bring their monastery within the circle of Fécamp reform.

---

[100] Cassandra Potts, 'The Earliest Norman Counts Revisited: The Lords of Mortain', *Haskins Society Journal*, 4 (1993), pp. 23–35, at p. 32.

[101] Fauroux no. 49; Potts, 'Counts Revisited'.

[102] Orderic, 2, p. 312 and 4, p. 98; Jumièges, GND, 2, pp. 126–27; Searle, *Predatory Kinship*, pp. 222–25. William's half-brother, Robert of Mortain, proved a stauncher ally to both the duke and the monastery of Mont-St-Michel, claiming in one charter, in fact, to have carried St Michael's banner into battle. *The Cartulary of St. Michael's Mount*, ed. P. L. Hull (Torquay, 1962), no. 3.

[103] Fauroux nos. 47, 49.

[104] Laporte, 'Séries', pp. 271–73. The confusion in the *Annals* is reflected in *Gallia*, 11, cols. 514–15.

And during Almod's abbacy Mont-Saint-Michel stood in precarious balance between Brittany and Normandy.

The only source for Robert the Magnificent's Breton war in the 1030s is William of Jumièges, and his account is not impartial. Jumièges echoes Dudo in describing Alan III, Count Geoffrey's heir, as carried away with arrogance, renouncing the service he owed the duke.[105] From the point of view of Brittany however, the war that followed was an effort by Alan of Rennes to assume his father's inheritance and resist Norman encroachment. The castle of Chérrueix which Robert constructed during this conflict lay within later Breton territory, so the Couesnon River was not yet seen as a demarcation between the two realms. Both princes no doubt intended to seize whatever territory they could; both would have sought to hold the abbey in peril of the sea.

Mont-Saint-Michel's allegiance during this conflict apparently lay with the house of Rennes. In 1030 Count Alan came to the Mont to confirm his father's donations and add gifts of his own. The monastery also received four more villages south-west of Dol during this period.[106] And in 1032, Almod approached Count Alan, requesting that he restore two churches and some property which had been usurped in the disruption.[107] These were timely benefactions of Breton property from the Breton lord to Mont-Saint-Michel. Moreover, Duke Robert's actions immediately after the war confirm where the community's loyalties had lain. After receiving Alan's homage at the Mont, he sent Almod packing up north to Cerisy and gave the monastery a new abbot, Suppo, another disciple of William of Dijon. Robert then granted the Mont several properties in the Cotentin, strengthening its ties to Normandy.[108]

Since Almod's roots lay in Maine, his readiness to ally with the count of Rennes might have been influenced by Alan III's assistance to Herbert of Maine against Fulk Nerra and the bishop of Le Mans in 1027.[109] But more important was the fact that the community had in the sixty-odd years since its refoundation developed stronger ties and interests in Brittany and Maine than in Normandy. Seen both in the context of the immediate local concerns of the community, and from the point of view of Rouen, still more distant

---

[105] Jumièges, GND, 2, pp. 56–59.
[106] Bibl. Avranches, ms. 210, fols. 45r–46r; BN, nouv. acq. fr. 21815, fols. 226v–227r. Morice, cols. 361–62, provides an extremely condensed copy of this act. See Laporte, 'Abbaye', p. 73; Michel Mollat, 'La Seigneurie maritime du Mont Saint-Michel', in *Millénaire*, 2, pp. 73–88, at p. 76. Three of the villages were in the parish of Miniac: *Tretgkented*, Kaibesgel and *Ros*; the other, in that of Mothoon: *Kainotker*. I have not been able to locate the latter parish.
[107] Bibl. Avranches, ms. 210, fols. 46r–47r; BN, coll. Moreau, 21, fols. 207r–209r and fols. 212r–214r. Morice, cols. 372–73, presents a condensed version of this charter.
[108] Fauroux nos. 65, 73, 76.
[109] Latouche, pp. 24, 28, note 3. Also see Bachrach, *Fulk Nerra*, pp. 188–89.

than Rennes in the third decade of the eleventh century, the Mont's alliance with Alan III made sense.

After the war, tensions persisted at Mont-Saint-Michel between the 'Fécampois' and the 'Montois' factions, that is between members of the community who supported Norman and specifically Fécamp influence, and those who resented what they perceived as encroachment of their liberties. Hostility within the monastery increased during the reign of Suppo whose ties with Fécamp were close. A kinsman of William of Dijon, Suppo had been born in Italy and was the abbot of Frutturia, William of Dijon's foundation in northern Italy, before coming to Normandy.[110] To Mont-Saint-Michel he brought many relics, books and ornaments. During his abbacy, the monastery gained considerable property.[111] Yet in 1048, faced with bitter opposition, Suppo resigned his office and returned to Frutturia.[112]

Duke William immediately placed another Fécamp monk, Ralph of Beau-

---

[110] Neustria, pp. 384–85; Gallia, 11, c. 515; Laporte, 'Séries', pp. 273–74; Laporte, 'Abbaye', pp. 74–76; Alexander, pp. 11–13.

[111] See the map of Mont-St-Michel's acquisitions, 1035–1066. During Suppo's abbacy, Mont-St-Michel acquired from William the Conqueror the islands of Serc and Aurigny in exchange for half of Guernsey: Fauroux no. 111, 1035–1048. The monastery also received La Croix Avranchin (canton St James) and its dependences, Villiers le Pré (canton St James), Ballant (canton Pontorson, commune Vessey), St Georges (placename disappeared, but canton St James), and three carrucates at Jersey with the rights attached of toll and usufruct from an individual named Adelelmus: Fauroux no. 110, 1037–1046. In Maine, the abbey acquired the monastery of St Victeur from Rainaldus, miles, and his mother Hersende (Broussillon, St-Victeur au Mans nos. 6 and 7, with a partial facsimile of the original = Gallia, 11, Instr. c. 106, 1040) as well as five arpents of vineyards nearby, from Odo and his wife (Broussillon, St-Victeur au Mans, no. 5 = Broussillon, Abbayette, no. 4, 1033–1040).

[112] According to Alexander, p. 13, Bibl. Avranches, ms. 213 explains that Suppo left Mont-St-Michel 'because of the hostility of the monks'. Gallia, 11, c. 515, claims that the monks accused Suppo of squandering the abbey's possessions: 'Post quindecim regiminis annos, a monachis de dilapidatione bonorum monasterii accusatus.' Fauroux no. 148, p. 332 provides some evidence to this view, in that Suppo was said to have sold the abbey's mill at Vains unjustly to Ranulf the moneyer: 'Sed Suppo ipsius loci abbas Ranulfo monetario monachis contradicentibus illud injuste vendiderat.' Another charter indicates that Suppo had entrusted St Benoît des Ondes to a lord named Rivallon, who subsequently sold it to another layman: Broussillon, Abbayette, no. 5. It is probable that this same Rivallon, 'a noble lord of Brittany', received Pontorson from Suppo as well to guard and defend (custodire ac defensare): ADCalvados, F 5276, coll. Beausse. Finally, Suppo is known to have given the tithes of half of Guernsey, the revenues of the churches and a carrucate of land to Hugh bishop of Avranches, on the condition that these possessions return to the Mont upon Hugh's death: Bibl. Avranches, ms. 210, fols. 87rv; published in Cartulaire de Jersey, Recueil de documents concernant l'histoire de l'île conservés aux archives du département de la Manche, in Société jersaise (Jersey, 1920), no. 149, pp. 227–28. Perhaps the monks considered these agreements which Suppo made with laymen mismanagement of the abbey's possessions. Alexander, pp. 12–13, suggests a relationship between Suppo's departure and the rebellion of Guy of Brionne in 1047, but there is no clear evidence to support this.

mont, in charge of Mont-Saint-Michel.[113] Ralph was the son of Humphrey of Vieilles and brother of Roger of Beaumont and therefore a member of one of the greatest families of Normandy. But he soon departed on a pilgrimage for Jerusalem and died in 1053 from the hardships of the journey. Perhaps the hostility of the monks to another 'Fécampois' prompted Ralph's departure, as it had led to Suppo's.[114] In the absence of sources, this suggestion cannot be proved, but it is evident that tensions remained high at the abbey. After Ralph's death, a dispute broke out between the monks of Mont-Saint-Michel and Duke William which led to a two-year vacancy at the Mont. Circa 1055, the monks elected Renouf of Bayeux, and soon thereafter forged the bull of Pope John XIII to support their claims to choose an abbot from their midst.[115] Although the Fécamp contingent accused Renouf of buying the duke's consent, he ruled the Mont until 1085.

During the abbacies of Ralph and Renouf, the monastery continued to gain property in Brittany and Maine as well as in Normandy. Ralph's reign witnessed the acquisition of Saint Colombe and Saint Germain sur Ay in the Cotentin,[116] as well as the land of La Perelle at Guernsey.[117] In Maine, the bishop of Rennes sold the Mont the churches of Villamée and Poilley for twenty *solidi Cenomannensium* and a good chestnut walking horse.[118] These churches supplemented holdings which the abbey had already gained in these areas.[119] Under Renouf, Mont-Saint-Michel recovered the mill of Vains which Duke Robert had given to the abbey and Suppo had sold, as well as Saint Benoît des Ondes, which Suppo had entrusted to a Breton named Rivallon. The Mont also gained property in Potrel,[120] Boucey,[121] Le

---

113 *Gallia*, 11, c. 515.
114 Laporte makes this suggestion: Laporte, 'Abbaye', pp. 76–77; Laporte, 'Séries', p. 273.
115 See above, notes 4 and 10.
116 For these properties, see the map of Mont-St-Michel's acquisitions, 1035–1066. St Colombe, canton St Sauveur le Vicomte: Fauroux no. 132; St Germain sur Ay (formerly *Fulquerevilla*), canton Lessay: Bibl. Avranches, ms. 210, fols. 34v–35r = BN, nouv. acq. fr. 21821, f. 167r = BN, nouv. acq. fr. 21815, fols. 223rv. This charter is mentioned in *Millénaire*, 1, p. 634, but Dubois cites the wrong folio number to ms. 210.
117 La Perelle, parish of St Sauveur: Fauroux no. 133.
118 Bibl. Avranches, ms. 210, fols. 62v–63v = BN, coll. Moreau, vol. 24, fols. 186r–188r; 189r–190r.
119 For Villamée: BN, nouv. acq. fr. 21821, f. 138rv = BN, nouv. acq. fr. 21821, f. 139rv = BN, ms. lat. 5430A, pp. 48–49 = BN, ms. lat. 10072, f. 3r = BN, coll. Moreau, 16, fols. 141r–143r. For Poilley: Bibl. Avranches ms. 210, fols 47r–48r = BN, ms. lat. 5430A, pp. 49–50 and 170–71 = BN, coll. Moreau, 40, fols. 196r–197v and 231r–232v. An undated charter indicates the abbey continued to acquire property at Poilley. An individual named Rannulf gave Mont-St-Michel three acres of land in the parish of Poilley in exchange for spiritual benefits and the promise that, if he should go to the Mont, the monks would provide him with bread and drink: Bibl. Avranches, ms. 210, fols. 79rv.
120 Potrel, canton Sartilly, commune Dragey: Fauroux 232.
121 Boucey (formerly *Calgeio*), canton Pontorson: Bibl. Avranches, ms. 210, fols. 76v–77v.

Luot[122] and several additional holdings outside Le Mans between 1055 and 1066.[123]

The charters which record these transfers of property indicate that Breton and Mançeaux lords continued to favor the Mont during the reign of William the Conqueror. They continued to visit the community, to join it, to find refuge there and to enter into agreements which covered several generations. Thus, Rivallon's son William returned St Benoît des Ondes to Mont-Saint-Michel, and his brother John confirmed the donations of his *fideles tam in Normannia quam in Brittania*, including one whose son entered the abbey as a monk.[124] And Vitalis, the priest of Danfront, offered his lands in Maine to the Mont as an entrance gift.[125] Another charter describes an agreement whereby Mont-Saint-Michel would come to the aid of a Breton lord if he was captured; the monks' assistance would be commensurate with the value of the land in Brittany which he had given them.[126]

Among Bretons who joined the community during the reign of the Conqueror, one lord from the diocese of Dol, Tréhan of Saint Broladre, entered too hastily, believing his death imminent. When he recovered his health, Tréhan returned his habit to the monks and resumed secular life, generously endowing the Mont.[127] But Trehan still retained the right to stay at the Mont in case of war, where he would receive daily as much bread and wine as one monk.[128] Tréhan's agreement with Mont-Saint-Michel, like Grallon's at the beginning of the century, underlines the significance of this abbey as a local institution with immediate responsibilities to its neighbors and benefactors outside as well as within Normandy.

The monks no doubt were aware of the violent interplay of regional ambitions that constituted statecraft in the first feudal age. The complex political ties binding the rulers of Normandy, Brittany, Maine, Anjou and

122 Le Luot, canton La Haye Pensnel: Bibl. Avranches, ms. 210, fols. 83v–84r.
123 Broussillon, *Saint-Victeur au Mans*, nos. 10, 11, 12.
124 This William later became the abbot of St Florent of Saumur. The charter of Rivallon's son John appears in Bibl. Avranches, ms. 210, fols. 66rv = BN, ms. lat. 5430A, pp. 58–59.
125 Broussillon, *Saint-Victeur au Mans*, no. 10.
126 Bibl. Avranches, ms. 210, f. 73v: '. . . de eodem adjutorio secundum hoc quod terra valebit et justum fuerit'.
127 Tréhan's history is found in Bibl. Avranches, ms. 210, fols. 44rv; 74rv; Bibl. Avranches, ms. 210, fols. 44rv; BN, ms. lat. 5430A, p. 288; BN, nouv. acq. fr. 21815, f. 226v: Caen, Musée des Beaux Arts, coll. Mancel, ms. 300, fols. 148rv. Tréhan is also discussed by Guillotin de Corson, 2, pp. 527–30; Dubois, 'Les Dépendances', pp. 643–44.
128 Bibl. Avranches, ms. 210, fols. 44rv: 'Hoc totum dono sancto Michaeli pro salute anime meae et antecessorum meorum et successorum, tali conditione quod quando perrexero ad sanctam Michaelem causa orationum habebo caritatem sancti Michaelis de pane et vino. Et si per querram mansero apud montem quandiu ibi fuero habebo cotidie de pane et potu quantum unus monachus et se forte voluero effici monachus aliquando, cum parte possessionis mee in omni re mobili et censu facient me monachi monachum.'

Blois-Chartres in a constantly shifting web of alliances and rivalries presented dangers as well as opportunities to the community. As the only community which did not shake off its ties to distant lands in the course of the eleventh century, Mont-Saint-Michel was an exception among Norman abbeys. This orientation was expressed liturgically as well: eleventh-century sacramentaries reveal very few Norman saints in the Mont's Sanctoral, in contrast to the preponderance of those from dioceses outside of Normandy.[129] At the junction of Normandy, Brittany and Maine, the community flourished as a rich and famous abbey, a site which drew pilgrims and gifts from afar. And when disputes occurred between the neighbors of Mont-Saint-Michel, conflicting loyalties placed the monastery in an awkward position.

The view of the monks of Mont-Saint-Michel as 'Norman pioneers at the borders of Brittany' does them disservice by oversimplifying their situation and underestimating their achievement. It implies a need to explain their apparent lapse in loyalty during the Breton wars of Robert the Magnificent, and it distorts our understanding of the monks' resistance to Norman domination during the second half of the century. Mont-Saint-Michel's efforts to maintain its independence from the rulers of Rouen and from the abbots of Fécamp had a long legacy by 1066; if relations between the Mont and the dukes deteriorated after 1085, it is nevertheless important to recognize the continuity of earlier tensions in that conflict. The monks at Mont-Saint-Michel should be seen not as pioneers at a Norman outpost but in their own context, endeavoring to fulfill complex social and spiritual commitments that crossed political and territorial boundaries which continually shifted as the duchy of Normandy took shape. In their efforts to balance these commitments, the monks at the Mont highlight the tensions at work in the formation of this region, reinforcing the conclusion that the advance of Norman ducal authority in the west was a more gradual process than the narrative sources suggest.

---

[129] Henri Tardif, 'La Liturgie de la messe au Mont Saint-Michel aux XIe, XIIe et XIIIe siècles', in Millénaire, 1, pp. 353–77, at pp. 368–69.

6

Private Monasteries and their Patrons

During the half century following 1030, the Norman aristocracy followed the example of their dukes, founding and restoring over twenty abbeys in Normandy. In his praise of this movement, Orderic Vitalis wrote that the Norman barons of the eleventh century had been 'inspired by the piety of their princes . . . Each magnate would have thought himself beneath contempt if he had not supported clerks and monks on his estates for the service of God.'[1] To evaluate the role which aristocratic abbeys played in the complementary processes of regional consolidation and monastic revival in Normandy, it is necessary to take a close look at the families that built these houses, their ties with the dukes and with the ducal monasteries. Orderic praised the pious zeal of the nobles who were responsible for the proliferation of non-ducal abbeys in Normandy after 1030. A more skeptical observer, however, would note that there were potential disadvantages – to ducal authority and to the cohesiveness of the duchy – associated with the rise of private monasteries.

After all, historians link the privatization of religious communities with the breakdown of royal control during the ninth and tenth centuries: private churches and abbeys are seen as both a consequence of and a contributory factor to the devolution of centralized power in the later Carolingian empire.[2] Likewise, the foundation of private monasteries in Normandy might have undermined the duke's control over the church. Moreover, several aristocratic monasteries were either founded on property or endowed with lands which had previously been in the possession of the ducal monastery of Fécamp. This raises the possibility that the new aristocratic foundations, in themselves potentially threatening to ducal authority, were established at the expense of the community most favored by the dukes in the early eleventh century. The monks of a monastery established and endowed by someone other than the duke would obviously be beholden to their founder and primary benefactor. If that lord were to rebel, the abbey could become a pocket of local resistance, refusing to open its doors to the duke. And as

---

[1] Orderic, 2, pp. 10–11.
[2] For a general description, see Lemarignier, 'Une Église', pp. 49–77, and Lemarignier, *Institutions et société*, pp. 190–203.

imposing buildings of stone, monasteries transformed readily into fortresses in which to garrison soldiers.

Given all these factors, it would make sense to view the appearance of private monasteries in Normandy as a danger to centralized authority. As David Bates observes, 'The establishment of "private" castles and monasteries were threats to some very basic aspects of ducal power.'[3] Since noble families did not begin establishing their own abbeys in Normandy until the reign of Robert the Magnificent (1027–1035), a ruler who faced rebellion and opposition on several fronts, it would also seem reasonable to consider them a symptom of the political instability during his time. In fact, however, a closer look at when these private monasteries appeared in Normandy and who built them argues against this conclusion. Instead, as non-ducal monasteries multiplied in Normandy after 1030, they supplemented the movement of monastic reform sponsored by the dukes, reinforcing the interconnections that gave cohesion to the duchy.

Although private monasteries did not appear in Normandy until Robert the Magnificent's reign, the majority were founded when ducal authority was relatively strong.[4] All five aristocratic houses built during Robert's reign, for example, arose between circa 1030 and 1035: they were not products of the earlier, rougher years of his rule.[5] The same was true during the reign of William the Conqueror. Of the thirteen private monasteries built between 1035 and 1066, all but one arose in the decade following William's victories at Val-ès-Dunes and the siege of Brionne.[6] No rash of endowments occurred while the dukes' position was the most insecure. Instead, non-ducal houses were products of more peaceful times, when ducal leadership was steady. Thus, the timing of these foundations argues against considering them threats to centralized authority.

[3] Bates, 1066, p. 121.
[4] On the difficulty of dating monastic foundations, see V. H. Galbraith, 'Monastic Foundation Charters of the Eleventh and Twelfth Centuries', Cambridge Historical Journal, 4 (1934), pp. 205–22.
[5] The first three years of Robert the Magnificent's reign were the worst. According to Jumièges, GND, 2, pp. 44–49, war broke out after the death of Richard II between his sons, and Jumièges attributes Richard III's sudden death (ut retulerunt plurimi) in 1027 to poison. Robert, who then succeeded his brother, began his reign facing internal rebellion as well as threats from outside Normandy. The most powerful bishops of Normandy and his father's closest advisors, Robert archbishop of Rouen and Hugh bishop of Bayeux, on separate occasions both struggled against the new duke. On Normandy's southern border, Robert fought with William of Bellême at the beginning of his reign, and he later entered a war with his cousin, Alan the III of Rennes, in the west. The five non-ducal abbeys that appeared during Robert's reign were: Trinité du Mont, Rouen; St Amand, Rouen; St Pierre, Preaux; Conches; Bec.
[6] The thirteen private abbeys which appeared between 1035 and 1066 were: St Pierre sur Dives; Fontenay; St Evroul; Lyre; Notre Dame du Pré, Lisieux; St Léger, Preaux; Grestain; Troarn; St Martin of Sées; Cormeilles; Le Tréport; Almenèches; St Sauveur, Evreux.

Furthermore, most of the monastery builders in Normandy before 1066 were men who surrounded the duke, signed his charters and provided him with counsel and aid.[7] Many were related to him by blood. The abbey of Saint Pierre of Préaux for example was built by Humphrey of Vieilles, first cousin of Richard II and patriarch of the great Beaumont family.[8] Humphrey's son Roger of Beaumont numbered third among the top attestors of Duke William's pre-Conquest charters, and the ship list appended to the *Brevis Relatio* records that Roger supplied his lord generously with ships on the eve of the Conquest.[9] An even stronger testimony to Roger's good faith is provided by William of Poitiers, who recalls that Duke William left Roger of

---

7 On the distribution of wealth and ties of kinship among the Norman aristocratic families, see C. Warren Hollister, 'The Greater Domesday Tenants-in-Chief', in *Domesday Studies*, ed. J. C. Holt (Woodbridge, 1987), pp. 219–48; Lucien Musset, 'L'Aristocratie normande au XIe siècle', in *La Noblesse au moyen âge, XIe–XVe siècles*, ed. Philippe Contamine (Paris, 1976), pp. 71–96.

8 Fauroux no. 89, p. 231 describes Humphrey of Vieilles as 'structor ejusdem ecclesie'. On the foundation of Préaux, see *Gallia*, 11, cols. 834–35; *Neustria*, pp. 505–07; Besse, pp. 198–99; Jacques Henry, 'Les Abbayes de Préaux', in *Normandie*, ed. Gaillard, pp. 191–227. According to these sources, St Pierre of Préaux was built on the site of a Merovingian monastery that had been destroyed by the Vikings. The evidence for Humphrey's connection to the ducal family comes from Robert of Torigny, who identifies Humphrey's mother as a sister of Gunnor, Richard I's wife. Although Torigny's genealogies have been criticized in the past, Elisabeth van Houts' recent analysis has demonstrated that they are fairly trustworthy. See Torigny, in Jumièges, *GND*, 2, pp. 268–69, and note 4; Elisabeth M. C. van Houts, 'Robert of Torigni as genealogist', in *Studies in Medieval History Presented to R. Allen Brown*, ed. C. Harper Bill, Christopher J. Holdsworth, and Janet L. Nelson (Woodbridge, 1989), pp. 215–33; G. H. White, 'The Sisters and Nieces of Gunnor, Duchess of Normandy', *The Genealogist*, 37 (1921), pp. 57–65, 128–32. For a genealogy and more general discussion of the kinship ties that bound the Norman aristocracy, see Searle, *Predatory Kinship*, Table 5, and pp. 98–107. The fortunes of the Beaumont family during the later eleventh and twelfth centuries are examined in Sally N. Vaughn, *Anselm of Bec and Robert of Meulan: The Innocence of the Dove and the Wisdom of the Serpent* (Berkeley, 1987); David Crouch, *The Beaumont Twins: The Roots and Branches of Power in the Twelfth Century* (Cambridge, 1986).

9 The top three attestors of Duke William's charters before 1066 were:
1. Roger II of Montgomery: Fauroux nos. 99, 105, 107, 113, 120, 122, 123, 133, 137, 140, 141, 142, 144, 145, 150, 151, 155, 156, 160, 161, 162, 163, 171, 172, 179, 194, 195, 198, 199, 203, 208, 218, 219, 220, 222, 223, 226, 228, 230, 231, 232, 233. (42 total)
2. William fitz Osbern: Fauroux nos. 96, 106, 113, 118, 119, 120, 123, 124, 126, 132, 138, 140, 155, 173, 175, 176, 179, 180, 181, 182, 188, 191, 193, 197, 198, 204, 212, 220, 226, 229, 231, 233, 234. (33 total)
3. Roger of Beaumont: Fauroux nos. 73, 88, 94, 96, 106, 107, 111, 123, 128, 129, 131, 133, 141, 145, 156, 179, 197, 208, 213, 218, 222, 228, 229, 232. (24 total)

For the general reliability of the ship list as a description of the 'minimum contribution' which Duke William sought from his men for the invasion of England, see Elisabeth M. C. van Houts, 'The Ship List of William the Conqueror', *Anglo-Norman Studies*, 10 (1988), pp. 159–83. Van Houts includes a facsimile and new edition of the ship list in her appendices. She also suggests, p. 168, that the monastery of Fécamp

Beaumont to safeguard Normandy as Duchess Matilda's chief advisor in 1066.[10]

During Robert the Magnificent's reign, two more abbeys, Trinité du Mont and Saint Amand, were founded by Goscelin *vicomte* of Rouen and his wife Emmeline in Rouen.[11] Located in Rouen, these two communities clearly enjoyed ducal favor, and Trinité du Mont far outdistanced other non-ducal monasteries as a recipient of ducal charters.[12] Goscelin obtained from the duke a promise of immunity and protection for Trinité du Mont before entering the monastery himself, thus placing the abbey directly under ducal care.[13] Later in the century, the monks at La Trinité wrote an account of the community's foundation which described Duke Richard II in glowing terms, emphasizing that Goscelin had been a close confidant of his.[14] Goscelin's continued loyalty to Richard II's son is seen in his frequent appearance in the attestation lists of Robert's charters. Witnessing charters for Mont-Saint-Michel and Fécamp as well as for his own houses, Goscelin numbered among the most frequent lay attestors of Robert the Magnificent's reign.[15]

provided the scribes that compiled this list. Also see Hollister, 'Domesday Tenants-in-Chief', pp. 221–26, where the ship list is discussed and its authenticity defended.

10 Poitiers, *Gesta Guillelmi*, p. 260: 'Optime quidem egerat in gubernaculo domina nostra Matildis, jam nomine divulgato regina etsi nondum coronata. Illius prudentiam viri adjuvere consilio utilissimi, in quibus locum dignitatis primum tenebat Rogerus de Bellomonte, Humfridi hominis generosissimi filius . . .'

11 On these abbeys, see: Fauroux nos. 60, 61, 62. On Trinité de Mont in particular, see A. Deville, ed., *Cartulaire de l'abbaye de la Sainte-Trinité du Mont de Rouen*, in *Cartulaire de Saint Bertin*, ed. B. Guérard (Paris, 1841); F. Pommeraye, *Histoire de l'abbaye de la très Sainte Trinité dite depuis de St Catherine du Mont de Rouen*, in Pommeraye, *Histoire de St-Ouen*. On St Amand in particular, see Marie-Josèphe le Cacheux, *Histoire de l'abbaye de Saint-Amand de Rouen, des origines à la fin du XVIe siècle*, published in BSAN, 44 (Caen, 1937). On the *vicomtes* of Rouen, see Jean-Michel Bouvris, 'Contribution à une étude de l'institution vicomtale en Normandie au XIe siècle, l'exemple de la partie orientale du duché: les vicomtes de Rouen et de Fécamp', *Cahier des Annales de Normandie*, 17 (1985), pp. 149–74.

12 Fauroux p. 36: In Fauroux's edition of ducal charters, Trinité du Mont was a recipient of twenty-two charters (nos. 60, 61, 81, 82, 83, 84, 96, 101, 104, 118, 119, 123, 130, 135, 138, 143, 200, 201, 202, 206, 221, 233), and St Amand was a recipient of eight genuine ducal charters and one probable forgery (nos. <62>, 116, 182, 183, 184, 185, 186, 187, 192). Their closest competitors among non-ducal Norman monasteries regarding the number of ducal *acta* were Bec (nos. 98, 178, 179, 180, 181, 189) and St Pierre, Préaux (nos. 88, 89, 97, 121, 174, 175), each with six charters.

13 Fauroux no. 61. The significance of this immunity is discussed by Yver, 'Absence d'avouerie', pp. 201–07. On the entrance of Goscelin and Emmeline into Trinité du Mont and St Amand, respectively, see Douglas, *William the Conqueror*, p. 115, note 5.

14 Poncelet, 'Sanctae Catharinae', pp. 427–28. On this text, also see Fawtier, 'Reliques rouennaises'.

15 Out of 30 authentic ducal charters from Robert I's reign, the top three lay attestors were:
1. Osbern the Steward (Fauroux nos. 65, 69, 70, 79, 80, 82, 85).
2. Goscelin of Rouen (Fauroux nos. 60, 61, 69, 73, 81, 84, 85).
3. Gilbert of Brionne (Fauroux nos. 64, 65, 66, 67, 70, 80, 85).

The founder of the abbey of Conches, Roger of Tosny, also came from a family whose members numbered among trusted ducal supporters.[16] In 1013 or 1014, Richard II committed his castle at Tillières to Roger and his father to hold and defend.[17] Roger himself spent a great deal of his later life adventuring in Spain, but he returned to Normandy toward the end of Robert's reign and died during the minority of William the Conqueror, killed by Roger of Beaumont in a private war.[18] The feud between the Tosny and the Beaumont families, symptomatic of the disruptions during Duke William's minority, did not poison the Tosny relations with the duke. Orderic refers to Roger's son Ralph of Tosny, who fought for the duke against the king of Francia in 1054 and against the king of England in 1066, as the 'standard bearer of the Normans'.[19]

The founder of the fifth private abbey begun during the reign of Robert the Magnificent, unlike Humphrey of Vieilles, Goscelin of Rouen and Roger of Tosny, was neither a member of the upper Norman aristocracy nor a prominent *fidelis* of the duke. Herluin, who had been a knight of Gilbert of Brionne, entered religious life as abbot of a monastic community that he established at Bonneville in 1034 and transferred to Bec, about 1039.[20] At its origins, Bec was humble and secluded. Orderic shows Lanfranc coming to Bec specifically because of its remoteness and poverty.[21] And at its peak when Bec stood as one of the most important monasteries in northern Francia, its leaders worked closely with the dukes of Normandy. Consequently, it would be difficult to consider Herluin's foundation a challenge to ducal control of the church.

The motivations of nobles for founding monasteries appear to have been both pious and practical, but not inimical to ducal interests. Tension existed

---

16 On the Tosny family, see Musset, 'Aux Origines d'une classe dirigeante', pp. 45–80; Jumièges, *GND*, 2, p. 95, note 6.

17 Jumièges, *GND*, 2, pp. 22–23.

18 Orderic, 2, pp. 40–41, and vol. 4, pp. 206–07; Jumièges, *GND*, 2, pp. 96–97. For a brief discussion of Roger of Tosny and his death, see Douglas, *William the Conqueror*, p. 85.

19 Orderic, 2, pp. 140–41: 'Normannorum signifer'.

20 The classic study of the abbey of Bec is that of Andrée Porée, *Histoire de l'abbaye du Bec*, 2 vols. (Evreux, 1901, rpt. 1980). The careers of Lanfranc and Anselm ensured that the monastery would be of continuing interest to historians, and consequently the bibliography on Bec is enormous. For general background and an introduction to more recent literature, see Margaret Gibson, *Lanfranc of Bec* (Oxford, 1978); Vaughn, *Anselm of Bec*; R. W. Southern, *Saint Anselm: A Portrait in a Landscape* (Cambridge, 1990); Thibaud Maze, 'L'Abbaye du Bec au XIe siècle', in *Normandie*, ed. Gaillard, pp. 229–47. The collected letters of Lanfranc and Anselm are particularly valuable resources for the study of Bec and of eleventh-century monasticism in general: *The Letters of Lanfranc, Archbishop of Canterbury*, ed. and trans. Helen Clover and Margaret Gibson (Oxford, 1979); *The Letters of Saint Anselm of Canterbury*, ed. and trans. Walter Frölich, 3 vols. (Kalamazoo, 1990–1995). Also see *The Monastic Constitutions of Lanfranc*, ed. David Knowles (London, 1951).

21 Orderic, 2, pp. 250–51: 'Coenobiolum Beccense in Normannia loci situ et paupertate elegit ...'

in medieval society between the aggressive vocation of knighthood and the peaceful tenets of Christianity. Consciousness of their guilt before God prompted these lords to seek absolution through charity and donations to the church.[22] An excellent way to gain personal redemption and demonstrate piety to one's neighbors was the foundation of a monastic house. The number of people who retired to spend their last years in the monasteries they had founded attests to their hope to find peace at the end of their days. Thus, Goscelin of Rouen and his wife entered the houses they had founded, while Humphrey of Vieilles and his son Roger of Beaumont both entered their abbey of Saint Pierre toward the end of their lives.[23] Herluin of Bec built his abbey specifically to commit himself to religious life, and he gave the new community all of his lands.

As was the case with ducal benefactions, worldly advantages supplemented the spiritual incentives that prompted nobles to found monasteries. Aristocratic families used their abbeys to gain status, to build up and preserve family patrimonies, to consolidate their domains and even to stake out claims in new regions. Monastic endowment *jure hereditario* underlined and confirmed the donor's inherited tenure.[24] As sources of literate men and of ready cash, private monasteries aided their lords in managing their estates, writing documents and mobilizing financial capital.[25] Moreover, a stately mausoleum with a community of monks to pray for their souls was an attractive prospect to those who could afford it. In an uncertain and violent age, a private monastery represented a solid and enduring monument to family identity; generations of benefactors might be buried side by side within its walls. Living descendants reaffirmed and expanded the donations of their ancestors, often joining the community toward the end of their days, and anticipated being buried alongside their relatives.[26] Vying with each other in the con-

---

[22] For an insightful analysis of the relationship between liturgy, patronage and lay guilt, see Barbara H. Rosenwein, 'Feudal War and Monastic Peace: Cluniac Liturgy as Ritual Aggression', *Viator*, 2 (1971), pp. 129–57.

[23] See above, note 13.

[24] J. C. Holt, 'Feudal Society and the Family in Early Medieval England: II. Notions of Patrimony', *TRHS*, 33 (1983), pp. 193–220. On this subject, also see Chibnall, 'Ecclesiastical Patronage', pp. 103–18. Chibnall suggests (p. 104) that the primary motive behind the foundation of churches was akin to Roman *pietas*: 'a desire to preserve the family patrimony and the family traditions.' Yet, when material and spiritual goals conflicted, tensions inevitably arose between patrons and monastic communities. The ambivalence of this relationship is explored further by Emma Mason, in *'Timeo barones et donas ferentes'*, *Studies in Church History*, 15 (1978), pp. 61–75.

[25] See above, Chapter Three especially pp. 56–58.

[26] At St Pierre of Préaux, for example, Robert of Beaumont was laid to rest in the chapter house in 1118 beside his father and uncle, the sons of the original founder, Humphrey of Vieilles. Robert's son Waleran became a monk at St Pierre of Préaux toward the end of his days, and was buried beside his father in 1166. Crouch, *Beaumont Twins*, pp. 3–4, 78–79.

struction of monasteries, Norman nobles therefore reinforced their place within the Christian community, erecting physical symbols of piety and prestige which people at all social levels understood. Thus private monasteries served nobles much as ducal monasteries served the dukes, affirming their rightful authority as Christian lords to those who lived on their lands and to those who lived beyond.

At their inception, therefore, aristocratic monasteries were not signs of defiance against ducal authority nor symbols of a breakdown of ducal control over the church. Their appearance coincided with periods of firm ducal authority, and they owed their existence to strong supporters of the dukes. Danger lay, however, in the direction these abbeys might take once started. During William's unsteady minority, this danger was especially high, and the years from 1035 to 1050 were hard on the Norman church. In the 1040s, for example, a bishop of Coutances was accused of having 'lavishly distributed' cathedral prebends among his relatives.[27] And an ecclesiastical synod in that decade suggests that the alienation of church property was perceived as a serious problem: the council of Rouen warned that bishops must not under any circumstances present stipends or lands of the church to laymen.[28] As lands were slipping out of control of the church, it would not have been surprising to see more and more private monasteries being built, independent of ducal control.

But in fact, only one new non-ducal abbey arose during William's minority. This was Saint Pierre sur Dives, founded around 1045 by Lesceline countess of Eu and the sister-in-law of Duke Richard II with her son Robert. Lesceline submitted the monastery to the protection of the duke, just as Goscelin *vicomte* of Rouen had committed Trinité du Mont to ducal guardianship. And before entering a different monastery she later founded, the countess paid off her heirs so that Saint Pierre sur Dives would be safe from any future claims based on hereditary right.[29] Lesceline's son Robert count of Eu fought for Duke William at the Battle of Mortemer where, according to William of Poitiers, his courage was equal to his high birth.[30] Robert provided sixty ships for the Conquest of England, and William of Poitiers shows Robert among the magnates whom the duke consulted before he left in 1066.[31]

---

27   *De statu*, cols. 154–55.
28   *Concilia Rotomagensis Provinciae*, ed. William Bessin (Rouen, 1717), p. 42; 'Concilium Rotomagense', in Joannes Dominicus Mansi, *Sacrorum Conciliorum*, 19 (Graz, 1960 reprint), col. 753.
29   *Gallia*, 11, *Instr.* cols. 154–55.
30   Poiters, *Gesta Guillelmi*, pp. 72–73; Orderic, 4, pp. 86–87. Lesceline's son William Busac gave his consent to having a priory established on his lands committed to the ducal abbey of St Ouen: Fauroux no. 107. Busac was, however, later expelled by the duke and received Soissons from the king of France. See Jumièges, *GND*, 2, pp. 128–29. Searle, *Predatory Kinship*, pp. 218, 319, note 11.
31   Van Houts, 'Ship List', pp. 175–76; *Brevis Relatio* in *Scriptores Rerum Gestarum Willelmi*

If non-ducal monasteries had undermined William the Conqueror's control of the church, we would expect to find more being established when he was weakest, that is before 1050 – but only one abbey, Saint Pierre sur Dives, appeared during William's minority. On the other hand, however, a sudden proliferation of non-ducal abbeys did accompany the re-emergence of strong ducal authority in the second half of the century. And in every case, they were built by families closely associated with ducal authority. In fact, the top three attestors of William's charters from his minority until 1066 were William fitz Osbern, who built houses at Lyre and Cormeilles, Roger II of Montgomery, founder of Troarn, Saint Martin of Sées and Almenèches, and Roger of Beaumont, whose father Humphrey of Vieilles had built Saint Pierre of Préaux and who himself founded Saint Léger of Préaux.[32] William fitz Osbern and Roger of Montgomery were both said to have provided their duke with sixty ships apiece for the Conquest of England, and the duke took counsel with William fitz Osbern and Roger of Montgomery, as well as Roger of Beaumont, before embarking in 1066.[33]

The families that built the other new abbeys were likewise close to the duke. The founder of Saint Pierre sur Dives, Lesceline countess of Eu, built Notre Dame du Pré with her son Hugh bishop of Lisieux circa 1050 and entered it herself. About ten years later, Robert count of Eu, whom William of Poitiers and Orderic Vitalis both praise for his loyalty to the duke, built the monastery of Tréport. The monastery of Fontenay was established by Ralph Taisson, the second highest attestor of ducal charters during William's minority.[34] According to Wace's late testimony, Ralph Taisson supported Duke William at the Battle of Mortemer.[35] The abbey of Grestain owed its existence to Herluin of Conteville, the husband of Duke William's mother, and their son Robert, William's half-brother, who received the county of Mortain from the duke.[36] And the monastery of Saint Sauveur was built by Richard

Conquestoris, ed. J. A. Giles (Caxton Society, 1845, rpt. 1967), p. 22; Poitiers, *Gesta Guillelmi*, pp. 72–73, 148–49.

32 See above, note 8.

33 Van Houts, 'Ship List', pp. 175–76; *Brevis Relatio*, p. 22; Poitiers, *Gesta Guillelmi*, pp. 148–49.

34 On the monastery of Fontenay, see de Farcy, vol. 3, pp. 1–4, 27–36; Lucien Musset, 'Autour des Origines de Saint-Etienne de Fontenay', BSAN, 56 (1953), pp. 11–41; Louis Gosselin, 'L'Abbaye de Saint-Etienne de Fontenay au début de sa fondation', in *Normandie*, ed. Gaillard, pp. 277–85.
   The two highest attestors of Duke William's charters, 1035–1050, were:
   1. William Fitz Osbern (Fauroux nos. 96, 99, 106, 113, 117, 118, 119, 120, 122).
   2. Ralph Taisson (Fauroux nos. 93, 98, 100, 103, 105, 115, 122).

35 *Le Roman de Rou de Wace*, ed. A. J. Holden, vol. 2 of 3 vols. (Paris, 1970–1973), p. 67, line 4829.

36 According to a later legend, Herluin of Conteville was instructed by the Virgin Mary in a dream to restore an ancient chapel at Grestain which had been destroyed. On the abbey of Grestain, see Louis de Saint Pierre, 'L'Abbaye de Grestain et ses fondateurs',

count of Evreux, the son of Duke William's great-uncle Robert archbishop of Rouen. Count Richard's son, William count of Evreux, fought in the ducal army at Hastings.[37]

In his account of the restoration of Saint Evroul, Orderic Vitalis provides the most detailed description of Norman lords seeking ducal support for their plans to revive a monastery. He also relates how the community suffered when the abbot of that community fell into the duke's disfavor. Initially, having decided to restore the community in 1050,

> ... William and Robert, the sons of Giroie, and Hugh and Robert, the sons of Robert of Grandmesnil, sought out William duke of Normandy and revealed their intentions to him, asking him to give his princely support to so worthy an undertaking. By common consent they gave the chosen site into his protection, free and quit from all customs and dues which anyone might try to exact from the monks or their men, saving only prayers. The duke gladly approved their good intention, and confirmed the charter of gifts which his magnates were giving to St. Évroul . . .[38]

This was clearly a project which the duke encouraged. Hugh and Robert of Grandmesnil then 'obtained ducal permission to choose an abbot'.[39] They visited the monastery of Jumièges and asked the abbot there to give them Thierry, a monk who had been trained by William of Dijon's disciple Thierry. Saint Evroul's patrons therefore sought the approval of Duke William at every stage, placing the community under his protection (*tutela*) and seeking his permission to appoint an abbot, which in itself underlines that this was a ducal right. By requesting Thierry from Jumièges, Hugh and Robert of Grandmesnil chose an abbot for Saint Evroul who was closely affiliated with the reform circle of ducal abbeys. Whatever the mixture of piety and pragmatism that motivated the sons of Giroie and Grandmesnil to restore Saint Evroul, this community clearly did not represent a threat to Duke William's authority in 1050.

---

in *Normandie*, ed. Gaillard, pp. 263–76; Charles Bréard, *L'Abbaye de Notre-Dame de Grestain de l'ordre de Saint-Benoît à l'ancien diocèse de Lisieux* (Rouen, 1904). A previously unknown *pancarte* from the abbey of Grestain has been recently discovered, and this document provides a great deal of information about the early years of the abbey of Grestain. For a description and analysis, see David Bates and Véronique Gazeau, 'L'Abbaye de Grestain et la famille d'Herluin de Conteville', AN, 40 (1990), pp. 5–30. On the earliest counts of Mortain, see Potts, 'Counts Revisited'. On the Conqueror's half-brother Robert of Mortain specifically, see most recently Brian Golding, 'Robert of Mortain', *Anglo-Norman Studies*, 13 (1991), pp. 119–44.

[37] Poitiers, *Gesta Guillelmi*, pp. 194–97.

[38] Orderic, 2, pp. 16–17. In addition to Chibnall's six-volume edition of Orderic Vitalis, for background on St Evroul see Chibnall, *World*, especially pp. 45–114. A brief summary of the monastery's history is also available in Jean-Marie Lamouroux, 'L'Abbaye de Saint-Evroult au XIe siècle', in *Normandie*, ed. Gaillard, pp. 249–61.

[39] Orderic, 2, pp. 16–17: 'Deinde Hugo et Rotbertus a duce accepta licentia eligendi abbatem Gemmeticum expetierunt.'

A decade later, William demonstrated his determination to keep the community under his authority when the monastery was embroiled in a conflict between the duke and his nobles, a dispute in which Robert and Hugh of Grandmesnil were implicated.[40] Robert by then had succeeded Thierry as abbot of the community, but this did not stop the duke from exiling him and his brother Hugh. The duke chose another monk named Osbern to be abbot of Saint Evroul, an appointment which the community accepted, despite some reservations, because they did not dare resist the duke. Robert of Grandmesnil then journeyed to Rome and appealed to the pope, who sided with the exiled abbot and sent him back to Normandy with two cardinals and a letter demanding Robert's reinstatement. According to Orderic,

> When the duke heard that Abbot Robert was approaching in the company of papal legates to claim the abbacy of St. Évroul and charge the duke's candidate Osbern with usurpation of his rights, he flew into a violent rage, declaring that he was ready to receive legates of the pope, their common father, in matters touching the Christian faith, but that if any monk from his duchy dared to bring a plea against him he would ignore his cloth and hang him by his cowl from the top of the highest oak-tree in the wood near by.[41]

On hearing of this threat, Robert and the papal cardinals turned tail and fled Normandy in haste. Osbern remained abbot of Saint Evroul, despite the papal opposition, and Robert of Grandmesnil found a new life among his kinsmen in Norman Italy.[42]

This example from Saint Evroul provides clear testimony to Duke William's willingness and ability to assert his supremacy over a private monastery. While Orderic might have put words in William's mouth when he recounted the duke's threat to hang Robert of Grandmesnil from the highest tree, he did not invent the duke's refusal to accept papal judgement in this case. The duke's priority was loyalty, and he would not permit a man he distrusted to remain in control of a monastery, even if it was a community that man had restored, and even if it meant disobeying the pope.

Like Saint Evroul, Troarn, Trinité du Mont of Rouen and Saint Pierre sur Dives were also placed under ducal protection.[43] This freed them from local subordination, as it promised that the duke would defend these communities

---

[40] For the discussion which follows, see Orderic, 2, pp. 90–115.

[41] Orderic, 2, pp. 94–95.

[42] Several of the monks from Saint Evroul joined Robert in Italy, where they resumed their vocation in a church donated by Robert Guiscard. Orderic, 2, pp. 100–01.

[43] The charter in which the duke extends his protection over Troarn is edited by Sauvage, *Troarn*, no. 2. For Trinité du Mont, see Fauroux no. 61; for St Pierre sur Dives, see *Gallia*, 11, *Instr.* cols. 153–56. For a fuller discussion of the significance of ducal protection, see Yver, 'Absence d'avouerie', in particular p. 201, note 32; Haskins, *Norman Institutions*, p. 36 and note 143.

against any lay lords who might be tempted to encroach upon their lands. Protection, however, carried its own price, and being placed under the ducal guard gave him the right of direct intervention.[44] By including non-ducal houses under the same guardianship he extended to all ducal houses, the duke publicly gained the right to exert his control over the growing network of monasteries in the duchy. This legitimized his involvement even in those cases where the communities themselves resisted him, as the monks of Saint Evroul learned under Duke William, and as the monks of Mont-Saint-Michel discovered during his father's reign.

The charters indicate that Norman magnates were eager to entrust the duke with their abbeys, but whether willing or forced, the result was that their communities became part of the expanding group of Norman monasteries connected to the dukes and their reformers. Modern college administrators can see reasons for private schools to establish relations with state universities; private abbeys in eleventh-century Normandy similarly gained more than simple protection through their association with the duke and his circle of monastic communities. Access to broader sources of funds, personnel and library collections were foremost among the additional advantages. Like today, however, the reverse of the coin was that the central authority of the state gained a greater right to intervene in their internal affairs, especially when political issues were at stake.

The ties between private monasteries and ducal abbeys in Normandy were further reinforced through a series of interconnections which linked the nobles who built them, the lands which supported them, and even the monks who filled them. With respect to their founders, it is not surprising that the families that founded and restored monasteries before the Conquest tended to be related to each other and to the duke. Lesceline and her sons, for example, who collectively founded three abbeys, were tied to the ducal house through Lesceline's marriage to Duke Richard II's half-brother, William count of Eu. William fitz Osbern, who built two abbeys, claimed kinship to the duke through both sides of his family. His father had been the son of Duchess Gunnor's brother Herfast, and his mother was the daughter of Ralph of Ivry, half brother of Duke Richard I.[45] The founder of Conches, Roger of Tosny, married his daughter to William fitz Osbern, and after Roger's death, his widow married the founder of Saint Sauveur, Richard count of Evreux, nephew of Duke Richard II. According to Robert of Torigny, the Beaumont family, responsible for two abbeys, and the Montgomery house, responsible for three, were related to the duke through the sisters of Duchess Gunnor.[46]

[44] Yver, 'Absence d'avouerie', p. 203. On this subject, also see Tabuteau, *Transfers*, pp. 202–04.

[45] David Douglas, 'The Ancestors of William fitz Osbern', *EHR*, 59 (1944), pp. 62–79.

[46] Jumièges, *GND*, 2, pp. 264–75. On the Beaumont family, see above note 8; on the Montgomery family, see J. F. A. Mason, 'Roger de Montgomery and his Sons (1067–1102)', *TRHS* 13 (1963), pp. 1–28.

And finally, Robert count of Mortain, half brother of Duke William and founder of Grestain, married a daughter of Roger II of Montgomery.[47]

As they helped bind the Norman aristocracy together, these ties of kinship also strengthened the cohesiveness of monasticism in Normandy. Families were willing to endow each others' monasteries; consequently, ducal and non-ducal monasteries received lands and monks from these lords. This passage of property and men kept communities from becoming isolated from each other, and the dukes participated by supporting and enriching private monasteries. Both Robert the Magnificent and William the Conqueror confirmed and approved the construction of non-ducal houses. William, moreover, donated churches and lands to Saint Pierre, Préaux, to Bec, to Notre Dame du Pré and to Tréport.[48] Throughout their reigns, Robert and William confirmed the charters of their subjects' donations to non-ducal abbeys.

Lords whose families founded private monasteries also appear donating to ducal and other non-ducal abbeys as well. Roger and Robert of Beaumont, for example, presented the ducal house of Saint Wandrille with churches and lands, and Jumièges received mills from Roger of Beaumont and Richard of Evreux.[49] Richard of Evreux was generous to Saint Taurin.[50] And Roger of Montgomery also donated an important burg with its dependencies to Saint Etienne, Caen.[51] Ralph II of Tosny gave a forest to the Saint Ouen priory, La Croix Saint Leuffroy, and his son Ralph III was a benefactor of Jumièges and La Croix Saint Leuffroy as well as the Grandmesnil house of Saint Evroul.[52] Robert of Grandmesnil, in turn, donated a manor to Saint Etienne, Caen.[53] The dukes, through their relations with ducal and non-ducal monasteries, and through their participation in the agreements between lords and religious houses, were able to direct this movement of wealth and lands.

Closer analysis helps clarify the significance of these land transfers. For example, one document from the 1040s describes the arrangements which Roger II of Montgomery made with the abbey of Jumièges when a vassal of his decided to retire and become a monk.[54] While in Roger's service, the vassal

47 Orderic, 3, pp. 138–39.
48 Fauroux nos. 97, 179, 140, 215, 216, 217.
49 Lot, Etudes critiques, no. 42 (this charter survives in original form at ADSM 16H 30); Fauroux nos. 128, 129, 213, 92.
50 ADEure H793, 'Petite cartulaire', f. 72v.
51 Musset, Abbayes caennaises, nos. 1, 3.
52 AD Eure, H 280. Ralph's charter survives in original form. It is edited by Prévost, Mémoires, pp. 459–60. On the benefactions of Ralph III of Tosny, see Douglas, William the Conqueror, p. 113. Douglas, however, skips a generation in the Tosny family tree, calling Ralph III the son rather than the grandson of Roger I of Tosny. See Musset, 'Aux Origines d'une classe dirigeante', p. 57 for an accurate Tosny genealogy.
53 BN, nouv. acq. lat. 1406, f. 50r.
54 Fauroux no. 113. This charter survives in original form at ADSM 9H 30.

had held some property of him in the *villa* of Fontaine in lower Normandy.[55] When he decided to enter Jumièges, he asked Roger to donate that property to the monastery as an entrance gift. Roger agreed, and in exchange he received a horse worth thirty pounds and a hauberk worth seven pounds from the abbot and the vassal. Thus, Roger, by giving up his vassal's former fief to Jumièges, managed to reward his man for his service and at the same time receive compensation for his loss of property. Roger's vassal was able to retire at a prestigious ducal monastery near Rouen, while the abbey itself received property over eighty kilometers away, in the vicinity of lands it had already acquired.[56]

Arrangements like this show how monasteries increased both the number of options within Norman society and the range of agreements involving lands and men. Since Fontaine was not far from property which Jumièges already owned in lower Normandy, which included the former monastic sites at Vimoutiers and Almenèches, it was especially desirable to the abbey, despite its distance from Rouen. This point underlines the importance of the expansion of monastic patrimonies across the duchy: if Jumièges had limited its interests to upper Normandy, the community would have been less interested in Fontaine, and Roger of Montgomery's vassal would also have been less likely to spend his last days at the ducal monastery. The passage of lands and men across the region reveals the growing perception of the duchy as a single pool of exchange. And the fact that this act, like so many others, was confirmed by William the Conqueror emphasizes the duke's role in an interchange which added one more connection between a ducal monastery and a noble who founded his own communities, and one more tie between upper and lower Normandy.[57]

Another area in which the dukes were able to exercise control was the passage of monks between abbeys, and this movement further strengthened the connections between ducal and non-ducal houses. It began with Fécamp during Richard II's reign as William of Dijon sent disciples to reform ducal houses, and then expanded to include the private foundations that appeared under Richard's son and grandson.[58] Thus, Fécamp provided the first two abbots as well as the monks for Roger of Tosny's Conches.[59] Fécamp also supplied the first abbot for the monastery of Troarn, founded by Roger II of Montgomery. Saint Ouen sent a monk to become abbot of Goscelin of Rouen's Trinité du Mont, and another to become abbot of the countess of

---

55 Fontaine-les-Bassets, canton Trun.
56 Almenêches, canton Mortrée; Vimoutiers, canton Vimoutiers: Fauroux nos. 34, 36.
57 As noted above, Roger II of Montgomery founded the monasteries of Troarn, Saint Martin of Sées and Almenêches.
58 The discussion which follows concerning the movement of monks between monasteries in Normandy is based primarily on Torigny, *De immutatione*, pp. 191–206. On the accuracy of Robert of Torigny's text, see Douglas, *William the Conqueror*, p. 112, note 2.
59 Musset, 'Aux Origines d'une classe dirigeante', p. 53.

Eu's Saint Pierre sur Dives. Jumièges gave Saint Evroul its first abbot, and Saint Wandrille provided the first abbot for Humphrey of Vieilles' Saint Pierre of Préaux. Saint Wandrille also established monks, as well as customs, at Herluin of Conteville's Grestain. Gerbert, a former monk from Fécamp, reformed Saint Wandrille itself in the early 1060s.

Once the aristocratic abbeys had become established, they continued to pass prelates among themselves. Trinité du Mont, for example, provided the first abbots for Cormeilles, Tréport, Saint Pierre sur Dives, Saint Evroul and Troarn. Saint Evroul sent the second abbots to Lyre and to Saint Pierre sur Dives, while Lyre sent the first abbot to Ralph Taisson's Fontenay.[60] The second abbot of Fontenay came from Troarn.[61] Ducal houses also on occasion received abbots from private abbeys. The abbey of Bernay, for instance, received its second abbot from Roger of Montgomery's Troarn, and the rule of Lanfranc of Bec at Duke William's Saint Etienne, Caen is renowned.[62]

The career of Isembert of Germany serves to illustrate the circulation of monks through the abbeys of eleventh-century Normandy. Having been a monk at the ducal monastery of Saint Ouen under the rule of Abbot Nicholas, son of Duke Richard III, Isembert was chosen in the 1030s to become the first abbot of Trinité du Mont, Goscelin of Rouen's foundation.[63] At Trinité du Mont, Isembert taught theology and music for some twenty years, having among his disciples Ainard who later became the abbot of Saint Pierre sur Dives, Osbern the future abbot of Saint Evroul, and Durand the nephew of Gerard of Saint Wandrille who later became the abbot of Troarn.[64] This chain was derived ultimately from Fécamp since Nicholas, Isembert's abbot at Saint Ouen, had been a disciple of John of Ravenna, William of Dijon's successor.[65]

As Isembert's career shows, ducal and non-ducal houses were clearly connected through the interchange of monks, and the school of reform generated by Fécamp reached out to abbeys founded by lords outside the ducal family. By virtue of his authority to appoint abbots, the duke was able to direct the movement of monks like Isembert and his pupils, and the range of their travels added to the cohesion of monastic life in Normandy.[66] Given these close relations, it is reasonable to conclude that non-ducal abbeys did not undermine ducal control of monasticism in Normandy. But the fact

---

[60] *Gallia*, 11, cols. 645, 730, 414; On the rivalry between Lyre and St Wandrille over Fontenay, see Musset, 'Fontenay', pp. 16–19.

[61] *Gallia*, 11, c. 414.

[62] *Gallia*, 11, cols. 831, 422; Gibson, *Lanfranc*, pp. 98–111.

[63] *Gallia*, 11, cols. 125–26.

[64] *Gallia*, 11, cols. 416, 177; Fournée, *La Spiritualité en Normandie*, pp. 16–17.

[65] *Gallia*, 11, cols. 141–42; Jumièges, *GND*, 2, pp. 46–47.

[66] A letter from John of Ravenna to William the Conqueror c. 1076 reveals that the duke continued to appoint abbots after the Conquest. Abbot John simply requested that he be consulted before the duke chose the monk who would become abbot of Bernay. The letter is edited by J. Mabillon, *Vetera analecta* (Paris, 1723), pp. 450–51.

remains that several aristocratic monasteries were established on property and endowed with estates which had previously been in the possession of the ducal monastery of Fécamp. Modern scholars have assumed that these lands were usurped by lords who later donated them to their own communities. A re-examination of the evidence, however, suggests that historians have been too hasty in assuming predation.

The three top attestors of William the Conqueror's charters before 1066, Roger II of Montgomery, William fitz Osbern and Roger of Beaumont, stood out among the lords who built abbeys, earning high praise from William of Poitiers and Orderic Vitalis. Among their achievements, these men and their families were responsible for the construction of seven abbeys before 1066.[67] Yet these men are all charged with having acquired lands at the expense of Fécamp. Lucien Musset has described the Montgomery family as being 'particularly violent in the scramble' for church lands at the beginning of Robert the Magnificent's reign and during the minority of his son.[68] And David Douglas, in his biography of the Conqueror, agrees that Fécamp, along with several other ducal monasteries, 'clearly had reason to regret the rise of Montgomery in the second quarter of the eleventh century'.[69]

The properties which this family allegedly usurped include Troarn, Almenèches and half the burg of Bernay, lands which all belonged to Fécamp at one point, and which are all later found in the possession of the Montgomeries. The *acta* which indicate the movement of Fécamp lands into Montgomery hands disclose few details. In 1025, Troarn and Almenèches

---

[67] Montgomery: St Martin of Sées, St Martin of Troarn and Almenèches; Beaumont: St Pierre and St Léger at Préaux; fitz Osbern: Lyre and Cormeilles.

[68] According to Musset, Roger I of Montgomery 'prevailed upon his kinsman, the abbot or rather the guardian of Bernay, Thierry, to cede to him half of the burg of Bernay. . . . He took into his hands the land of Troarn, a dependence of Fécamp, while Hugh, bishop of Bayeux, related to the ducal family, usurped that of Argences close by. It is probable that Almenèches was usurped in the same way.' Lucien Musset, 'Les Premiers Temps de l'abbaye d'Almenèches', in *L'Abbaye d'Almenèches-Argentan et Sainte Opportune*, ed. Yves Chaussy (Paris, 1970), pp. 11–36, at pp. 20–21. Musset reaffirms this conclusion of usurpation in the following articles: Musset, 'Une Nouvelle Charte de Robert le Magnifique', pp. 142–53; Musset, 'Les Fiefs de deux familles vicomtales', pp. 342–43. More recently, David Bates, 1066, p. 100, also describes a 'feast on church property' during the early years of Robert's reign, and he includes members of the Montgomery family among the alleged despoilers of Fécamp's lands.

[69] Douglas, *William the Conqueror*, p. 91. An older school of historians was not so quick to accuse the Montgomery family. Over a century ago, A. Goujon wrote that Roger I of Montgomery was a protector of Bernay, chosen by the Fécamp guardian Thierry, rather than a predator. R. N. Sauvage, writing before World War I, likewise saw no reason to assume that Roger I of Montgomery acquired Troarn without the permission of Fécamp. And in 1020, Henri du Motey suggested that Troarn and Almenèches were simply bought rather than usurped from Fécamp. See A. Goujon, *Histoire de Bernay et de son canton touchant à l'histoire générale de la Normandie* (Evreux, 1875), p. 53; Sauvage, *Troarn*, pp. 10–12; Du Motey, *Origines*, p. 101.

were listed among the donations made to Fécamp by Richard II.[70] Troarn then reappeared in 1059 when Roger II of Montgomery endowed his new abbey Saint Martin of Troarn.[71] If we accept Roger II's claim that Troarn came 'de mea hereditate', then the elder Montgomery must have acquired it sometime between 1025 and his death around 1040.

Almenèches is harder to pin down. After the duke's donation to Fécamp of 'the residence which is called Almenèches, with the church and everything pertaining' in 1025, this land does not reappear in any surviving *acta* until 1178, when Alexander III confirmed the estates of the nunnery of Almenèches in a papal bull.[72] Since Robert of Torigny leaves no doubt that the ancient abbey of Almenèches was rebuilt by Roger II of Montgomery around 1060, the property must have changed hands sometime between 1025 and roughly 1060.[73] The editors of the *Gallia Christiana* believed that Fécamp gave Almenèches to Roger II of Montgomery specifically to rebuild the ancient nunnery there.[74] But the only sure conclusion that can be drawn from these few surviving documents is that Troarn and Almenèches passed from Fécamp to Roger I and Roger II of Montgomery, who chose these sites for two of the family's three monastic foundations.

Although modern historians assume wrongdoing, the fortunes of Bernay likewise provide no clear evidence of foul play. In 1025, Richard II founded the abbey of Bernay, entrusting it to the abbot of Fécamp, William of Dijon, and his successors.[75] Since William of Dijon had little time to devote to the new community, he delegated the responsibility of *custos* of Bernay to Thierry, the prior of Fécamp.[76] Robert of Torigny, the only source which mentions Montgomery's stake in Bernay, writes simply that Thierry gave half the burg of Bernay to Roger I of Montgomery 'so that he could provide for himself when he came to Bernay'.[77]

---

70 Fauroux no. 34.

71 Fauroux no. 144: '. . . res proprias de mea hereditate trado Deo omnipotenti et Sancto Martino de Truardo ipsum in primis Truardum ex integro . . .'

72 Fauroux, no. 34, p. 130: '. . . masnile quod dicitur Almanniscus, cum aecclesia et omnibus ejus pertinentiis.' The papal bull is printed in Musset, 'Almenèches', pp. 33–36.

73 Jumièges, *GND*, 2, pp. 132–33. The editors of *Neustria*, p. 366, also place the foundation of Almenèches about 1060.

74 *Gallia*, 11, c. 736: '. . . Richard II anno 1026 Almaniscas Fiscannensibus monachis largitus est, qui parthenonis restituendi cupido Rogerio jura sua cessere anno 1070.' It is not possible to date precisely the foundation for Almenèches since the abbey's archives were completely destroyed by fire. We can only assume that the house existed before 1070 since the first abbess, Adelasia, attested a charter with Ivo, bishop of Sées, who died in 1070. Musset, 'Almenèches', p. 23.

75 Fauroux no. 35.

76 Bulst, *Untersuchungen*, pp. 173–76.

77 Torigny, *De immutatione*, p. 194: 'Hujus custodes fuerunt Rodulfus, abbas Sancti Michaelis, et post ipsum Theodericus Gemmeticensis, quorum prior dedit Uticum et Bellum Montellum Hunfrido de Vetulis, sequens vero medietatem burgi Bernaii patri

Since Thierry died about 1027, the arrangement between Roger and Bernay's *custos* would have taken place around the time of Richard II's death, Richard III's short rule and his brother's accession. There is no doubt that the church, secular and regular, suffered in this unsettled period. Duke Robert himself admitted that he had distributed property belonging to Fécamp and Montivilliers to his knights when he first became duke, and that he had wrenched lands from Saint Wandrille.[78] Later charters also confirm the restoration of various possessions local lords had seized unjustly from Trinité du Mont and the cathedral in Rouen.[79] Similarly, the bishop of Coutances was found early in Robert's reign dividing the prebends of his cathedral among his relatives.[80]

Roger I of Montgomery is thought to have coerced Thierry, whom Torigny calls his kinsman (*propinquus*), to grant this land to him, perhaps even seizing it by force.[81] Like the duke, Roger admitted to having mistreated monastic property in the early years of Robert's reign when he transferred a market which belonged to Jumièges into his own domain.[82] Jumièges later regained its market and received compensation from Roger for revenue the abbey had lost. This incident indicates that Roger I of Montgomery was willing to exploit the opportunity when ducal protection of monasticism lapsed. Had he usurped half the burg of Bernay, however, an outcry from Fécamp would be expected. As the reaction of Jumièges demonstrates, Norman monks did not suffer their lands to be taken quietly, and in the more settled times which followed they frequently demanded restitution, clearly identifying the culprits.[83] Of all the monasteries in Normandy which could have raised its voice against lords who despoiled its lands, Fécamp was in the best position, especially during the reign of John the Ravenna, an efficient administrator close to the duke. Consequently, the silence regarding Montgomery's alleged plunder of Bernay should not be simply dismissed as a failure of monks to complain or of records to survive. The assumption of modern historians that the transfer of an estate from a ducal monastery to a ducal *fidelis* automatically signals plunder is too simplistic.

It might be argued that Thierry was an irresponsible guardian of Bernay who took advantage of his position to enrich a powerful relative. But this view of Thierry does not match the picture of him presented elsewhere. It was this monk who accompanied Richard II to the peace assembly at Com-

Rogerii de Monte Gommerici, qui erat propinquus ejus, ut inde se procuraret quando Bernaium venisset.' As Bulst points out, *Untersuchungen*, p. 174, Torigny reversed the order of *custodes*: Thierry was first, and Rodulf followed him.
78 Fauroux nos. 70, 80, 95.
79 Fauroux nos. 201, 66.
80 *Gallia*, 11, col. 869; *De statu*, col. 218.
81 See above, note 77.
82 Fauroux no. 74. This charter survives in original form at ADSM 9H 30.
83 See, for example, Fauroux nos. 49, 70, 74, 80, 95, 148, 201.

piègne in 1023 where they met with Robert king of Francia, Baldwin of Flanders, the emperor Henry II and Lédvin of Saint Vaast.[84] And it was also this monk, in charge of Jumièges in 1017 and Mont-Saint-Michel in 1022, whom William of Dijon designated as his right-hand man in Normandy – a distinction that speaks highly for Thierry's character and ability.[85] Moreover, if he had been an untrustworthy *custos* of Bernay, it is unlikely that Orderic Vitalis would have placed such emphasis on the close, personal ties between Thierry, whom he considered both 'reverend' and 'venerable', and the first abbot of Saint Evroul.[86] It is also worth noting that the editors of *Neustria Pia* and *Gallia Christiana* saw no grounds for suspicion in the grant of half the burg of Bernay to Montgomery, just as they saw nothing amiss in the foundations of Saint-Martin of Troarn and Almenèches on lands previously held by Fécamp.[87]

More importantly, Fécamp itself played an active role in the Montgomery abbeys. As Orderic recalls, Roger II of Montgomery sought out Gilbert, a former Fécamp monk, and entrusted him with the reform of Troarn, 'driving out the twelve canons whom his father Roger had established there'.[88] Following Gilbert as abbot of Troarn was Durand, another monk from Fécamp who had carried the crosier for John of Ravenna. Durand was also the nephew of Gerard, abbot of Saint Wandrille, and the disciple of Isembert, abbot at Trinité du Mont.[89] Clearly, he was well-connected with the reform movement based in upper Normandy. Orderic reports that Saint Martin of Troarn, as well as Roger II's later foundation Saint Martin of Sées, 'both owed their foundation to the same lord and their monastic customs and ritual to the same source. Roger of Montgomery established monks in both; and the custom of Fécamp provided them with their monastic rites.'[90]

All this argues for good relations between the ducal abbey of Fécamp and the Montgomery monasteries. A later charter, moreover, shows the abbeys of Fécamp and Troarn collaborating on the maintenance of a road which ran between Troarn and the Fécamp priory of Argences.[91] Nor did William the Conqueror treat Roger II of Montgomery as someone who had seized lands from Fécamp. On the contrary, the duke enlisted his help in his efforts to expand monasticism in Normandy, delegating to Roger the protection of the

---

84 Lemarignier, 'Paix et réforme monastique', p. 453.
85 Chanteux, 'L'Abbé Thierry', pp. 67–72; Bates, 1066, pp. 195–96.
86 Orderic, 2, pp. 18–19, 74–75.
87 *Neustria*, pp. 400, 558, 366; *Gallia*, 11, cols. 831, 416, 736.
88 Orderic, 2, pp. 20–21.
89 Orderic, 4, pp. 162–65; Sauvage, *Troarn*, pp. 287–88.
90 Orderic, 4, pp. 164–65: '. . . et Fiscannensis norma utrumque monachico ritui applicavit'.
91 Sauvage, *Troarn*, no. 6, pp. 364–65 (dated 1066–1083). On the subject of public roads in Normandy, see Lucien Musset, 'Voie publique et chemin du roi en Normandie du XIe au XIIIe siècle', in *Autour du pouvoir*, pp. 95–111.

new priories Saint Martin of Ecajeul and Sainte Barbe en Auge.[92] Moreover, Roger's own community of Troarn numbered among the private abbeys which received promises from the duke of protection against all adversaries.[93]

Rather than assume that Roger I or Roger II usurped these lands against Fécamp's will, we should consider the problem more carefully from Fécamp's point of view. When the possessions of this monastery are mapped, the distance between Troarn, Almenèches and even Bernay from Fécamp and the majority of its holdings is striking. And a comparison with the lands of other monasteries in Normandy underlines their isolation. Besides Fécamp and Saint Taurin, only Mont-Saint-Michel held interests as far west as Troarn when Richard II gave this property to Fécamp in 1025, and no upper Norman monastery possessed lands as far south as Almenèches, so close to the Bellême stronghold of Alençon. A charter from the 1020s, in which William of Bellême restores three burgs with their dependencies to the cathedral of Sées, shows that the Bellême family was aggressive in its acquisition of lands in this area.[94] No doubt the only reason William of Bellême decided to return these lands to the church was because the bishop of Sées at that time was his kinsman, Sigefridus. It is worth noting that all three of the burgs which William of Bellême returned were within ten kilometers of Almenèches.[95] Their proximity emphasizes that Almenèches was deep in Bellême territory; from Fécamp's perspective, the monastery's chances of defending this distant possession were low.

Indeed, the most recent scholarship on the Bellême lordship suggests that Almenèches itself was part of the patrimony of the first lordship of Bellême.[96] At the time of Richard II's donation of Almenèches to Fécamp, the bishopric of Sées had passed from the Bellême Sigefridus to Radbod, a local lord with close ties to the Norman court.[97] Perhaps the duke thought he could get away with granting Bellême lands to Fécamp, as long as the monks could rely on support from the local bishop. But when Ivo of Bellême gained the episcopal seat of Sées in the next decade, Fécamp's hold on Almenèches must have become tenuous indeed. Given these considerations, the reappearance of Almenèches in Montgomery possession a few decades later appears much less sinister, at least from the point of view of Fécamp.

In the heart of Bellême territory, Almenèches was a difficult property for Fécamp to maintain in the best of times; with Ivo of Bellême on the episcopal

---

[92] Fauroux no. 222; *Regesta* no. 72.

[93] Sauvage, *Troarn*, no. 2, pp. 350–51: '. . . ut Sancti Martini Troarnensis abbas et monachi eas firmiter teneant in perpetuo et quiete maneant sub defensione mea et heredum meorum contra omnes adversarios . . .'

[94] Fauroux no. 33.

[95] Chailloué, Boiville and Giberville are today approximately eight, eight and a half, and ten kilometers from Almenèches, respectively.

[96] Louise, *Bellême*, 1, p. 390.

[97] See above, Chapter Four, note 49.

seat, Fécamp's hold would have been in danger of slipping entirely. It is therefore possible that Fécamp accepted the acquisition of these lands by Montgomery sometime in the second quarter of the century when Robert the Magnificent established Roger I of Montgomery as *vicomte* of this *pagus* to counter Bellême encroachment.[98] This would make it easier to understand the close ties between the Montgomery monasteries: the ducal abbey encouraged, even sponsored, the new foundations. Fécamp may have made an arrangement with Montgomery that the monastery would not dispute his possession of Troarn and Almenèches on the condition that abbeys be constructed there. There is no way of knowing for certain what happened, given the gaps in our sources, but the context argues that the acquisition of these lands by Montgomery was not a case of simple theft from Fécamp.

Robert of Torigny's terse statement that Roger I of Montgomery received half of Bernay 'to provide for himself' can and has been read many ways. Bernay, like Troarn and Almenèches, was south of Fécamp, and the *Gallia Christiana* editors recorded that it had fallen into the hands of the counts of Alençon when it was granted to Roger.[99] Since the counts of Alençon at this time could only mean the Bellême family, this statement has far-reaching implications, suggesting urgent need for a local protector. This may have provided sufficient incentive for Thierry to grant half the town to Roger I of Montgomery. Robert the Magnificent gave back to Fécamp half the vill of Bernay, with all its appurtenances, between 1032 and 1035.[100] No mention is made of Montgomery – it is not even certain that this was his half – but it seems possible that Fécamp no longer felt it needed a local guardian at Bernay during the more settled times toward the end of Robert's reign, and therefore reasserted direct control of its holdings there.

Also accused of predation is Roger of Beaumont's father Humphrey of Vieilles, who is thought to have stolen from Bernay its property at Beaumont and Vieilles. Again, however, the case is not persuasive.[101] The foundation charter of Bernay recalls that Richard II gave Beaumont and Vieilles to the

---

98   Kathleen Thompson, 'The Norman Aristocracy before 1066: the Example of the Montgomerys', *Historical Research*, 60 (1987), pp. 251–63. Thompson points out that Roger I of Montgomery fell out of favor during Duke William's minority. The *vicomté* of the Hiémois was handed over to Thurstin Goz about 1035–1043, and Roger I of Montgomery was banished to Paris in this period. According to Thompson, Roger II's foundation of Troarn about 1050 was therefore a means to retain influence over ducal lands formerly in his father's charge. However Thompson notes, p. 260, 'It is interesting that Fécamp never challenged the legality of the Montgomerys' seizure of their lands.' Ockham's razor suggests that Fécamp did not contest the Montgomery's possession of Troarn because the abbey did not object to it.

99   *Gallia*, 11, c. 831: '. . . quae in Alenconiorum comitum manus delapsa.'

100 Fauroux no. 85, p. 225: 'Reddidi etiam totam medietatem Bernai villae, cum omnibus que ad ipsam medietatem pertinent ex integro.'

101 Accusations appear in Douglas, *William the Conqueror*, pp. 90–91; Bates, *1066*, p. 100.

new community in 1025.[102] Robert of Torigny records that the Fécamp *custos* of Bernay gave Beaumont to Humphrey, lord of Pont Audemer.[103] The *Gallia Christiana* editors, seeing a connection between this grant and the property Montgomery gained, explained that these transfers took place 'since they [Roger of Montgomery and Humphrey of Vieilles] had to take care of things'.[104] It seems reasonable to suggest that the Fécamp *custos* of Bernay was again ceding property, in this case Beaumont, to secure the protection of a local lord against external threats.[105] There was no outcry, and the monks of Fécamp gave no indication in any of the extant ducal charters that the *caput* of the Beaumont family was seized against their wishes. The sources do not tell how Humphrey received Vieilles from Bernay. The earliest evidence of this surname appears in an extant original charter from the 1030s.[106] And so, he must have become associated with Vieilles sometime in the decade following its dedication to Bernay. In the cases of both Beaumont and Vieilles, however, silence argues against theft, and it seems ill-advised to assume foul play when neither Bernay nor Fécamp complained.

Unlike the Montgomery acquisitions of Troarn and Almenèches, Beaumont and Vieilles did not reappear as monastic foundations or as benefactions, but Humphrey of Vieilles' cooperation with Saint Wandrille in the establishment of his monastery Saint Pierre, Préaux, is reminiscent of Roger II of Montgomery's enlistment of Fécamp's help in founding his houses. Saint Pierre, Préaux, was built around 1035 with the counsel of Gradulf, abbot of the ducal house of Saint Wandrille, and the new abbey received its first abbot and monks from Saint Wandrille.[107] Having been reformed by Gerard, the founder of Crépy in the Ile de France, Saint Wandrille stood outside the Fécamp network until the 1060s, yet the abbey was also closely allied with

---

102 Fauroux no. 35.

103 Torigny, *De immutatione*, p. 194; *Gallia*, 11, c. 515 records that the *custos* at the time was Ralph of Beaumont, a Fécamp monk.

104 *Gallia*, 11, c. 831: 'At dum monasterii res curare debuissent, Radulfus dedit Bellummontellum Humfrido de Vetulis, factus postea abbas sancti Michaelis, et Theodoricus medietatem burgi Bernaici patri Rogerii de Montegomerici, quae in Alenconiorum comitum manus delapsa, comitatus titulum accepit.'

105 David Bates, *1066*, p. 101, has pointed out that Humphrey of Vieilles extended his lands south from Pont Audemer toward Conches; it is likely that Neubourg, close to Bernay, was also in Humphrey's hands.

106 In Fauroux no. 85: *Unfredus vetulus*. See Jumièges, *GND*, 2, p. 96, note 3. He is also called *Hunfridus de Vetulabus* in Fauroux no. 50, a twelfth-century copy of a charter dated 1017–1026, but if the toponym were actually contemporary, it would mean that Humphrey received Vieilles no less than a year after its dedication to Bernay. It is likely that the twelfth-century scribe simply added *de Vetulabus* when he rewrote the document.

107 *Gallia*, 11, cols. 834–35: 'Quamobrem accersito Gradulfo Fontanellae abbate cui valde familiaris erat, ejus consilio novi monasterii aedificia disposuit, brevique multum promovit eidemque locum regendum commisit. Mox adducti e Fontanella monachi quibus sui vice Gradulfus praefecit Ansfridum abbatem.'

the dukes and figured prominently in the ducal charters.[108] The nunnery Saint Léger appeared beside Saint Pierre at Préaux around 1050, and the generosity of Humphrey's son, Roger, to Saint Wandrille in 1086 suggests that good relations continued between the family and the ducal abbey.[109]

Humphrey of Vieilles and his sons also established ties with Fécamp. The most interesting case involves an arrangement in 1034 or 1035 by which a monk named Peter moved from Fécamp to Humphrey's abbey of Saint Pierre of Préaux. With the permission of the duke, the abbot and monks of Fécamp, and Humphrey's son Roger, Peter donated considerable property to Préaux, lands which he held as a benefice of Roger.[110] This is significant in itself since it indicates that Peter had been Roger of Beaumont's man when he entered Fécamp, and that his gift to Préaux came from the benefice he still held of Roger, who was after all the son of the Préaux's founder.[111] Peter did not join Préaux immediately, however. Instead, 'he at first withdrew from them to the church of Saint Martin de Flaville in the woods of Bonneville', roughly twenty kilometers west of Préaux, where he lived in seclusion with a few brothers. When he was ready to leave this hermitage, Peter then moved to Préaux, donating additional properties to the monastery. The cell in the woods of Bonneville continued after Peter's departure, and by 1066 it had grown into the Fécamp priory of Saint Martin du Bosc.[112]

Thus, Fécamp gained a new priory which flourished in the woods of Bonneville, and Préaux accepted a monk from Fécamp who brought to Préaux his benefice from the Beaumont lordship. There are several possible interpretations of this sequence of events. On one hand, the abbot of Fécamp, John of Ravenna, might have decided to found a new priory for Fécamp near Beaumont, so he sent Peter to lay the groundwork since he already had local connections. On the other hand, it is also possible that Peter himself sought the move, and that he withdrew to the woods of Bon-

---

108 Lot, *Etudes critiques*, pp. liv–cxii; Fauroux nos. 7, <27>, 30, 46, 46b, 52, 55, 69, 80, 95, 102, 106, 108, 109, 124, 125, 126, 128, 129, 134, 152, 153, 154, 177, 190, 207, 234.

109 Torigni, *De immutatione*, p. 199; *Gallia*, 11, c. 853; Lot, *Etudes critiques*, no. 41.

110 Fauroux no. 88, p. 230: 'Quidam Fiscannensis monachus nomine Petrus dedit Sancto Petro Pratelli mediam ecclesiam Sancte Oportune Exnutriville, et decimam mediam ejusdem ville, et XLVI acros terre, ut ibi efficeretur reclusus. Quod et factum est. Hoc autem egit, jubente inclito rege Anglorum Willelmo et Rogero Bellimontis, de quo idem Petrus suprascriptum benefitium tenebat, et concedente Johanne abbate Fiscanni com (*sic*) omni congregatione sua; eorum enim monachus fuerat professus, et eorum licentia, postquam ab eis recessit primo, in silva Boneville in ecclesia Sancti Martini Flaviville (*sic*), cum quibusdam fratribus habitavit. Inde vero ut reclusus sicut dictum est efficeretur, Pratellum venit. Dedit etiam cum supra scriptis decimam piscium Weneburgi maris mediam tamen ex ea parte quam tenuerat Gaufridus et emerat idem Petrus ab eodem Gaufrido ut cetera omnia.' The earliest extant copy of this charter dates from the thirteenth century.

111 Humphrey attested the charter: 'Signum Hunfridi constructori (*sic*) loci.'

112 Fauroux no. 218. The charter of St Martin du Bosc exists in original form at ADSM 7H 12.

neville because he knew the area and continued to hold property nearby. It is even possible that Roger of Beaumont initiated the arrangement because he wanted Préaux to receive the benefice that Peter held of him. These scenarios are all worth considering since it is clear that this charter, which survives as an imperfect thirteenth-century cartulary copy, does not tell the whole story.[113] What is certain is that Roger of Beaumont, Fécamp and Préaux all approved of Peter's move, that Préaux's support was ensured by the initial gift of Peter's benefice from Roger of Beaumont, and that this marked the beginning of a Fécamp priory near the lordship of Beaumont.

This example offers insight into the variety and complexity of agreements which lords and monasteries formed in early Normandy. It also provides clear testimony that there was more going on than meets the modern eye. Complicated arrangements took place and sometimes only a few clues survive, a point which warns against assuming that movements of lands which our sources do not explain automatically signal theft. More specifically, with respect to the charges of predation which historians have raised against Humphrey of Vieilles, Peter's story argues that John of Ravenna was willing to strike deals to gain local protectors for Fécamp's interests. It seems reasonable to suggest, therefore, that he instructed the Fécamp *custos* of Bernay to cede Vieilles and Beaumont from Bernay's patrimony to Humphrey to secure his support for the new community. This conclusion explains the lack of contemporary outcry against Humphrey's alleged theft, and it fits best with Robert of Torigny's claim that the Fécamp *custos* of Bernay simply gave Beaumont to Humphrey. Thus, the editors of *Gallia Christiana* were probably right: Humphrey of Vieilles, like Robert of Montgomery, would have received this property so that he would 'take care of things'.

Finally, among the lords charged with usurping Fécamp's lands is Bishop Hugh of Bayeux, the son of Ralph of Ivry, half brother of Duke Richard I.[114] Since Hugh's lands passed down to his nephew, William fitz Osbern, the second highest attestor of Duke William's pre-Conquest charters, the case made against Hugh deserves re-examination.[115] It concerns a single, albeit important, piece of property in the Bessin: the domain of Argences, about fifteen kilometers south-east of Caen. In 990, Richard I gave Argences with all its appurtenances to Fécamp.[116] The confirmation charter of his son

---

113 A reference to Duke William as the king of England further confuses the chronology in the act. Since the signatures of Robert the Magnificent and Humphrey of Vieilles appear beside William's, it seems likely that a post-Conquest scribe recopied the charter, adding the duke's new title, while preserving the original attestation list.

114 On this bishop, see David Bates, 'Notes sur l'aristocratie normande: Hugues, évêque de Bayeux (1011 env. –1049)', AN, 23 (1973), pp. 7–38.

115 For Fitz Osbern's attestations, see above, note 9. On the descent of these lands, see Bates, 1066, p. 119; Bates, 'Hugues, évêque de Bayeux'.

116 Fauroux no. 4, p. 73: '. . . confero ei in hoc loco, qui dicitur Fiscannus . . . Argentias etiam cum omnibus appenditiis suis'. William of Malmesbury, *De gestis regum anglorum*, ed. Stubbs, vol. 90 (Rolls Series), p. 210, relates a story about Fécamp's

Richard II shows that by 1025 Argences was already a commercial center with a weekly public market.[117] Then, regretting that he had distributed possessions of Fécamp to his knights in his younger and more desperate days, Robert the Magnificent restored Argences to the abbey between 1028 and 1034.[118] Fécamp therefore temporarily lost Argences sometime toward the beginning of Robert the Magnificent's reign, only to regain it again in the final years of his rule.

Bishop Hugh of Bayeux meanwhile had quarrelled violently with Robert when the young duke first assumed power. William of Jumièges explains that the bishop, angry at Robert for ignoring his advice, secretly introduced arms and supplies into the castle of Ivry which he had inherited from his father, Duke Robert's uncle.[119] The bishop then rushed off to gather knights outside of Normandy to lead against the duke, but Robert anticipated trouble, successfully laid seige to Ivry, and forced Hugh into exile for some years.[120] Charter evidence supports the story William of Jumièges tells: Hugh bishop of Bayeux disappears from the witness lists from 1025–1026 to 1030–1032.[121]

When Hugh returned in the early 1030s he regained favor with the duke, attesting ducal *acta* until his death in 1049. In 1034, Robert the Magnificent confirmed an agreement between the bishop of Bayeux and the abbey of Fécamp in which the monks agreed to exchange their possessions at Ar-

acquisition of Argences. He writes that the sacristan at Fécamp struck Richard II, not knowing who he was, when the duke tried to interrupt and join the monks during matins. Pretending to be very angry, Richard II ordered the monk to stand before him while he described the encounter to his court. After keeping the poor man in terrified suspense for a considerable period of time (*et prae metu pene exanimato*), the duke turned the jest into an occasion of compassion, adding the village of Argences, where the best wine is said to be, with all its appurtenances to the sacristan's office.

117 Fauroux no. 34, p. 130: 'Concedo etiam apud Argentias mercatum forense per singulas anni ebdomadas . . .'

118 Fauroux no. 70, pp. 206–07: 'Ego Robertus . . . transtuli ad militiam nostram quasdam possessiones monasterii sancte Trinitatis. Tactus vero respectu Dei, cum juvenilis ætatis ingreder evum, . . . vestivi cum omni integritate praedicta ecclesiae quas abstulerant villas, et in perpetuum restitutas omni auctoritate censeo: id est Argentia cum omni integritate . . .'

119 Jumièges, *GND*, 2, pp. 52–53: 'Interea dum hec geruntur perspiciens Baiocasine urbis presul Hugo, Rodulfi comitis filius, prudentium consilia ducem velle sectari, suaque destitui, quadam usus versutia doli Ibroicum castrum clam armis alimoniisque sufficienter munivit.'

120 Jumièges, *GND*, 2, pp. 52–53: 'Et custodibus positis Franciam ocius adiit, ut inde milites sibi conduceret, qui illum ad repugnandum viriliter juvarent. Cuius molimina fraudis dux accelerans anticipare, contractis Normannorum copiis, idem castellum preoccupavit obsidione, clausa egrediendi ab eo sive ingrediendi omnibus hominibus facultate.'

121 Fauroux nos. 55 (original act, 1025 or 1026, *Signum Hugonis Baiocensis episcopus*); 61 (eleventh-century copy, 1030, *S. Hugonis, episcopi* – this could be a different Bishop Hugh); 64 (thirteenth-century copy, 1032, *Signum Hugonis Bajocensis episcopi*).

gences for one hundred rural tenants, three churches, woods, meadows and all the dependencies, along with twenty freemen at three coastal towns near Dieppe: Biville, Brunville and Penly, in the north-east corner of the duchy. The bishop also agreed to give Fécamp a fishing port between Tréport and Dieppe, as well as the vill of Vieux Rouen with a mill, about forty kilometers inland from Tréport.[122] At Hugh's death, Argences with all its appurtenances would return to Fécamp, and the abbey would permanently keep the men and lands the bishop had traded. For Lucien Musset this act incriminates Bishop Hugh, whom he sees among the ranks of the predators of Fécamp's lands. Musset writes that Duke Robert forced the monks to agree to this exchange which was not in their interests as a favor to Hugh, with whom the duke had recently been reconciled.[123]

The charter does show that Hugh initiated the transaction and that the Fécamp monks at first hesitated to accept the trade, but there is no reason to assume that the final agreement represented Hugh's first offer. The monks' initial hesitation may have been simply to bargain for better terms. More importantly, the exchange outlined in the charter made sense for both parties. As the bishop of Bayeux, Hugh could conveniently administer Argences which was in his diocese and far from the abbey; Fécamp, on the other hand, was in a natural position to manage its new holdings in the Pays de Talou. Moreover, there was an escape clause in the charter stating that the monks would automatically regain Argences, whether or not Hugh was still alive, if they had any difficulty claiming their new possessions in the north.[124] But

---

122 Fauroux no. 71, pp. 208–09: 'Fecerunt itaque per tales tamen convenientias: episcopus debet dare monachis centum hospites ad presens . . . et tres ecclesias, et XX francos homines in locis qui appellantur Boiavilla, Brumvilla, Penloi, Lexartum cum portu piscatorio, cum silvis, pascuis, et omnibus pertinentiis suis et villam quae dicitur Vetus Rodum cum molendino et omnibus appendiciis ejus; et debet recipere ab ipsis monachis predictam terram, id est Argentias, per tale conventum ut usque dum vixerit teneat, et post obitum ejus, monachi eam statim recipiant, id est ipsam villam Argentias, per meam licentiam sine contradictione alicujus potestatis cujuslibet ordinis, seu magnae parvaeque personae, sic ex integro cum terris, vineis, modendinis, silvis, pratis, aquis, et mercato forensi, seu omnibus appendiciis ejus absque ulla calumnia, sicut unquam melius tenuerunt; et ipsos centum hospites quos episcopus donat, sicut praedictum est, in prenominatis locis, cum omnibus suis appendiciis, similiter cum ipsa, post obitum episcopi teneant et possideant jure hereditario in alodum, ex mea parte concessum sicut predictum est.'

123 Musset, 'Contribution de Fécamp', p. 62; Musset, 'Une Nouvelle Charte de Robert le Magnifique', pp. 149–50.

124 Fauroux no. 71, p. 209: 'Notum quoque esse volo quia illa terra, quam dat episcopus, quorumdam hominum calumniis refutata est a monachis postquam has convenientias incepimus antequam perficeremus, et postea a me et ab ipso episcopo tali convenientia est data et ab eis recepta ut si per illam calumniam dammum aliquod ipsi monachi habuerint, duas reclamationes in mea corte vel curia faciant, et si tunc ego et episcopus non acquitaverimus eam, monachi per meam licentiam, sine contradictione vel malivolentia episcopi, vel alicujus hominis reveniant ad villam suam Argentias et recipiant eam et teneant et possideant absque ullo deinceps cambio.'

the strongest bonus for Fécamp was that the abbey was to recover Argences at Hugh's death in any case, while keeping the lands which he had given, *jure hereditario in alodum*. Contrary to Musset's conclusion, this trade between Fécamp and Hugh bishop of Bayeux seems to have been very much in the monks' favor.[125]

The view of Hugh usurping Fécamp's property, moreover, is not consistent with the picture of him presented in other sources. It was this bishop who raised his voice against *raptores ecclesiae* during William's minority.[126] And Bishop Hugh was generous to the ducal house of Jumièges, as well as to the aristocratic foundation of Saint Amand where his sister Emma, the wife of Osbern the Steward and mother of William fitz Osbern, became abbess after her husband's murder.[127] Nor should the bishop's quarrel with his cousin at the beginning of Robert's reign be counted against Hugh. The new duke also besieged and exiled their uncle Robert archbishop of Rouen in the same period. William of Jumièges is careful to blame their dispute on the 'counsel of depraved men' and records that the archbishop retaliated by placing Normandy under interdict.[128] The charters also ascribe Duke Robert's appropriation of church lands to the 'counsel of evil men' in the early years of his reign.[129] Since Hugh's complaint at this time was that the duke did not listen to his advice, the bishop should not be associated with Robert's distribution of ecclesiastical benefices among his knights. In fact, considering Hugh's reaction to the depredation of church lands during William's minority, Robert's misuse of ecclesiastical property may have been a cause of their conflict.

William fitz Osbern, then, inherited no stain on his family record from his

---

125 It is not clear from subsequent charters if this exchange actually occurred. A charter (Fauroux no. 85), dating from 1031 to 1035, shows Fécamp holding Argences, but this could indicate possession either before or after the trade between Fécamp and the bishop of Bayeux was to have taken place. Musset ('Contribution de Fécamp', p. 62 and 'Une Nouvelle Charte de Robert le Magnifique', p. 150) assumes that the deal failed since Robert the Magnificent soon died, but there is no way to confirm his assumption. There are no references to Biville, Brunville, Penly or Vieux-Rouen in later Fécamp charters before 1066, but neither are there any general confirmations of Fécamp properties, so the failure of these lands to reappear is not conclusive.

126 *Antiquus Cartularius ecclesiae Baiocensis (Livre Noir)*, ed. V. Bourrienne, 1 (Rouen, 1902), no. 21: 'Hoc ergo felici et divino accensus commercio, videns quosdam raptores ecclesiae qui, post excessum Ricardi comitis ejusque filii Rotgerti, omni postposita aequitate, jure quodam tirannico terras Sanctae Mariae plurimas Baiocacensis ecclesiae quia vi abstulerant, dolui, quod multum diu ferre non potui . . .' Hugh's outrage in this passage makes it hard to consider him a predator of church lands.

127 For Jumièges, see Vernier no. 8. This charter survives in original form at ADSM 9H 27. For St Amand, see Fauroux no. 116.

128 Jumièges, *GND*, 2, pp. 48–49: 'Quamobrem diutine pacis oblectamento semper meruit frui, preter id quod pravorum consultu sponte sibi delegit.'

129 Fauroux nos. 70, 74, 80, 95; *Inventio*, p. 47.

uncle, the bishop of Bayeux. And the rest of his family's participation in the revival of monastic life in Normandy was considerable. William's grandfather, Ralph of Ivry, and his father, Osbern the Steward, richly endowed the ducal abbey of Saint Ouen, while William himself donated to Saint Amand where his mother ruled after Osbern's death.[130] Both he and his brother Osbern were benefactors of Trinité du Mont, Rouen, granting lands to the community themselves and endorsing donations of their men.[131] William fitz Osbern also endowed Bec and La Trinité, Caen.[132] He was personally responsible for two new monastic foundations, Lyre and Cormeilles 'on his own estates,' as Orderic writes, about twenty-four kilometers south-east of Bernay, and fifteen kilometers south-west of Pont Audemer, respectively.[133] Moreover, like Roger II of Montgomery, William fitz Osbern was entrusted by the duke to guard and protect monastic properties – in fitz Osbern's case, the Norman possessions of the monastery of Saint Denis.[134]

There is no doubt that the church, secular and regular, suffered when Robert the Magnificent assumed his brother's place as duke in the late 1020s, and also when he died in 1035, leaving the seven-year-old William as his successor. Monastic property was particularly vulnerable when ducal authority waned, and later reclamations indicate that some lands were lost in the disruption. But it is not safe to assume theft whenever charters show the property of one monastery later in the patrimony of another, especially when those houses maintained close relations. We do not know the full story behind these transfers of property from Fécamp to the families of Montgomery, Beaumont and fitz Osbern, but sufficient evidence exists to revise current assumptions of usurpation. The variety of deals which Fécamp was willing to cut with local lords to protect and promote its interests shows that it was not a passive victim of aristocratic depredation. Instead, Fécamp contributed to the connections between private and ducal monasteries by weaving a complex web of agreements with the nobles of the region.

The monasteries which noble families began building in Normandy after 1030, therefore, were not established at the expense of Fécamp. Nor did they undermine the ducal program of monastic reform. Instead, they contributed to the unity of the duchy through the ties they formed and the customs they shared. Established by nobles within the ducal circle, private monasteries

---

[130] Fauroux nos. 13, 193, 182.
[131] Fauroux nos. 96, 118; Deville, *Cartulaire*, no. 55.
[132] Fauroux nos. 180, 181, 231.
[133] Orderic, 2, pp. 12–13; Fauroux no. 120. Two copies of the foundation charter for the abbey of Lyre survive at AD Eure, H 438. For a study of this monastery, see C. Guéry, *Histoire de l'abbaye de Lyre* (Evreux, 1917), but Fauroux's edition of the foundation charter is to be preferred to Guéry's, pp. 562–64. For Cormeilles, see Jacques Henry, 'L'Abbaye Notre-Dame de Cormeilles', in *Normandie*, ed. Gaillard, pp. 305–21.
[134] Bates, *1066*, p. 207.

appeared during periods of strong central authority and were often subordinated to ducal protection. Their founders were related by blood and willing to endow each other's communities, as well as ducal houses. The movement of men and property between all these communities, ducal and non-ducal, further reinforced the connections which increasingly bound the duchy together.

7

Conclusion

The rulers of Normandy performed a complex juggling act: starting from a pagan Norse military power base around Rouen, they built an accepted political entity within the boundaries of the Christian state their ancestors had invaded. In establishing this new realm, they melded together disparate peoples, customs and traditions. By 1066, the region under Norman control stretched from the Bresle and the Epte Rivers to the west coast of the Cotentin, and it had taken on an identity all its own. In the face of internal and external threats, the Normans' successful creation of a unified polity shows the resourcefulness which characterized their reign. Indeed, they succeeded so far as to undertake and prevail in the Conquest of England. In this process of state-building within Normandy, the revival and reform of monasticism was a key component.

In Dudo's version of Normandy's past, Rollo's son William Longsword wished as a youth 'to forsake this transient age and to become a monk at Jumièges'.[1] Only the urgent protests of the abbot of Jumièges dissuaded the young count: 'Defender of this homeland, why do you wish to do such things? Who will sustain the clergy and the people? Who will rule the people vigorously by ancestral law? To whom will you commit and commend the herd?'[2] No matter how William longed for the perfect life of the cloister, the abbot explained, he would best serve the monastery outside its walls, as its protector and as its duke. However unlikely it was that Rollo's son actually desired monastic retirement, Dudo's story nevertheless underlines the association between ducal authority and monasticism which was true in his own day – and remained so. Approximately a century after Dudo, Orderic Vitalis praised William the Conqueror:

> For he founded many monasteries and enlarged and enriched other men's foundations, lavishing treasure upon them and granting them his patronage against all their enemies.[3]

---

[1] Dudo, p. 180: 'Cupiebat labile linquere saeculum, seque Gimegias fieri monachum.'
[2] Dudo, p. 201: ' "Defensor hujus patriae, cur talia rimatus es facere? Quis fovebit clerum et populum? Quis contra nos ingruentium paganorum exercitui obstabit? Quis paternis legibus reget strenue populum? Cui gregem committes et commendabis?" '
[3] Orderic, 2, pp. 190–91.

While no one in the ninth century would have expected the sons of Vikings to join hands with monks, this partnership in Normandy had far-reaching consequences in the tenth and eleventh centuries.

Besides spiritual benefits, what did the Norman dukes gain from their support of monasticism? Important benefits included prestige and broader credibility. It was largely through their patronage of the church that the Norman lords changed their image in the eyes of the Franks from Viking marauders to Christian princes. To achieve this goal they adopted a strategy which gained them recognition inside and outside their realm. They appealed to local loyalties by enriching monasteries which their Viking ancestors had raided and by encouraging indigenous cults of Merovingian saints.[4] At the same time, they gained respect beyond their borders by enlisting the support of reformers of the highest caliber. There is every reason to suspect that the Norman leaders appreciated the benefits of playing to both audiences: the Normans had a keen sense of the power of public perception.[5] By supporting the efforts of well-known monastic reformers, the dukes spread the word that they were on the right side of God. As Barbara Rosenwein has written about Cluny, the Normans 'affirmed stability in the face of change' through their revival of ancient monasteries.[6]

Just as significant was the role that monasticism played in the extension of Norman authority geographically, to areas distant from Rouen, and socially, to classes below the aristocracy. The spread of monastic patrimonies across the region paralleled and reinforced political expansion. Monastic estates in lower Normandy not only provided the dukes with *postes avancés*, they also represented enduring centers of Norman support which reinforced ducal

---

4   This point is discussed in greater detail in Potts, 'When the Saints'. It is worth noting here, however, that scholars have seen a similar trend in England after 1066. Although later writers like Eadmer and William of Malmesbury denigrated Anglo-Saxon monasticism, Antonia Gransden has demonstrated that the Normans worked with Anglo-Saxons after 1066 'in preserving tradition and continuity' (p. 201). With respect to saints' cults, Susan Ridyard has also shown the fallacy of the view that the Normans were disrespectful toward Anglo-Saxon saints. She argues that 'Norman churchmen . . . perceived the usefulness of the English saints' and concludes, 'In terms of both publicity and of veneration the Norman Conquest was perhaps one of the better things ever to happen to the saints of the Anglo-Saxons.' (pp. 205–06). Just as Merovingian saints received new *vitae* under the Normans before 1066, the lives and miracle stories of Anglo-Saxon saints were revised and updated after 1066. Thus, the Normans continued in England an attitude of respect toward indigenous religious traditions that they had practiced in Normandy. See Antonia Gransden, 'Traditionalism and Continuity during the Last Century of Anglo-Saxon Monasticism', *Journal of Ecclesiastical History*, 40 (1989), pp. 159–207; S. J. Ridyard, '*Condigna Veneratio*: Post-Conquest Attitudes to the Saints of the Anglo-Saxons', *Anglo-Norman Studies*, 9 (1987), pp. 179–206.

5   Consider, for example, the propaganda generated over Harold Godwinson's alleged perjury to the Norman duke. See Douglas, *William the Conqueror*, pp. 175–78, 187–88.

6   Rosenwein, *Rhinoceros Bound*, p. 107.

authority. Since monks interacted with people on all levels of the social ladder, moreover, they generated support for the Norman lords among the broader populace. This point is underlined by the monasteries' involvement with the laity at the local level and by the great number of parish churches held by ducal monasteries. By the reign of William the Conqueror, 'Norman' was a designation which included members of all classes in the new realm, not just the aristocratic descendants of the original *northmanni*. The unity of the duchy was strengthened by the economic, administrative and religious ties that linked monastic lands. Thus, as monastic interests expanded, they contributed to the connections that bound the peripheries of the realm and the center.

How did the revival of monasticism in Normandy compare with other movements of monastic reform? It is possible to see many parallels. It was certainly not unusual for lords intent on restoring monasteries to appeal to respected reform abbots.[7] By the end of the tenth century, Cluniac monks were receiving requests from lay lords throughout Francia for assistance in monastic reform. Charters and saints' lives also provide examples of monasteries in other regions regaining possession of lands that had been lost during the Viking raids.[8] The dominance in one area of a reform center, like Fécamp, that trained monks and sent them out to be abbots of other communities – this too had precedents elsewhere. Indeed, this was the primary way that monastic reforms spread before the twelfth century.[9] Beyond these parallels, there is an underlying pattern that needs to be emphasised: monastic reform flourished in those areas where strong territorial princes offered protection from local interests. From Burgundy to Lotharingia to Dunstan's reforms in Anglo-Saxon England, this point holds true.[10] And so, when the pope referred to Fécamp as Richard II's church, he was simply acknowledging a state of affairs that existed at reform centers elsewhere.

The second half of the eleventh century brought important changes to Norman monasticism. On one hand, the appointment of Maurilius, a former monk of Fécamp, as archbishop of Rouen in 1055 signaled the reform of the secular church. In the decade that followed, the ecclesiastical province of Rouen entered the age of reforming synods. No longer was the reform of the

---

[7] To cite just one example, before William of Dijon became abbot of Fécamp, the count of Burgundy convinced him to leave Cluny to reform St Benigne.

[8] *Coutansais*, pp. 4–21.

[9] See Constance B. Bouchard, 'Merovingian, Carolingian and Cluniac Monasticism: Reform and Renewal in Burgundy', *Journal of Ecclesiastical History*, 41 (1990), pp. 365–88; Dauphin, 'Monastic Reforms'.

[10] Constance B. Bouchard, 'Laymen and Church Reform around the year 1000: the Case of Otto-William, Count of Burgundy', *Journal of Medieval History*, 5 (1979), pp. 1–10; D. A. Bullough, 'The Continental Background of the Reform', in *Tenth-Century Studies: Essays in Commemoration of the Millenium of the Council of Winchester and Regularis Concordia* (Sussex, 1975), pp. 20–36; Steven Fanning, *A Bishop and his World before the Gregorian Reform: Hubert of Angers, 1006–1047* (Philadelphia, 1988), p. 88.

Norman church the sole domain of the regular clergy, and bishops soon began challenging the right of monasteries to hold churches exempt from episcopal authority.[11] Moreover, a shift of influence occurred as the network of Bec monks gradually eclipsed that of Fécamp. The abbey of Bec, following the example of Fécamp, sent out monks to head other houses – Lanfranc himself stands as the best example, ruling the duke's new abbey at Caen in the 1060s, and following him to England as archbishop of Canterbury in 1070. Indeed, many of the greatest churchmen of the post-Conquest Anglo-Norman realm were former monks of Bec.[12] The difference between the two reform movements should not be exaggerated; the austerity of Bec would have certainly pleased William of Dijon. Yet it is nevertheless significant that it was to be monks from Bec rather than monks of Fécamp who filled so many of the episcopal and abbatial posts in the Anglo-Norman realm.[13]

Perhaps the greatest change to the monastic order of Normandy, however, came with the Conquest of England itself. As the duke and his men endowed abbeys in their homeland with English property they created vast cross-channel estates for the Norman monasteries. By William's death in 1087, the ducal abbeys of Caen, Jumièges, Saint Wandrille, Fécamp, Bernay, Montivilliers and Mont-Saint-Michel had all gained English lands, as had many of the family monasteries of his vassals.[14] Given a stake in the new lands, these abbeys established administrative lines across the channel through which Norman traditions and customs, as well as men, passed. The orientation of many Norman abbeys therefore turned to the west, toward England where their new commitments lay.[15] By bringing competent and qualified abbots

---

11 Raymonde Foreville, 'The Synod of the Province of Rouen in the Eleventh and Twelfth centuries', in *Church and Government in the Middle Ages: Essays Presented to C. R. Cheney on his Seventieth Birthday*, ed. C. N. L. Brook et al. (Cambridge, 1976), pp. 19–39.

12 Their numbers included Gundulf bishop of Rochester, Fulk bishop of Beauvais, Gilbert Crispin abbot of Westminster, Roger abbot of Lessay, Richard abbot of Chester, William abbot of Cormeilles, Henry prior of Canterbury, John abbot of Telese, and Durand abbot of Ivry. This list appears in Vaughn, *Anselm of Bec*, p. 71. According to Vaughn, 'Bec's influence was swiftly eclipsing that of the old Fécamp network' by the 1090s.

13 Vaughn, *Anselm of Bec*, pp. 70–73; C. Warren Hollister, 'St Anselm on Lay Investiture', *Anglo-Norman Studies*, 10 (1988), pp. 145–58.

14 These included St Evroul, Troarn, St Martin of Sées, Almenêches, Tréport, Cormeilles, St Pierre sur Dives, Grestain and Préaux. On this subject, see Donald Matthew, *Norman Monasteries and their English Possessions* (Oxford, 1962), pp. 27–39, especially pp. 30–32.

15 Le Patourel, *Norman Empire*, pp. 36–40, 250–54. More recently on the impact of the Conquest of England on Norman monasteries, see Marjorie Chibnall, 'Monastic Foundations in England and Normandy, 1066–1189', in *England and Normandy in the Middle Ages*, ed. David Bates and Anne Curry (London, 1994), pp. 37–49; Marjorie Chibnall, 'Some Aspects of the Norman Monastic Plantation in England', in *Normandie*, ed. Gaillard, pp. 399–415; Véronique Gazeau, 'The Effect of the Conquest of 1066 on

from Normandy to head the monasteries of England, William achieved a double objective – ensuring the allegiance of English abbeys while enhancing his own spiritual prestige. The new king thereby turned the rising current of ecclesiastical reform to political advantage and colonized English houses with monks loyal to the new regime. By using Norman monasteries as instruments of colonization and consolidation in England, William was following a precedent established by his predecessors in the duchy. The English lands William the Conqueror donated to Norman abbeys and the Norman reformers he imported to England strengthened the ecclesiastical and political coherence of the lands he ruled on both sides of the channel. As he pursued this course, the new king owed a debt to the dukes before him who had employed the same tactics under similar circumstances to confirm the Norman conquest of Normandy.

Monasticism in Normandy: The Abbeys of the Risle Valley', in *England and Normandy in the Middle Ages*, pp. 131–42.

Appendix

The new numbering system for the Fécamp charters at the Musée Bénédictine in Fécamp

In the decades since Fauroux's edition of ducal charters was published, a new numbering system has been created for the Fécamp charters at the Musée Bénédictine in Fécamp. The first number given below is the designation according to the new system; the second number refers to the former numbering system.

1 = 2: 1006 charter of Robert II, king of France; ed. *Gallia*, 11, *Instr.* cols. 8–9, no. 4; *Recueil des historiens des Gaules et de la France*, 10, pp. 587–88; Mabillon, *Annales ordinis sancti Benedicti*, 4, p. 185.

2 = 1: 1007 charter of Robert II, king of France, in which he concedes Villers St Paul to the abbey of Fécamp = BN, coll. Moreau, v. 341, f. 12r; ed. *Receuil des historiens des Gaules et de la France*, 10, p. 587.

3 = 1 bis: 1006 charter of Richard II duke of Normandy; ed. Fauroux no. 9, facsimile in Haskins, *Norman Institutions*, pl. 1.

4 = 2 bis: 1017–1025 charter of Richard II duke of Normandy; ed. Fauroux no. 31, facsimile in Haskins, *Norman Institutions*, pl. 2.

5 = 28: 1023 charter of Waleran of Meulan; ed. Fauroux no. 25.

6 = 2 ter: 1025 'Propicia' charter of Richard II; ed. Fauroux no. 34, facsimile in Haskins, *Norman Institutions*, pl. 3.

7 bis = 3 bis: 1031–1035 charter of Robert the Magnificent; ed. Fauroux no. 85, facsimile in Haskins, *Norman Institutions*, pls. 4 and 5.

8 = 5 bis: William of Arques, count of Talou, confirms the donation made by his father = BN, coll. Moreau, v. 341, fols. 17r–v.

9 = 7: William the Conqueror confirms English lands to Fécamp; ed. *Monasticon*, 7, 1082; *Regesta* 1, no. 112; *Neustria*, p. 223, partial copy. Haskins, *Norman Institutions*, p. 264, explains why he considers it a forgery: 'The style of the charter and the extraordinary privileges which it purports to grant are sufficient to condemn it, quite apart from the appearance of the pretended original.'

10 = unnumbered: forged charter of William the Conqueror confirming Fécamp's possession of Saint Gervais, free of all subjection to the archbishop; ed. Delisle, St. Sauveur, pièce no. 43. Haskins, Norman Institutions, p. 263 declares the charter 'a rank fabrication of a later age'. See also, Monasticon, 7, 1082; Regesta, no. 112; Neustria, p. 223; Round, Calendar, no. 113.

11 = 6a: 1088 charter of Robert Curthose in which he returns to Fécamp lands his father had confiscated. This charter is discussed and edited by Haskins, Norman Institutions, Appendix E, no. 4.

12 = 83: 1027–1059, concession of free travel over Beaumont by Yves II count of Beaumont = BN, coll. Moreau, v. 21 fols. 28r–v; ed. Depoin, Les Comtes de Beaumont-sur-Oise, appendix 2, no. 1, pp. 117–18.

13 = 85: donation to Cluny from Adelaide, copy from the mid-eleventh century. See Laporte, 'Romainmôtier', pp. 415–29.

44 = 2: Letter of John of Ravenna naming the next abbot of Blangy: ed. PL, 147, c. 474; Thesaurus novus anecdotorum, 1, cols. 153–54.

45 = 3: c. 1139 letter of Hugh archbishop of Rouen confirming the monks of Fécamp in their exemption, original.

99 = unnumbered: 1141, Letter of Hugh Candavène confirming Fécamp's ancient right over Sainte Berthe de Blangy.

Bibliography

PRIMARY SOURCES

A. *Manuscripts*
Principal archival collections consulted for this study

Archives départementales du Calvados
  collection Beausse: Mont-St-Michel
  legs Hunger: 'abbayes de la Manche'

Archives départementales de l'Eure
  H 123: Bernay
  H 793: 'petite cartulaire' of St Taurin
  H 794: 'grand cartulaire' of St Taurin

Archives départementales de l'Orne
  H421: St Etienne, Caen

Archives départementales de la Seine Maritime
  7H: Fécamp
  9H: Jumièges
  14H: St Ouen
  16H: St Wandrille
  54 H: Montivilliers

Archives nationales de Paris
  Semilly, collection Mathan, vols. 70, 72, 73, 76

Bibliothèque municipale d'Avranches
  ms. 210: cartulary of Mont-St-Michel

Bibliothèque municipale de Rouen
  ms. Y51 (1207): cartulary of Fécamp
  ms. Y188 (1210): copy of ms. Y51
  ms. Y201 (1235): 'cartulaire de Normandie' for Cerisy

Bibliothèque nationale, Paris
  collection Moreau: vols. 16, 18, 19, 21–23, 25, 27–41, 341, 391

Bibliothèque nationale, Paris
  fonds français, nouvelle acquisition:
    ms. 20219: St Etienne and La Trinité, Caen (de la Rue)

ms. 21659: Cerisy (Delisle)
ms. 21807: Bernay (Delisle)
ms. 21808: Cerisy (Delisle)
ms. 21811: Jumièges (Delisle)
ms. 21812: Montivilliers; Mont-St-Michel (Delisle)
ms. 21815: St Ouen; Mont-St-Michel; St Taurin (Delisle)
ms. 21816: St Wandrille (Delisle)
ms. 21819: Fécamp (Delisle)
ms. 21821: Mont-St-Michel (Delisle)
ms. 21822: Mont-St-Michel (Delisle)
fonds latin:
ms. lat. 1939: Fécamp
ms. 2294: *Sacramentaria ad usum Parisiensem*
ms. 5423: St Ouen (Gaignières)
ms. 5424: Jumièges (Gaignières)
ms. 5425: St Wandrille (Gaignières)
ms. 5430A: Mont-St-Michel (Gaignières)
ms. 5650: St Etienne, Caen (Gaignières)
ms. 10072: Mont-St-Michel (Léchaudé d'Anisy)
ms. 16738: original charters of St Wandrille
ms. 17132: 'cartulaire de Paris' for St Wandrille
fonds latin, nouvelle acquisition:
ms. 1024: Mont-St-Michel
ms. 1245–1246: 'diverses chartes normandes' (Deville)
ms. 1406: St Etienne, Caen (Hippeau)

Bibliothèque de l'Université de Caen
cartulary of St Etienne, Caen, copied by Henri Toustain, *cote* 1702 (N. RB. II, d3).

Musée de la bénédictine de Fécamp
The Fécamp charters at the Musée bénédictine have received a new numbering system since Fauroux's edition of ducal charters. See Appendix.

Musée des Beaux Arts, Caen
collection Mancel: 'Répertoire ou recueil de chartes extraites de cartulaires ou dépots publiés et particuliers du département de la Manche'.

B. Record and Cartulary Sources

Antiquus Cartularius ecclesiae Baiocensis (Livre Noir). Ed. V. Bourrienne. Rouen: 1902.
Archives de Normandie et de la Seine-Inférieure: Recueil de facsimilés d'écritures. Ed. P. Chevreux and J. Vernier. Rouen: 1911.
Cartulaire de Jersey, Recueil de documents concernent l'histoire de l'île conservés aux archives de la Manche. Ed. Société Jersiaise. Jersey: 1918–1920.
Cartulaire de l'abbaye de Saint-Père de Chartres. Ed. M. Guérard. Paris: 1840.

Cartulaire de Saint-Michel de l'Abbayette, prieuré de l'Abbaye du Mont-Saint-Michel. Ed. Bertrand de Broussillon. Paris: 1894.

Cartulaire de Saint-Victeur au Mans. Ed. Bertrand de Broussillon. Paris: 1894.

Concilia Rotomagensis Provinciae. Ed. Guillaume Bessin. Rouen: 1717.

Deville, A. 'Cartulaire de l'abbaye de la Sainte-Trinité du Mont de Rouen.' *Cartulaire de Saint Bertin.* Ed. B. Guérard. Paris: 1841.

Fauroux, Marie. *Recueil des actes des ducs de Normandie de 911 à 1066. Mémoires de la société des antiquaires de Normandie.* vol. 36. Caen: 1961.

Gallia Christiana. vols. 11, 14. Paris: 1715, rpt. 1967.

Halphen, Louis, and Ferdinand Lot. *Recueil des actes de Lothaire et de Louis V, rois de France (954–987).* Paris: 1908.

Hull, P. L. *The Cartulary of St. Michael's Mount.* Torquay: 1962.

Lot, Ferdinand. *Etudes critiques sur l'abbaye de Saint-Wandrille.* Paris: 1913.

Lot, Ferdinand, and Philippe Lauer. *Recueil des actes de Charles III le Simple, roi de France (893–923).* Paris: 1949.

Mabillon, J. *Vetera analecta.* Paris: 1723.

Mansi, Joannes Dominicus. *Sacrorum conciliorum nova et amplissima collectio.* vol. 19. Graz: 1774–1775, rpt. 1960.

Missal of Robert of Jumièges. Ed. H. A. Wilson. London: 1896.

Monastic Constitutions of Lanfranc. Ed. David Knowles. London: 1951.

Monasticon Anglicanum. Ed. W. Dugdale. 6 vols. London: 1817–1830.

Morice, Hyacinthe. *Mémoires pour servir de preuves à l'histoire ecclésiastique et civile de Bretagne.* 3 vols. Paris: 1742–1746, rpt. 1974.

Musset, Lucien. *Les Actes de Guillaume le Conquérant et de la reine Mathilde pour les abbayes caennaises.* Caen: 1967.

Neustria Pia. Ed. Arthur du Monstier. Rouen: 1663.

Regesta Regum Anglo-Normannorum, 1066–1154. Ed. H. W. C. Davis. vol. 1. Oxford: 1913.

Round, John Horace. *Calendar of Documents Preserved in France Illustrative of the History of Great Britain and Ireland.* London: 1899.

Soehnée, Frédéric. *Catalogue des actes d'Henri Ier, roi de France (1031–1060).* Paris: 1907.

Tessier, Georges. *Recueil des actes de Charles II le Chauve, roi de France.* 2 vols. Paris: 1952.

Thesaurus novus anecdotorum. Ed. Edmund Martène and Ursin Durand. 5 vols. Paris: 1717, rpt. 1968.

Vernier, Jules. *Chartes de l'abbaye de Jumièges (v. 825 à 1204).* 2 vols. Rouen: 1916.

Vernier, Jules. *Recueil de fac-similés de chartes normandes.* Rouen: 1919.

C. Annals, Narratives and Literary Sources

Adémar de Chabannes. *Chronicon.* Ed. Jules Chavanon. Paris: 1897.

Annales de Saint Bertin, Ninth-Century Histories, Volume I. Ed. and trans. Janet L. Nelson. Manchester and New York: 1991.

Anselm of Canterbury. *The Letters of Saint Anselm of Canterbury.* Ed. and trans. Walter Fröhlich. 3 vols. Kalamazoo: 1990–1995.

Benoît. *Chronique des ducs de Normandie.* Ed. F. Michel. 3 vols. Paris: 1836–1843.

Chronicon Fiscamnense. Patriologia Latina. Vol. 147. Cols. 479–86.

Chronicon Fontanellense: les premières annales de Fontenelle. Ed. Jean Laporte. *Mélanges: documents,* Societé de l'histoire de Normandy, 15e série. Rouen: 1951.

Complainte sur l'assassinat de Guillaume Longue-épée, duc de Normandie. Ed. Jules Lair. *Bibliothèque de l'ecole des chartes.* vol. 31.

Dudo of Saint Quentin. *De Moribus et actis primorum Normanniae ducum.* Ed. Jules Lair. Caen: 1865.

Flodoard. *Les Annales de Flodoard.* Ed. Philippe Lauer. Paris: 1906.

Hugh of Flavigny. *Chronicon. Monumenta Germaniae Historica. Scriptores.* vol. 9.

Introductio monachorum and *Revelatio,* in Thomas le Roy: *Livre des curieuses recherches du Mont-Sainct-Michel. Mémoires de la société des antiquaires de Normandie.* vol. 29. Ed. Eugène de Robillard de Beaurepaire. 1876.

Inventio et miracula Sancti Vulfranni. Ed. Jean Laporte. Rouen: 1938.

La Chanson de Sainte Foi d'Agen. Ed. Antoine Thomas. Paris: 1925.

La Chronique de Nantes. Ed. and trans. René Merlet. Paris: 1896.

Lanfranc, archbishop of Canterbury. *The Letters of Lanfranc, Archbishop of Canterbury.* Ed. and trans. Helen Clover and Margaret Gibson. Oxford: 1979.

Mabillon, J. *Annales Ordinis Sancti Benedicti.* vol. 4. Paris: 1713.

Migne, J. P. *Patrologiae cursus completus: series latina.* Paris: 1844–1864.

Orderic Vitalis. *The Ecclesiastical History of Orderic Vitalis.* Ed. and trans. Marjorie Chibnall. 6 vols. Oxford: 1969–1980.

Rodulfus Glaber Opera. Ed. and trans. John France, Neithard Bulst and Paul Reynolds. Oxford: 1989.

Rodulfus Glaber. *Les Cinq Livres de ses histoires, 900–1044.* Ed. Maurice Prou. Paris: 1886.

Recueil des historiens des Gaules et de la France. Ed. M. Bouquet. New edition, ed. Léopold Delisle. 24 vols. Paris: 1869–1904.

Richer. *Histoire de France, 888–995.* Ed. and trans. Robert Latouche. 2 vols. Paris: 1930.

Robert of Torigny. *Chronique de Robert de Torigni, abbé du Mont Saint Michel.* Ed. Léopold Delisle. 2 vols. Rouen: 1872–1873.

Le Roman de Rou de Wace. Ed. A. J. Holden. Paris: 1970–1973.

'Sanctae Catharinae virginis et martyris: translatio et miracula rotomangensia saec. XI.' Ed. Albert Poncelet. *Analecta Bollandiana* 22 (1903): 423–38.

Scriptores Rerum Gestarum Willelmi Conquestoris. Ed. J. A. Giles. London: 1845, rpt. 1967.

Vie de Saint Alexis: poème du XIe siècle. Ed. Gaston Paris. Paris: 1933.

'Vita Sancti Gildardi episcopi Rothomagensis et ejusdem translatio Suessiones, anno 838–840 facta.' Ed. Albert Poncelet. *Analecta Bollandiana* 8 (1889): 389–405.

Warner of Rouen. *Moriuht.* Ed. and trans. Christopher J. McDonough. Toronto: 1995.

William of Jumièges. *The* Gesta Normannorum Ducum *of William of Jumièges, Orderic Vitalis, and Robert of Torigni.* Ed. and trans. Elisabeth van Houts. 2 vols. Oxford: 1992–1995.

William of Jumièges. *Gesta Normannorum Ducum.* Ed. Jean Marx. Rouen: 1914.

William of Malmesbury. *De gestis regum anglorum. Rolls Series.* vol. 90. Ed. W. Stubbs. 1887–1889.

William of Poitiers. *Gesta Guillelmi ducis Normannorum et regis Anglorum.* Ed. and trans. Raymonde Foreville. Paris: 1952.

SECONDARY WORKS

Adigard des Gautries, Jean. 'Les Noms de lieux de la Manche attestés entre 911–1066.' *Annales de Normandie* 1 (1951): 9–44.

Adigard des Gautries, Jean. 'Les Noms de lieux de la Seine-Maritime attestés entre 911 et 1066.' *Annales de Normandie* 6 (1956): 119–34, 223–44; 7 (1957): 135–58; 8 (1958): 299–322; 9 (1959): 151–67, 273–83.

Adigard des Gautries, Jean. *Les Noms de personnes scandinaves en Normandie de 911 à 1066.* Lund: 1954.

Alexander, J. J. G. *Norman Illumination at Mont-St-Michel, 966–1100.* Oxford: 1970.

Andrieu, Lucien, ed. *Les Abbayes de Normandie: actes du XIIIe congrès des sociétés historiques et archéologiques de Normandie.* Rouen: 1979.

Anisy, Léchaudé d.' *Les anciennes abbayes de Normandie.* 2 vols. Caen: 1834.

Arnoux, Mathieu. 'Classe agricole, pouvoir seigneurial et autorité ducale: l'évolution de la Normandie féodale d'aprés le témoignage de chroniqueurs (Xe–XIIe siécles).' *Le Moyen Age* 98 (1992): 35–60.

Avril, François. 'La Décoration des manuscrits au Mont Saint-Michel (XIe–XIIe siécles).' *Millénaire monastique du Mont Saint-Michel.* 2 vols. Paris: 1967. 2: 203–38.

Bachrach, Bernard S. *Fulk Nerra, the Neo-Roman Consul, 987–1040.* Berkeley: 1993.

Banton, Nicholas. 'Monastic Reform and the Unification of Tenth-Century England.' *Studies in Church History* 18 (1982): 71–85.

Barth, Fredrik. *Ethnic Groups and Boundaries: The Social Organization of Culture Difference.* Boston: 1969.

Bates, David, and Véronique Gazeau. 'L'Abbaye de Grestain et la famille d'Herluin de Conteville.' *Annales de Normandie* 40 (1990): 5–30.

Bates, David. 'The Conqueror's Charters.' *England in the Eleventh Century: Proceedings of the 1990 Harlaxton Symposium.* Ed. Carola Hicks. Stamford, Lincolnshire: 1992. 1–15.

Bates, David. 'Four Recently Discovered Norman Charters.' *Annales de Normandie* 45 (1995): 35–48.

Bates, David. 'Lord Sudeley's Ancestors: The Family of the Counts of Amiens, Valois and the Vexin in France and England during the 11th Century.' *The Sudeleys: Lords of Toddington.* London: 1987. 34–47.

Bates, David. 'Normandy and England after 1066.' *English Historical Review* 104 (1989): 851–80.

Bates, David. *Normandy Before 1066.* London: 1982.

Bates, David. 'Notes sur l'aristocratie normande: Hugues, évêque de Bayeux (1011 env. –1049).' *Annales de Normandie* 23 (1973): 7–38.

Bates, David. 'West Francia: The Northern Principalities.' *The New Cambridge Medieval History*. Vol. 3. Cambridge: forthcoming.

Baylé, Maylis. 'Interlace Patterns in Norman Romanesque Sculpture: Regional Groups and their Historical Background.' *Anglo-Norman Studies* 5 (1983): 1–20.

Beaurepaire, François de. 'La Toponymie de la Normandie: méthods et applications.' *Cahiers Lépold Delisle* 18 (1969): 1–86.

Beaurepaire, François de. 'Les Noms d'Anglo-Saxons contenus dans la toponymie normande.' *Annales de Normandie* 10 (1960): 307–16.

Beaurepaire, François de. *Les Noms des communes et anciennes paroisses de l'Eure*. Paris: 1981.

Beaurepaire, François de. *Les Noms des communes et anciennes paroisses de la Manche*. Paris: 1986.

Beaurepaire, François de. *Les Noms des communes et anciennes paroisses de la Seine-Maritime*. Paris: 1979.

Beaurepaire, François de. 'Quelques Finales anglo-saxonnes dans la toponymie normande.' *Annales de Normandie* 13 (1963): 219–36.

Beaurepaire, François de. 'Toponymie et évolution du peuplement sur le pourtour de la baie du Mont Saint-Michel.' *Millénaire monastique du Mont Saint-Michel*. 2 vols. Paris: 1967. 2: 49–72.

Bénet, Armand. 'Etude sur la diplomatique des ducs de Normandie.' Thesis, Ecole des Chartes: 1881.

Berlière, Ursmer. 'L'Exercice du ministère paroissial par les moines dans le haut moyen-âge.' *Revue Bénédictine* 39: 227–50.

Berman, Constance. 'Land Acquisition and the Use of the Mortgage Contract by the Cistercians of Berdoes.' *Speculum* 57 (1982): 250–66.

Berthelier, Simone. 'L'Expansion de l'ordre de Cluny et ses rapports avec l'histoire politique et économique du Xe au XIIe siècle.' *Revue archéologique* 11 (1938): 319–26.

Besse, J. M. *Province ecclésiastique de Rouen. Abbayes et prieurés de l'ancienne France*. Vol. 7. Paris: 1914.

Bilson, John. 'Nouvelles Observations sur l'église abbatiale de Bernay.' *Bulletin monumental* 75 (1911): 396–422.

Bischoff, Bernard. *Paléographie d l'antiquité romaine et du moyen âge occidental*. Trans. Hartmut Atsma and Jean Vezin. Paris: 1985.

Blair, John, and Richard Sharpe, ed. *Pastoral Care Before the Parish*. Leicester: 1992.

Bloc, Marc. *Feudal Society*. London: 1961.

Borderie, Arthur de la. *Essai sur la géographie féodale de la Bretagne*. Rennes: 1889.

Boüard, A. de. *Manuel de diplomatique française et pontificale*. 2 vols. Paris: 1948.

Boüard, Michel de. 'A Propos de la datation du Hague-Dike.' *Annales de Normandie* 14 (1964): 270–71.

Boüard, Michel de. 'De la Neustrie Carolingienne à la Normandie féodale: continuité ou discontinuité?' *Bulletin of the Institute of Historical Research* 28 (1955): 1–14.

Boüard, Michel de. *Documents de l'histoire de la Normandie*. Toulouse: 1972.

Boüard, Michel de. 'La Hague, camp retranché des Vikings?' *Annales de Normandie* 3 (1953): 3–14.

Boüard, Michel de. *Le Château de Caen*. Caen: 1979.

Boüard, Michel de. 'Le Hague-Dike.' *Cahiers Archéologiques: fin de l'antiquité et moyen âge* 8 (1956): 117–45.

Bouchard, Constance B. 'Laymen and Church Reform around the Year 1000: the Case of Otto-William, Count of Burgundy.' *Journal of Medieval History* 5 (1979): 1–10.

Bouchard, Constance B. 'Merovingian, Carolingian and Cluniac Monasticism: Reform and Renewal in Burgundy.' *Journal of Ecclesiastical History* 41 (1990): 365–88.

Bouchard, Constance B. *Sword, Miter, and Cloister: Nobility and the Church in Burgundy, 980–1198.* Ithaca: 1987.

Bouet, G. 'L'Abbaye de Bernay.' *Bulletin monumental* 31 (1865): 95–100.

Bouet, Pierre. 'Dudon de Saint-Quentin et Virgile: L'*Enéide* au service de la cause normande.' *Recueil d'études en hommage à Lucien Musset.* Caen: 1990. 215–36.

Bourgeois-Lechartier, Michel. 'A la Recherche du scriptorium de l'abbaye du Mont Saint-Michel.' *Millénaire monastique du Mont Saint-Michel.* 2 vols. Paris: 1967. 2: 171–202.

Boussard, Jacques. 'La Seigneurie de Bellême aux X et XI siècles.' *Mélanges d'histoire du moyen âge dédiés à la mémoire de Louis Halphen.* Paris: 1951. 43–54.

Boussard, Jacques. 'Le Comté de Mortain au XIe siècle.' *Moyen Age* 58 (1952): 253–79.

Bouvris, Jean-Michel. 'La Renaissance de l'abbaye de Montivilliers et son développement jusqu'à la fin du XIe siècle.' *L'Abbaye de Montivilliers à travers les âges: actes du colloque organisé à Montivilliers le 8 mars 1986.* Recueil de l'association des amis du vieux Havre. Le Havre: 1988. 46: 17–84.

Bouvris, Michel. 'Contribution à une étude de l'institution vicomtale en Normandie au XIe siècle, l'exemple de la partie orientale du duché: les vicomtes de Rouen et de Fécamp.' *Cahier des Annales de Normandie* 17 (1985): 149–74.

Branch, Betty. 'Inventories of the Library of Fécamp from the Eleventh and Twelfth Century.' *Manuscripta* 23 (1979): 159–72.

Bréard, Charles. *L'Abbaye de Notre-Dame de Grestain de l'ordre de Saint-Benoît à l'ancien diocèse de Lisieux.* Rouen: 1904.

Breese, Lauren. 'Richard II, Duke of Normandy.' Dissertation, University of California, Los Angeles: 1967.

Brooke, Christopher. 'Princes and Kings as Patrons of Monasteries: Normandy and England.' *Il monachesimo e la riforma ecclesiastica (1049–1122), Miscellanea del centro di studi medioevali* 6 (Milan, 1968): 125–52.

Brown, R. Allen. *The Norman Conquest. Documents of Medieval History* 5. London: 1984.

Brown, R. Allen. *The Normans and the Norman Conquest.* London: 1969.

Brown, R. Allen. 'Some Observations on Norman and Anglo-Norman Charters.' *Tradition and Change: Essays in Honour of Marjorie Chibnall presented by her friends on the occasion of her seventieth birthday.* Ed. Diana Greenway, Christopher Holdsworth, and Jane Sayers. Cambridge: 1985. 145–63.

Bullough, D. A. 'The Continental Background of the Reform.' *Tenth-Century Studies: Essays in Commemoration of the Millennium of the Council of Winchester and Regularis Concordia.* Ed. David Parsons. Sussex: 1975.

Bulst, Neithard. 'La Réforme monastique en Normandie: étude prosopographique sur la diffusion et l'implantation de la réforme de Guillaume de Dijon.' Trans.

Victor Saxer. *Etudes Anselmiennes: les mutations socio-culturelles au tournant des XIe–XIIe siècles* 4 (1984): 317–30.

Bulst, Neithard. 'Untersuchungen zu den Klosterreformen Wilhelms von Dijon.' *Pariser Historische Studien.* Bonn: 1973. 11: 147–85.

Bur, Michel. *La Formation du comté de Champagne, v. 950–1150.* Nancy: 1977.

Burckard, François. 'Chartes, cartulaires et archives des abbayes.' *Trésors des abbayes normandes.* Rouen: 1979. 59–83.

Carabie, Robert. *La Propriété foncière très ancien droit normand (XIe–XIIIe siècles).* Caen: 1943.

Chandler, Victoria. 'Lordship, Prestige and Piety: Charitable Donations of the Anglo-Norman Aristocracy.' Dissertation, University of Virginia: 1979.

Chandler, Victoria. 'Politics and Piety: Influences on Charitable Donations during the Anglo-Norman Period.' *Revue Bénédictine* 90 (1980): 63–71.

Chanteux, H. 'L'Abbé Thierry et les églises de Jumièges, du Mont-Saint-Michel et de Bernay.' *Bulletin Monumental* 98 (1939): 67–72.

Chaplais, Pierre. 'Une Charte originale de Guillaume le Conquérant.' *L'Abbaye bénédictine de Fécamp: ouvrage scientifique du XIIIe centenaire.* 3 vols. Fécamp: 1959. 1: 93–104.

Chappell, David A. 'Ethnogenesis and Frontiers.' *Journal of World History* 4 (1993): 267–75.

Chapron, Martine, and Véronique Vecile. *Le Temporel de l'abbaye de St-Taurin d'Evreux du X siècle au XV siècle (vers 965–1400).* Mémoire de maîtrise, U. E. R. des lettres et sciences humaines. Rouen: 1979.

Charpillon, M. *Dictionnaire historique de toutes les communes du département de l'Eure.* Les Andelys: 1868–1879.

Chassant, L.-Alph. *Dictionnaire des abréviations latines et françaises.* Evreux: 1846, rpt. 1980.

Chaume, M. 'Les Origines paternelles de Saint Guillaume de Volpiano.' *Revue Mabillon* 14 (1924): 68–77.

Chazelas, Jean. 'Jumièges au XIe siècle.' *La Normandie bénédictine au temps de Guillaume le Conquérant.* Ed. J. Daoust and L. Gaillard. Lille: 1967. 107–16.

Chédeville, A. 'Les Restitutions d'églises en faveur de l'abbaye de Saint-Vincent du Mans.' *Cahiers de civilisation médiévale, Xe–XIIe siècles* 3 (1960): 209–17.

Chesnel, P. *Le Cotentin et l'Avranchin sous les ducs de Normandie (911–1204).* Caen: 1912.

Chevrier, G. 'Evolution de la notion de donation dans les chartes de Cluny du IXe du XIIe siècle.' *A Cluny, congrès scientifique.* Dijon: 1950. 203–9.

Cheyette, Frederic L. '*Suum cuique tribuere.*' *French Historical Studies* 6 (1970): 287–99.

Chibnall, Marjorie. *Anglo-Norman England, 1066–1166.* Oxford: 1986.

Chibnall, Marjorie. 'Ecclesiastical Patronage and the Growth of Feudal Estates at the Time of the Norman Conquest.' *Annales de Normandie* 8 (1958): 102–18.

Chibnall, Marjorie. 'The Empress Matilda and Church Reform.' *Transactions of the Royal Historical Society* 38 (1988): 107–30.

Chibnall, Marjorie. 'The Merovingian Monastery of St Evroul in the Light of Conflicting Traditions.' *Studies in Church History* 8 (1972): 31–40.

Chibnall, Marjorie. 'Monastic Foundations in England and Normandy, 1066–1189.' *England and Normandy in the Middle Ages.* Ed. David Bates and Anne Curry. London: 1994. 37–49.

Chibnall, Marjorie. 'Monks and Pastoral Work: a Problem in Anglo-Norman History.' *Journal of Ecclesiastical History* 18 (1967): 165–72.

Chibnall, Marjorie. 'Orderic Vitalis and Robert of Torigni.' *Millénaire monastique du Mont Saint-Michel.* 2 vols. Paris: 1967. 2: 133–39.

Chibnall, Marjorie. 'Some Aspects of the Norman Monastic Plantation in England.' *La Normandie bénédictine au temps de Guillaume le Conquérant.* Ed. J. Daoust and L. Gaillard. Lille: 1967. 399–415.

Chibnall, Marjorie. *The World of Orderic Vitalis.* Oxford: 1984.

Clanchy, M. T. *From Memory to Written Record: England, 1066–1307.* Cambridge, Ma.: 1979.

Cloke, Paul, Chris Philo and David Sadler. *Approaching Human Geography: An Introduction to Contemporary Theoretical Debates.* New York: 1991.

Constable, Giles. 'Monastic Possession of Churches and 'Spiritualia' in the Age of Reform.' *Il Monachesimo e la riform ecclesiastica (1049–1122).* Milan: 1971. 304–31.

Constable, Giles. *Monastic Tithes From Their Origins to the Twelfth Century.* Cambridge: 1964.

Cote, Albert Simeon, Jr. 'The Anglo-Saxon and Norman "Eigenkirche" and the Ecclesiastical Policy of William I.' Dissertation, Louisiana State University: 1982.

Cottineau, L. H. *Répertoire topo-bibliographique des abbayes et prieurés.* 2 vols. Mâcon: 1939.

Coupland, Simon. 'The Rod of God's Wrath or the People of God's Wrath? The Carolingian Theology of the Viking Invasions.' *Journal of Ecclesiastical History* 42 (1991): 535–54.

Coupland, Simon. 'The Vikings in Francia and Anglo-Saxon England to 911.' *The New Cambridge Medieval History.* Vol. 2. Ed. Rosamond McKitterick. Cambridge: 1995.

Cousin, Patrice. 'L'Abbaye Notre-Dame de Bernay au XIe siècle.' *La Normandie bénédictine au temps de Guillaume le Conquérant.* Ed. J. Daoust and L. Gaillard. Lille: 1967. 141–51.

Coutansais, Françoise. 'Les Monastéres du Poitou avant l'An Mil.' *Revue Mabillon* 53 (1963): 1–21.

Cowdrey, Herbert. 'The Anglo-Norman *Laudes regiae.*' *Viator* 12 (1981): 37–78.

Crouch, David. *The Beaumont Twins: The Roots and Branches of Power in the Twelfth Century.* Cambridge: 1986.

Daoust, Joseph. 'Normandie Bénédictine.' *La Normandie bénédictine au temps de Guillaume le Conquérant.* Ed. J. Daoust and L. Gaillard. Lille: 1967. 25–53.

Dauphin, Hubert. *Le Bienheureux Richard: Abbé de Saint-Vanne de Verdun.* Louvain: 1946.

Dauphin, Hubert. 'Monastic Reforms from the Tenth Century to the Twelfth.' *The Downside Review* 70 (1952): 62–74.

Davies, Wendy. *Small Worlds: The Village Community in Early Medieval Brittany.* Berkeley: 1988.

Davis, R. H. C. *The Normans and their Myth.* London: 1976.

Debidour, Louis. *Essai sur l'histoire de l'abbaye bénédictine de St-Taurin d'Evreux.* Evreux: 1908.

Delisle, Léopold. *Etudes sur la condition de la classe agricole et l'état de l'agriculture en Normandie au moyen âge.* Evreux: 1851.

Delisle, Léopold. *Histoire du château et des sires du Saint-Sauveur-le-Vicomte.* Valognes: 1867.

Delisle, Léopold, and Louis Passy, ed. *Mémoires et notes de M. Auguste le Prévost pour servir á l'histoire du département de l'Eure.* 3 vols. Evreux: 1862–1869.

Delisle, Léopold. 'Vie de Gauzelin abbé de Fleury et archevêque de Brouges.' *Société archéologique et historique de l'Orléanais, Mémoires* 2 (1853): 282–83.

Depoin, Joseph. *Les Comtes de Beaumont-sur-Oise et la prieuré de Sainte-Honorine de Conflans.* Pontoise: 1911.

Devailly, Guy. 'Les Dépendances bretonnes des abbayes normandes (Xe–XIIIe siècles).' *Aspects du monachisme en Normandie (IVe–XVIIIe siécles): Actes du colloque scientifique de l' 'année des abbayes normandes'.* Ed. Lucien Musset. Paris: 1982. 115–24.

Deville, Etienne. 'Notices sur quelques manuscrits normands conservés à la Bibliothèque Sainte-Geneviève.' *Revue catholique de Normandie* 14 (1904): 197–209, 269–324; 15 (1905): 17–42.

Dolley, Michael, and Jacques Yvon. 'A Group of Tenth-Century Coins Found at Mont-Saint-Michel.' *The British Numismatic Journal* 40 (1971): 1–16.

Doubleday, H. A., and Howard de Walden, ed. *The Complete Peerage.* London: 1929.

Douglas, David. 'The Ancestors of William fitz Osbern.' *English Historical Review* 59 (1944): 62–79.

Douglas, David. 'Companions of the Conqueror.' *History* 28 (1943): 129–47.

Douglas, David. 'The Earliest Norman Counts.' *English Historical Review* 61 (1946): 129–56.

Douglas, David. 'The Rise of Normandy.' *Time and the Hour: Some Collected Papers of David C. Douglas.* London: 1977. 95–119.

Douglas, David. 'Rollo of Normandy.' *English Historical Review* 57 (1942): 417–36.

Douglas, David. 'Some Problems of Early Norman Chronology.' *English Historical Review* 65 (1950): 289–303.

Douglas, David. *William the Conqueror: the Norman Impact upon England.* Berkeley: 1964.

Dubois, Jacques. 'La Vie des moines dans les prieurés du moyen âge.' *Histoire monastique en France au XIIe siècle.* London: 1982. 10–33.

Dubois, Jacques. 'Les Dépendances de l'abbaye du Mont Saint-Michel et la vie monastique dans les prieurés.' *Millénaire monastique du Mont Saint-Michel.* 2 vols. Paris: 1967. 1: 619–76.

Dubois, Jacques. 'Les Listes épiscopales témoins de l'organisation ecclésiastique et de la transmission des traditions.' *Revue d'histoire de l'église de France* 62 (1976): 9–23.

Dubois, Jacques. 'Les Moines dans la société du moyen âge (950–1350).' *Histoire monastique en France au XIIe siècle.* London: 1982. 5–37.

Duby, Georges. 'Economie domaniale et économie monétaire: le budget de l'abbaye de Cluny entre 1080 et 1155.' *Annales: économies, sociétés, civilisations* 7 (1952): 155–71.

Duby, Georges. *La Société aux XIe et XIIe siècles dans la région mâconnaise.* Paris: 1971.

Dufief, André. 'La Vie monastique au Mont Saint-Michel pendant le XIIe siècle (1085–1186).' *Millénaire monastique du Mont Saint-Michel.* 2 vols. Paris: 1967. 1: 81–126.

Dumas-Dubourg, Françoise. *Le Trésor de Fécamp et le monnayage en Francie occidentale pendant la second moitié du Xe siècle.* Paris: 1971.

Dumont, Ernest. *L'Abbaye de Montivilliers.* Rouen: 1876.

Duval, Georges. 'L'Abbaye de Cerisy.' *La Normandie bénédictine au temps de Guillaume le Conquérant.* Ed. J. Daoust and L. Gaillard. Lille: 1967. 179–85.

Evans, Gillian R. 'Mens Devota: The Literary Community of the Devotional Works of John of Fécamp and St. Anselm.' *Medium Ævum* 43 (1974): 105–15.

Fallue, Léon. *Histoire de la ville et de l'abbaye de Fécamp.* Rouen: 1841.

Fanning, Steven. *A Bishop and his World before the Gregorian Reform: Hubert of Angers, 1006–1047.* Philadelphia: 1988.

Farcy, Paul de. *Abbayes de l'éveché de Bayeux.* 3 vols. Laval: 1887–1888.

Farmer, Sharon. *Communities of Saint Martin: Legend and Ritual in Medieval Tours.* Ithaca: 1991.

Fauroux, Marie (as Marie Le Roy-Ladurie). 'Rôle des abbayes du Val de Loire dans la colonisation monastique normande (Xe–XIe siècle).' *Revue historique de droit français et étranger* 31 (1953): 322–23.

Fawtier, Robert. *The Capetian Kings of France: Monarchy and Nation 987–1328.* Trans. Lionel Butler and R. J. Adam. London: 1960, rpt. 1982.

Fawtier, Robert. 'Les Reliques rouennaises de sainte Catherine d'Alexandrie.' *Analecta Bollandiana* 41 (1923): 357–68.

Fellows-Jensen, Gillian. 'Viking Settlement in Normandy: The Place-Name Evidence as seen from the Danelaw.' *Souvenir Normand.* Copenhagen: 1979. 15–24.

Finberg, H. P. R. *Tavistock Abbey: A Study in the Social and Economic History of Devon.* Cambridge: 1951.

Fisher, D. J. V. 'The Anti-Monastic Reaction in the Reign of Edward the Martyr.' *The Cambridge Historical Journal* 10 (1950–1952): 254–70.

Flach, Jacques. *Les Origines de l'ancienne France, X et XI siècles.* 4 vols. Paris: 1886–1917.

Foreville, Raymonde. 'Robert de Torigni et "Clio".' *Millénaire monastique du Mont Saint-Michel.* 2 vols. Paris: 1967. 2: 141–53.

Foreville, Raymonde. 'The Synod of the Province of Rouen in the Eleventh and Twelfth Centuries.' *Church and Government in the Middle Ages: Essays Presented to C. R. Cheney on his 70th Birthday.* Cambridge: 1976. 19–39.

Fournée, Jean. *La Spiritualité en Normandie au temps de Guillaume le Conquérant.* Flers: 1987.

Fournée, Jean. *Le Culte populaire des saints en Normandie.* Paris: 1973.

Gaiffier d'Hestroy, Baudouin de. 'L'Hagiographe et son public au XIe siécle.' *Miscellanea Historica in honorem Leonis van der Essen.* Brussels and Paris, 1947. 1: 135–66.

Gaillard, L., and J. Daoust, ed. *La Normandie bénédictine au temps de Guillaume le Conquérant.* Lille: 1967.

Galbraith, V. H. 'Monastic Foundation Charters of the Eleventh and Twelfth Centuries.' *Cambridge Historical Journal* 4 (1934): 205–22.

Gazeau, Véronique. 'The Effect of the Conquest of 1066 on Monasticism in Normandy: The Abbeys of the Risle Valley.' *England and Normandy in the Middle Ages.* Ed. David Bates and Anne Curry. London: 1994. 131–42.

Geary, Patrick J. *Furta Sacra: Thefts of Relics in the Central Middle Ages.* Princeton: 1978, revised edn 1990.

Génestal, R. *Rôle des monastères comme établissements de crédit, étudié en Normandie du XIe à la fin du XIIIe siècle*. Paris: 1901.

Genouillac, Gourdon de. *Histoire de l'abbaye de Fécamp et de ses abbés*. Paris: 1875.

Gibson, Margaret. *Lanfranc of Bec*. Oxford: 1978.

Golding, Brian. 'Robert of Mortain.' *Anglo-Norman Studies* 13 (1991): 119–44.

Gosselin, Louis. 'L'Abbaye de Saint-Etienne de Fontenay au début de sa fondation.' *La Normandie bénédictine au temps de Guillaume le Conquérant*. Ed. J. Daoust and L. Gaillard. Lille: 1967. 277–85.

Goujon, A. *Histoire de Bernay et son canton touchant à l'histoire générale de la Normandie*. Evreux: 1875.

Goyau, Georges. *La Normandie bénédictine: pirates, vikings et moines normandes*. Paris: 1940.

Gransden, Antonia. 'Traditionalism and Continuity during the Last Century of Anglo-Saxon Monasticism.' *Journal of Ecclesiastical History* 40 (1989): 59–207

Green, Judith A. 'Lords of the Norman Vexin.' *War and Government in the Middle Ages: Essays in Honour of J. O. Prestwich*. Ed. John Gillingham and J. C. Holt. Woodbridge: 1984. 46–63

Grémont, Denis, and Lin Donnat. 'Fleury, le Mont Saint-Michel et l'Angleterre à la fin du Xe et au début du XIe siècle à propos du manuscrit d'Orleans no. 127 (105).' *Millénaire monastique du Mont Saint-Michel*. 2 vols. Paris: 1967. 1: 751–93.

Guéry, C. *Histoire de l'abbaye de Lyre*. Evreux: 1917.

Guillot, Olivier. 'La Conversion des Normands peu après 911: des reflets contemporains á l'historiographie ultérieure (Xe–XIe s.).' *Cahiers de civilisation médiévale* 24 (1981): 101–16, 181–219.

Guillot, Olivier. 'La Libération de l'église par le duc Guillaume avant la conquête.' *Histoire religieuse de la Normandie*. Ed. Guy-Marie Oury. Chambray: 1981. 71–85.

Guillot, Olivier. *Le Comte d'Anjou et son entourage au XIe siècle*. Paris: 1972.

Guillotin de Corson, A. *Pouillé historique de l'archevêché de Rennes*. 6 vols. Rennes: 1880–86.

Haenens, Albert d'. *Les Invasions normandes en Belgique au IXe siècle: le phénomène et sa répercussion dans l'historiographie médiévale*. Louvain: 1967.

Hallam, Elizabeth. *Capetian France, 987–1328*. New York: 1980.

Hallam, Elizabeth. 'The King and the Princes in Eleventh-Century France.' *Bulletin of the Institute of Historical Research* 53 (1980): 143–56.

Halphen, Louis. *Le Comté d'Anjou au XIe siècle*. Geneva: 1906, rpt. 1974.

Hanawalt, Emily Albu. 'Dudo of Saint-Quentin: The Heroic Past Imagined.' *Haskins Society Journal* 6 (1995): 111–18

Harper-Bill, Christopher. 'The Piety of the Anglo-Norman Knightly Class.' *Anglo-Norman Studies* 2 (1980): 63–77, 173–76.

Harper-Bill, Christopher. 'The Struggle for Benefices in Twelfth-Century East Anglia.' *Anglo-Norman Studies* 11 (1989): 113–32.

Hart, Cyril. 'The Mersea Charter of Edward the Confessor.' *Essex Archaeology and History* 12 (1980): 94–102.

Hartigan, Francis. 'Reform of the Collegiate Clergy in the Eleventh Century: The Case of Saint-Nicholas at Poitiers.' *Studies in Medieval Culture* 6 and 7 (1976): 55–62.

Haskins, Charles Homer. 'A Charter of Canute for Fécamp.' *English Historical Review* 33 (1918): 342–44.

Haskins, Charles Homer. *Norman Institutions*. Cambridge: 1918.

Haskins, Charles Homer. *The Normans in European History*. New York: 1915, rpt. 1966.

Head, Thomas. *Hagiography and the Cult of Saints: The Diocese of Orléans, 800–1200*. Cambridge: 1900.

Heene, Katrien. 'Merovingian and Carolingian Hagiography: Continuity or Change in Public and Aims?' *Analecta Bollandiana* 107 (1989): 415–28.

Henry, Jacques. 'L'Abbaye Notre-Dame de Cormeilles.' *La Normandie bénédictine au temps de Guillaume le Conquérant*. Ed. J. Daoust and L. Gaillard. Lille: 1967. 305–21.

Henry, Jacques. 'Les Abbayes de Préaux.' *La Normandie bénédictine au temps de Guillaume le Conquérant*. Ed. J. Daoust and L. Gaillard. Lille: 1967. 191–227.

Herval, René. 'L'Abbaye du Mont-Saint-Michel.' *La Normandie bénédictine au temps de Guillaume le Conquérant*. Ed. L. Gaillard and J. Daoust. Lille: 1967. 117–36.

Herval, René. 'Un Moine de l'an mille: Guillaume de Volpiano, 1er abbé de Fécamp.' *L'Abbaye bénédictine de Fécamp: ouvrage scientifique du XIIIe centenaire*. 3 vols. Fécamp: 1959. 1: 27–44.

Hill, Bennet D. *English Cisterician Monasteries and their Patrons in the Twelfth Century*. Urbana: 1968.

Hippeau, Célestin. *L'Abbaye de Saint-Etienne de Caen, 1066–1790*. Caen: 1855.

Hippeau, Célestin. *Dictionnaire topographique du Calvados*. Brionne: rpt. 1981.

Hollister, C. Warren. 'The Greater Domesday Tenants-in-Chief.' *Domesday Studies*. Ed. J. C. Holt. Woodbridge: 1987. 219–48.

Hollister, C. Warren. 'St Anselm on Lay Investiture.' *Anglo-Norman Studies* 10 (1988): 145–58.

Holt, J. C. 'Feudal Society and the Family in Early Medieval England: II. Notions of Patrimony.' *Transactions of the Royal Historical Society* 33 (1983): 193–220.

Hourlier, Jacques. 'Le Mont Saint-Michel avant 966.' *Millénaire monastique du Mont Saint-Michel*. 2 vols. Paris: 1967. 1: 13–28.

Hourlier, Jacques. 'Les Sources écrites de l'histoire montoise antérieure à 966.' *Millénaire monastique du Mont Saint-Michel*. 2 vols. Paris: 1967. 2: 121–32.

Huisman, Gerda. 'Notes on the Manuscript Tradition of Dudo of St. Quentin's *Gesta Normannorum*.' *Anglo-Norman Studies* 6 (1984): 122–36.

Howe, John. 'The Date of the "Life" of St. Vigor of Bayeux.' *Analecta Bollandiana* 102 (1984): 303–12.

Iogna-Prat, Dominique. 'Le Monachisme autour l'an mil en quelques questions.' *Religion et culture autour de l'an mil: royaume capétien et Lotharingie*. Ed. Dominique Iogna-Prat and Jean-Charles Picard. Auxerre: 1990. 13–15.

John, Eric. 'The King and the Monks in the Tenth-Century Reformation.' *Orbis Britanniâe and Other Studies*. Leicester: 1966. 154–80.

Jordan, Victoria B. 'The Role of Kingship in Tenth-Century Normandy: Hagiography of Dudo of Saint Quentin.' *Haskins Society Journal* 3 (1992): 53–62.

Johnson, Penelope D. *Prayer, Patronage, and Power: The Abbey of la Trinité, Vendôme, 1032–1187*. New York: 1981.

Kemp, B. R. 'Monastic Possession of Parish Churches in England in the Twelfth Century.' *The Journal of Ecclesiastical History* 31 (1980): 133–60.

Keynes, Simon. *The Diplomas of King Æthelred 'the Unready' 978–1016: a Study in their Use as Historical Evidence*. Cambridge: 1980.

Keynes, Simon. 'Regenbald the Chancellor (sic).' *Anglo-Norman Studies* 10 (1988): 185–222.

Kimble, George H. T. 'The Inadequacy of the Regional Concept.' *London Essays in Geography*. Ed. Rodwell Jones. Cambridge: 1951. 151–74.

Knowles, David. 'Great Historical Enterprises, I. The Bollandists.' *Transactions of the Royal Historical Society* 8 (1958): 147–66.

Knowles, David. 'Great Historical Enterprises, II. The Maurists.' *Transactions of the Royal Historical Society* 9 (1959): 169–87.

Knowles, David. *The Monastic Order in England*. Cambridge: 1941, second edition, 1963.

Lair, Jules. *Etude sur la vie et la mort de Guillaume Longue-Epée, Duc de Normandie*. Paris: 1893.

La Roque, André de. *Histoire généalogique de la maison de Harcourt*. 4 vols. Paris: 1662.

Lamouroux, Jean-Marie. 'L'Abbaye de Saint-Evroult au XIe siècle.' *La Normandie bénédictine au temps de Guillaume le Conquérant*. Ed. J. Daoust and L. Gaillard. Lille: 1967. 249–61.

Laporte, Jean. 'Gérard de Brogne à Saint-Wandrille et à Saint-Riquier.' *Revue Bénédictine* 70 (1960): 142–66.

Laporte, Jean. 'L'Abbaye du Mont Saint-Michel aux Xe et XIe siècles.' *Millénaire monastique du Mont Saint-Michel*. 2 vols. Paris: 1967. 1: 53–80.

Laporte, Jean. 'La Date de l'exode de Jumièges.' *Jumièges: congrès scientifique du XIIIe centenaire*. 2 vols. Rouen: 1955. 1: 47–48.

Laporte, Jean. 'Les Listes abbatiales de Jumièges.' *Jumièges: congrès scientifique du XIIIe centenaire*. 2 vols. Rouen: 1955. 1: 435–66.

Laporte, Jean. 'Les Origines du monachisme dans la province de Rouen.' *Revue Mabillon* 31 (1941): 1–68.

Laporte, Jean. 'Les Séries abbatiale et priorale du Mont Saint-Michel.' *Millénaire monastique du Mont Saint-Michel*. 2 vols. Paris: 1967. 1: 267–81.

Laporte, Jean. 'Un Diplôme pour Romainmôtier dans les archives de Fécamp.' *Bulletin de la société des antiquaires de Normandie* 56 (1963): 415–29.

Latouche, Robert. *Histoire du comté du Maine pendant le Xe et le XIe siècle*. Paris: 1910.

Lauer, Philippe. *Le Règne de Louis IV d'Outremer*. Paris: 1900, rpt. 1976.

Lauer, Philippe. 'Les Translations des reliques de Saint Ouen et de Saint Leufroy du IXe au Xe siècles et les deux abbayes de La Croix-Saint-Ouen.' *Bulletin philologique et historique du comité des travaux historiques et scientifiques* (1921): 119–36.

Le Cacheux, Marie-Josèphe. *Histoire de l'abbaye de Saint-Amand de Rouen des origines à la fin du XVI siècle. Bulletin de la société des antiquaires de Normandie*. Vol. 44. Caen: 1937.

Le Cacheux, Paul. 'La Baronnie de Saint-Ouen de Rouen.' *Bulletin de la société des antiquaires de Normandie* 47 (1940): 63–81.

Le Cacheux, Paul. *L'Exemption de Montivilliers*. Caen: 1929.

Le Cacheux, Paul. 'Une Charte de Jumièges concernant l'épreuve par le fer chaud (fin du XIe siècle).' *Société de l'histoire de Normandie, mélanges* 11 (1927): 205–16.

Le Maho, Jacques. 'L'Abbaye de Montivilliers et l'aristocratie locale aux XIe et XIIe siècles.' *L'Abbaye de Montivilliers à travers les âges: actes du colloque organisé à Montivilliers le 8 mars 1986. Recueil de l'association des amis du vieux Havre.* Le Havre: 1988. 46: 1–16.

Le Patourel, John. 'Geoffrey of Montbray, Bishop of Coutances.' *English Historical Review* 59 (1944): 129–61.

Le Patourel, John. *The Norman Empire.* Oxford: 1976.

Le Prévost, Auguste. *Mémoires et notes pour servir à l'histoire du départment de l'Eure.* Ed. Léopold Delisle and Louis Passy. 3 vols. Evreux: 1862–1869.

Le Roux, R. 'Guillaume de Volpiano: son cursus liturguque au Mont Saint-Michel et dans les abbayes normandes.' *Millénaire monastique du Mont Saint-Michel.* 2 vols. Paris: 1967. 1: 267–81.

Le Roy, Thomas. *Livre des curieuses recherches du Mont-Sainct-Michel.* Ed. Eugène de Robillard de Beaurepaire. Caen: 1876.

Lebeurier, Pierre-François. *Notice sur l'abbaye de la Croix-Saint-Leufroy.* Rouen: 1866.

Leclercq, Jean, and Jean-Paul Bonnes. *Un Maître de la vie spirituelle au XIe siècle: Jean de Fécamp.* Paris: 1946.

Legris, Canon. 'L'Exode des corps saints au diocèse de Rouen (IXe–XIe siècles).' *Revue Catholique de Normandie* 28 (1919): 125–36, 168–74, 209–21.

Lelegard, M. 'Saint Aubert.' *Millénaire monastique du Mont Saint-Michel.* 2 vols. Paris: 1967. 1: 29–52.

Lemarignier, Jean-François. 'Aspects politiques des fondations de collégiales dans le royaume de France au XIe siècle.' *La vita comune del clero nei secoli XI e XII, Miscellanea del centro di studi medioevali* 3 (1962): 19–40.

Lemarignier, Jean-François. *Etude sur les privilèges d'exemption et de juridiction ecclésiastique des abbayes Normandes depuis les origines jusqu'en 1140.* Paris: 1937.

Lemarignier, Jean-François. *La France médiévale: institutions et société.* Paris: 1970.

Lemarignier, Jean-François. *Le Gouvernement royal aux premiers temps capétiens (987–1108).* Paris: 1965.

Lemarignier, Jean-François. 'Le Monachisme et l'encadrement religieux des campagnes du royaume de France situées au nord de la Loire, de la fin du X à la fin du XI siècle.' *Settimana internazionale di studio* 6 (1974): 357–98.

Lemarignier, Jean-François, Evelyne Lamon, and Véronique Gazeau. 'Monachisme et aristocratie autour de Saint-Taurin d'Evreux et du Bec (Xe–XIIe siècles).' *Aspects du monachisme en Normandie (IVe–XVIIIe siècles): Actes du colloque scientifique de l' 'année des abbayes normandes'.* Ed. Lucien Musset. Paris: 1982. 177–205.

Lemarignier, Jean-François. 'Paix et réforme monastique en Flandre et en Normandie autour de l'année 1023: quelques observations.' *Droit privé et institutions régionales: études historiques offertes à Jean Yver.* Paris: 1976. 443–68.

Lemarignier, Jean-François. *Recherches sur l'hommage en marche et les frontières féodales.* Lille: 1945.

Lemarignier, Jean-François. 'Une Eglise de premier âge féodal.' *Histoire des institutions françaises au moyen âge.* Ed. Ferdinand Lot and Robert Fawtier. Paris: 1962. 3: 44–77.

Lesne, Emile. *Les Eglises et les monastères: centres d'accueil, d'exploitation et de peuplement.* Vol. 6 of *Histoire de la propriété ecclésiastique en France.* 6 vols. Lille: 1910–1943.

Lestocquoy, J. 'Abbayes et origines des villes.' *Revue d'histoire de l'église de France* 33 (1947): 108–12.

Letort, Jean. 'L'Abbaye de la Croix-Saint-Leufroy au XIe siècle.' *La Normandie bénédictine au temps de Guillaume le Conquérant*. Ed. J. Daoust and L. Gaillard. Lille: 1967. 187–89.

Lewis, Patricia. 'Mortgages in the Bordelais and Bazadais.' *Viator* 10 (1979): 23–38.

Leyser, Henrietta. *Hermits and the New Monasticism: A Study of Religious Communities in Western Europe, 1000–1150*. London: 1984.

Licquet, Th. *Histoire de Normandie depuis les temps les plus reculés jusqu'à la conquête de l'Angleterre en 1066*. 2 vols. Rouen: 1835.

Lifshitz, Felice. 'Beyond Positivism and Genre: "Hagiographical" Texts as Historical Narrative.' *Viator* 25 (1994): 95–113.

Lifshitz, Felice. 'The Dossier of Romanus of Rouen: The Political Uses of Hagiographical Texts.' Unpublished dissertation, Columbia University: 1988.

Lifshitz, Felice. 'Dudo's Historical Narrative and the Norman Succession of 996.' *Journal of Medieval History* 20 (1994): 101–20.

Lifshitz, Felice. 'The "Exodus of Holy Bodies" Reconsidered: The Translation of the Relics of St. Gildard of Rouen to Soissons.' *Analecta Bollandiana* 110 (1992): 329–40.

Lifshitz, Felice. 'The Migration of Neustrian Relics in the Viking Age: the Myth of Voluntary Exodus, the Reality of Coercion and Theft.' *Early Medieval Europe* 4 (1995): 175–92.

Lifshitz, Felice. *The Norman Conquest of Pious Neustria: Historiographic Discourse and Saintly Relics, 684–1090*. Toronto: 1995.

Lobel, M. D. 'The Ecclesiastical Banleuca in England.' *Oxford Essays in Medieval History Presented to Herbert Edward Salter*. Oxford: 1934. 122–40.

Lobineau, Guy Alexis. *Histoire de Bretagne*. 2 vols. Paris: 1707.

Lot, Ferdinand. *Etudes sur le règne de Hugues Capet et la fin du Xe siècle*. Geneva: 1903, rpt. 1975.

Lot, Ferdinand. 'La Grande invasion normande de 856–862.' *Bibliothèque de l'école des chartes* 69 (1908): 5–62.

Lot, Ferdinand. *Les Derniers Carolingiens: Lothaire, Louis V, Charles de Lorraine 954–991*. Paris: 1891, rpt. 1975.

Loth, Julien. *Histoire de l'abbaye royale de Saint-Pierre de Jumièges*. 3 vols. Rouen: 1882–1885.

Loud, G. A. 'The "Gens Normannorum" – Myth or Reality?' *Anglo-Norman Studies*, 4 (1982): 104–209.

Louise, Gérard. *La Seigneurie de Bellême Xe–XIIe siècles: dévolution des pouvoirs territoriaux et construction d'une seigneurie de frontière aux confins de la Normandie et du Maine à la charnière de l'an mil*. 2 vols. Flers: 1992–1993.

Lund, Neils. 'Allies of God or Man? The Viking Expansion in a European Perspective.' *Viator* 20 (1989): 45–59.

Lynch, Joseph. 'Monastic Recruitment in the Eleventh and Twelfth Centuries: Some Social and Economic Considerations.' *American Benedictine Review* 26 (1975): 425–47.

Mabille, Micheline. 'Le Temporel de l'abbaye de Fécamp des origines à la fin du XIIIe siècle.' Thesis, Ecole des Chartes. 1953.

Magnou-Nortier, Elisabeth. *La Société laïque et l'église dans la province ecclésiastique de Narbonne, de la fin du VIIIe à la fin du XIe siècle*. Toulouse: 1974.

Martin, Charles Trice. *The Record Interpreter*. Chichester: 1982.

Mason, Emma. 'Pro statu et incolumnitate regni mei: Royal Monastic Patronage, 1066–1154.' *Studies in Church History* 18 (1982): 99–117.

Mason, Emma. 'Timeo barones et donas ferentes.' *Studies in Church History* 15 (1978): 61–75.

Mason, J. F. A. 'Roger de Montgomery and his Sons (1067–1102).' *Transactions of the Royal Historical Society* 13 (1963): 1–28.

Matthew, Donald. *Norman Monasteries and their English Possessions*. Oxford: 1962.

Mathon, Gérard. 'Jean de Fécamp théologien monastique? (Notes de lecture de *Confessio fidei*, III, 36–40).' *La Normandie bénédictine au temps de Guillaume le Conquérant*. Ed. L. Gaillard and J. Daoust. Lille: 1967. 485–500.

Mayer, Theodor. 'The State of the Dukes of Zahringen.' *Mediaeval Germany, 911–1250: Essays by German Historians*. Ed. and trans. Geoffrey Barraclough. 2 vols. Oxford: 1948. 2: 175–202.

Maze, Thibaud. 'L'Abbaye du Bec au XIe siècle.' *La Normandie bénédictine au temps de Guillaume le Conquérant*. Ed. L. Gaillard and J. Daoust. Lille: 1967. 229–47.

McCulloh, John M. 'Historical Martyrologies in the Benedictine Cultural Tradition.' *Benedictine Culture, 750–1050*. Ed. W. Lourdaux and D. Verhelst. Leuven, Belgium: 1983. 114–31.

McKitterick, Rosamond. *The Carolingians and the Written Word*. Cambridge: 1989.

McKitterick, Rosamond. *The Frankish Church and the Carolingian Reforms, 789–895*. London: 1977.

McKitterick, Rosamond. *The Frankish Kingdoms under the Carolingians, 751–987*. London: 1983.

Mesnel, J. B. *Les Saints du diocèse d'Evreux*. Evreux: 1914.

Miller, David Harry. 'Ethnogenesis and Religious Revitalization beyond the Roman Frontier: The Case of Frankish Origins.' *Journal of World History* 4 (1993): 277–85.

Mollat, Michel. 'La Seigneurie maritime du Mont Saint-Michel.' *Millénaire monastique du Mont Saint-Michel*. 2 vols. Paris: 1967. 2: 73–88.

Mostert, Marco. *The Political Theology of Abbo of Fleury*. Hilversum: 1987.

Motey, Henry Renault du. *Origines de la Normandie et du duché d'Alençon*. Paris: 1920.

Motte-Collas, Marie de la. 'Les Possessions territoriales de l'abbaye de Saint-Germain-des-Prés du début du IXe au début du XII siècle.' *Revue d'histoire de l'église de France* 43 (1957): 49–80.

Musset, Lucien. 'A-t-il existé en Normandie au XIe siècle une aristocratie d'argent?' *Annales de Normandie* 9 (1959): 285–99.

Musset, Lucien. 'Actes inédits du XIe siècle, l'abbaye de Saint Ouen de Rouen et la ville de Caen.' *Bulletin de la société des antiquaires de Normandie* 58 (1968): 119–26.

Musset, Lucien. 'Actes inédits du XI siècle: II, une nouvelle charte de Robert le Magnifique pour Fécamp.' *Bulletin de la société des antiquaires de Normandie* 52 (1955): 142–53.

Musset, Lucien. 'Actes inédits du XIe siècle: I, les plus anciennes chartes du prieuré de Saint-Gabriel (Calvados).' *Bulletin de la société des antiquaires de Normandie* 52 (1955): 117–41.

Musset, Lucien. 'Actes inédits du XIe siècle: III, les plus anciennes chartes normandes de l'abbaye de Bourgueil.' *Bulletin de la société des antiquaires de Normandie* 54 (1959): 15–54.

Musset, Lucien. 'Aperçus sur le dîme ecclésiastique en Normandie au XIe siècle.' *Revue historique de droit français et étranger* 52 (1974): 544–45.

Musset, Lucien. 'Autour des modalités juridiques de l'expansion normande au XIe siècle: le droit d'exil.' *Autour du pouvoir ducal normand, Xe–XIIe siècles.* Ed. Lucien Musset, Jean-Michel Bouvris and Jean-Marie Maillefer. Cahier des Annales de Normandie. Caen: 1985. 17: 45–59.

Musset, Lucien. 'Autour des origines de Saint-Etienne de Fontenay.' *Bulletin de la société des antiquaires de Normandie* 56 (1963): 11–41.

Musset, Lucien. 'Aux Origines d'une classe dirigeante: les Tosny, grands barons normands du Xe au XIIIe siècle.' *Francia* 5 (1977): 45–80.

Musset, Lucien. 'Aux Origines de la féodalité normande: l'installation par les ducs de leurs vassaux normands et bretons dans le comté d'Avranches (XIe siècle).' *Revue historique de droit français et étranger* 29 (1951): 150.

Musset, Lucien. 'Considerations sur la genèse et le trace des frontières de la Normandie.' *Media in Francia . . . Recueil de mélanges offert à Karl Ferdinand Werner à l'occasion de son 65 anniversaire par ses amis et collègues français.* Maulévrier: 1989. 309–18.

Musset, Lucien. 'Foires et marchés en Normandie à l'époque ducale.' *Annales de Normandie* 26 (1976): 2–23.

Musset, Lucien. 'L'Abbaye de Saint-Etienne du Plessis-Grimoult.' *Art de Basse-Normandie* 27 (1962): 9–16.

Musset, Lucien. 'L'Aristocratie normande au XIe siècle.' *La Noblesse au moyen âge, Xe–XVe siècles.* Ed. Philippe Contamine. Paris: 1976. 77–81.

Musset, Lucien. 'L'Exode des reliques du diocèse de Sées au temps des invasions normandes.' *Bulletin de la société archéologique et historique de l'Orne* 83 (1970): 3–33.

Musset, Lucien. 'La Contribution de Fécamp à la reconquête monastique de la basse-Normandie.' *L'Abbaye bénédictine de Fécamp: ouvrage scientifique du XIIIe centenaire.* 3 vols. Fécamp: 1959. 1: 57–66, 341–43.

Musset, Lucien. 'La Vie économique de l'abbaye de Fécamp sous l'abbatiat de Jean de Ravenne (1028–1078).' *L'Abbaye bénédictine de Fécamp: ouvrage scientifique du XIIIe centenaire.* 3 vols. Fécamp: 1959. 1: 67–79.

Musset, Lucien. 'Le Problème de la continuité monastique en Normandie entre l'époque franque et l'époque ducale: les apports de l'épigraphie.' *Histoire religieuse de la Normandie.* Ed. Guy-Marie Oury. Chambray: 1981. 57–70.

Musset, Lucien. 'Les Abbayes normandes au moyen âge: position de quelques problèmes.' *Les Abbayes de Normandie, actes du XIIIe congrès des sociétés historiques et archéologiques de Normandie.* Ed. Lucien Andrieu et al. Rouen: 1979. 13–26.

Musset, Lucien. *Les Actes de Guillaume le Conquérant et de la reine Mathilde pour les abbayes caennaises.* Caen: 1967.

Musset, Lucien. 'Les Destins de la propriété monastique durant les invasions normands (IXe–XIe s.): l'exemple de Jumièges.' *Jumièges: Congrès scientifique du XIIIe centenaire.* 2 vols. 1955. 1: 49–55.

Musset, Lucien. 'Les Domaines de l'époque franque et les destinées du régime domanial du IXe au XIe siècle.' *Bulletin de la société des antiquaires de Normandie* 49 (1946): 7–97.

Musset, Lucien. 'Les Fiefs de deux familles vicomtales de l'Hiémois au XIe siècle, les Goz et les Montgommery.' *Revue historique de droit français et étranger* 48 (1970): 342–43.

Musset, Lucien. 'Les Origines du prieuré de Saint-Fromond: un acte négligé de Richard II.' *Bulletin de la société des antiquaires de Normandie* 53 (1957): 475–89.

Musset, Lucien. 'Les Premiers Temps de l'abbaye d'Almenèches des origines au XIIe siècle.' *L'Abbaye d'Almenèches-Argentan et Sainte Opportune.* Ed. Yves Chaussy. Paris: 1970.

Musset, Lucien. 'Les Sépultures des souverains normands: un aspect de l'idéologie du pouvoir.' *Autour du pouvoir ducal normand, Xe–XIIe siècles.* Ed. Lucien Musset, Jean-Michel Bouvris and Jean-Marie Maillefer. *Cahier des Annales de Normandie.* Caen: 1985. 17: 19–44.

Musset, Lucien. 'Monachisme d'époque franque et monachisme d'époque ducale en Normandie: le problème de la continuité.' *Aspects du monachisme en Normandie (IVe–XVIIIe siècles): actes du colloque scientifique de l' 'Année des Abbayes Normandes'.* Ed. Lucien Musset. Paris: 1982. 55–74.

Musset, Lucien. 'Naissance de la Normandie (Ve–XIe siècles).' *Histoire de la Normandie.* Ed. Michel de Boüard. Toulouse: 1970. 75–130.

Musset, Lucien. 'Notes sur l'ancienne abbaye de Deux-Jumeaux.' *Bulletin de la société des antiquaires de Normandie* 53 (1957): 405–21.

Musset, Lucien. 'Notules fécampoises.' *Bulletin de la société des antiquaires de Normandie* 54 (1959): 584–98.

Musset, Lucien. 'Observations sur l'histoire et la signification de la frontière normande (Xe–XIIe siècles).' *Revue historique de droit français et étranger* 41 (1963): 545–46.

Musset, Lucien. 'Origines et nature du pouvoir ducal en Normandie jusqu'au milieu de XIe siècle.' *Les Principautés au Moyen-Age: Communications du Congrès de Bordeaux en 1973.* Bordeaux: 1979. 47–59.

Musset, Lucien. 'Peuplement en bourgage et bourgs ruraux en Normandie du Xe au XIIIe siècle.' *Cahiers de civilisation médiévale, Xe–XIIe siècles* 9 (1966): 177–205.

Musset, Lucien. 'Recherches sur la consistance géographique des patrimoines monastiques normands: Iles Britanniques et Continent de l'époque Franque au XIIIe siècle.' *Annales de Normandie* 8 (1958): 185–86.

Musset, Lucien. 'Recherches sur le tonlieu en Normandie à l'époque ducale.' *Autour du pouvoir ducal normand, Xe–XIIe siècles.* Ed. Lucien Musset, Jean-Michel Bouvris and Jean-Marie Maillefer. Cahier des Annales de Normandie. Caen: 1985. 17: 61–76.

Musset, Lucien. 'Recherches sur les communautés des clercs séculiers en Normandie au XIe siècle.' *Bulletin de la société des antiquaires de Normandie* 55 (1961): 5–38.

Musset, Lucien. 'Recherches sur les pèlerins et les pèlerinages en Normandie jusqu'à la Première Croisade.' *Annales de Normandie* 12 (1962): 127–50.

Musset, Lucien. 'Voie publique et chemin du roi en Normandie du XIe au XIIIe siècle.' *Autour du pouvoir ducal normand, Xe–XIIe siècles.* Ed. Lucien Musset,

Jean-Michel Bouvris and Jean-Marie Maillefer. Cahier des Annales de Normandie. 17. Caen: 1985.

Navel, Henri. 'Les Vavassories du Mont-Saint-Michel à Bretteville-sur-Odon et Verson (Calvados).' *Bulletin de la société des antiquaires de Normandie* 45 (1937): 137–65.

Nortier, Geneviève. *Les Bibliothèques médiévales des abbayes bénédictines de Normandie.* Caen: 1966.

Omont, Henri. *Catalogue générale des manuscrits des bibliothèques publiques de France: departements.* Paris: 1886–1888.

Ortenberg, Veronica. *The English Church and the Continent in the Tenth and Eleventh Centuries: Cultural, Spiritual and Artistic Exchanges.* Oxford: 1992.

Oury, Guy-Marie. *Histoire religieuse de la Normandie.* Chambray: 1981.

Oury, Guy-Marie. 'La Reconstruction monastique dans l'ouest: L'Abbé Gauzbert de Saint-Julien de Tours (v. 990–1007).' *Revue Mabillon* 54 (1964): 69–124.

Paxton, Frederick S. *Christianizing Death: The Creation of a Ritual Process in Early Medieval Europe.* Ithaca: 1990.

Pfister, Christian. *Etudes sur le règne de Robert le Pieux (996–1031).* Paris: 1885, rpt. 1974.

Pigeon, E. A. *Histoire de la cathédrale de Coutances.* Coutances: 1876.

Poly, Jean-Pierre. *La Provence et la société féodale (879–1166).* Paris: 1976.

Pommeraye, F. *Histoire de l'abbaye de la très Sainte Trinité dite depuis de St Catherine du Mont de Rouen. Histoire de l'abbaye royale de St-Ouen de Rouen.* Ed. F. Pommeraye. Rouen: 1662.

Pommeraye, F. *Histoire de l'abbaye royale de St-Ouen de Rouen.* Rouen: 1662.

Poncelet, Albert, ed. 'Catalogus Codicum Hagiographicorum Latinorum Bibliothecae Publicae Rotomagensis.' *Analecta Bollandiana* 23 (1904): 251–75.

Porée, A. A. *Histoire de l'abbaye de Bec.* 2 vols. Evreux: 1901, rpt. 1980.

Potts, Cassandra. '*Atque unum ex diversis gentibus populum effecit*, Historical Tradition and the Norman Identity.' *Anglo-Norman Studies* 18 (1996): 139–52.

Potts, Cassandra. 'The Earliest Norman Counts Revisited: The Lords of Mortain.' *Haskins Society Journal* 4 (1993): 23–35.

Potts, Cassandra. 'The Early Norman Charters: A New Perspective on an Old Debate.' *England in the Eleventh Century: Proceedings of the 1990 Harlaxton Symposium.* Ed. Carola Hicks. Stamford, Lincolnshire: 1992. 25–40.

Potts, Cassandra. 'Les Ducs normands et leurs nobles: le patronage monastique avant la conquête de l'Angleterre.' *Etudes normandes* 3 (1986): 29–37.

Potts, Cassandra. 'Normandy or Brittany? A Conflict of Interests at Mont Saint Michel (996–1035).' *Anglo-Norman Studies* 12 (1990): 135–56.

Potts, Cassandra. 'When the Saints go Marching: Religious Connections and the Political Culture of Early Normandy.' *Anglo-Norman Political Culture and the Twelfth Century Renaissance: Proceedings of the Borchard Conference on Anglo-Norman History.* Ed. C. Warren Hollister. Woodbridge: 1997. 17–31.

Power, D. J. 'The Norman Frontier in the Twelfth and Early Thirteenth Centuries.' Unpublished Ph.D. thesis, University of Cambridge: 1994.

Power, D. J. 'What did the Frontier of Angevin Normandy Comprise?' *Anglo-Norman Studies* 17 (1995): 181–201.

Prentout, Henri. *Essai sur les origines et la fondation du duché de Normandie.* Paris: 1911.

Prentout, Henri. *Etude critique sur Dudon de Saint-Quentin et son histoire des premiers ducs normands*. Caen: 1915.

Prentout, Henri. 'Le Règne de Richard II duc de Normandie, 996–1027: son importance dans l'histoire.' *Academie nationales des sciences arts et belles-lettres de Caen* 5 (1929): 57–104.

Priem, Georges. 'L'Abbaye royale de Montivilliers.' *La Normandie bénédictine au temps de Guillaume le Conquérant*. Ed. J. Daoust and L. Gaillard. Lille: 1967. 153–77.

Prou, Maurice. *Manuel de paléographie latine et française*. Paris: 1924.

Raftis, J. A. 'Western Monasticism and Economic Organization.' *Comparative Studies in Society and History: An International Quarterly* 3 (1961): 452–59.

Ramsay, Nigel, Margaret Sparks, and Tim Tatton-Brown, ed. *St Dunstan: His Life, Times and Cult*. Woodbridge: 1992.

Renaud, Jean. *Les Vikings et la Normandie*. Ouest-France: 1989.

Renault, M. 'Essai historique sur la paroisse et l'abbaye de la Croix-St-Leufroi.' *Mémoires de la société des antiquaires de Normandie* 25 (1863): 652–98.

Renoux, Annie. 'Fouilles sur le site du château ducal de Fécamp (Xe–XIIe siecle): bilan provisoire.' *Anglo-Norman Studies* 4 (1982): 133–52, 221–23.

Renoux, Annie. 'Le Château des ducs de Normandie à Fécamp (IXe–XIe s.): Quelques données archéologiques et topographiques.' *Archéologie médiévale* 9 (1979): 5–35.

Renoux, Annie. 'Le Monastère de Fécamp pendant le haut Moyen âge (VIIe–IXe siècle). Quelques données historiques et archéologiques.' *Les Abbayes de Normandie, actes du XIIIe congrès des sociétés historiques et archéologiques de Normandie*. Ed. L. Andrieu. Rouen: 1979. 115–33.

Renoux, Annie. 'Le Palais des ducs de Normandie à Fécamp: bilan récent des fouilles en cours.' *Académie des inscriptions et belles-lettres: comptes rendus des séances de l'année 1982*. Paris: 1982. 6–30.

Reuter, Timothy. 'Plunder and Tribute in the Carolingian Empire.' *Transactions of the Royal Historical Society* 35 (1985): 75–94.

Reynolds, Susan. 'Medieval *origines gentium* and the Community of the Realm.' *History* 68 (1983): 375–90.

Riché, Pierre. 'Consequences des invasions normandes sur la culture monastique dans l'occident franc.' *I Normanni e la loro espansione in Europa nell'alto medioevo*. Spoleto: 1969. 705–26.

Riché, Pierre. *Education and Culture in the Barbarian West, Sixth through Eighth Centuries*. Trans. John J. Contreni. Columbia, SC: 1976.

Ridyard, Susan J. '*Condigna Veneratio*: Post-Conquest Attitudes to the Saints of the Anglo-Saxons.' *Anglo-Norman Studies* 9 (1987): 179–206.

Rosenwein, Barbara. 'Feudal War and Monastic Peace: Cluniac Liturgy as Ritual Agression.' *Viator* 2 (1971): 129–57.

Rosenwein, Barbara H. *To Be the Neighbor of Saint Peter: The Social Meaning of Cluny's Property, 909–1049*. Ithaca: 1989.

Rosenwein, Barbara H. *Rhinoceros Bound: Cluny in the Tenth Century*. Philadelphia: 1982.

Round, John Horace. *Calender of Documents Preserved in France Illustrative of the History of Great Britain and Ireland*. London: 1899, rpt. 1967.

Roux, R. le. 'Guillaume de Volpiano: son cursus liturgique au Mont Saint-Michel et dans les abbayes normandes.' *Millénaire monastique du Mont Saint-Michel*. 2 vols. Paris: 1967. 1: 417–72.

Sabbe, E. 'Etude critique sur la biographie et la réforme de Gérard de Brogne.' *Mélanges Félix Rousseau*. Brussels: 1958. 497–524.

Saint Pierre, Louis de. 'L'Abbaye de Grestain et ses fondateurs.' *La Normandie bénédictine au temps de Guillaume le Conquérant*. Ed. J. Daoust and L. Gaillard. Lille: 1967. 263–76.

Samaran, Charles, and Robert Marichal. *Catalogue des manuscrits en écriture latine*. Paris: 1959–1984.

Sauvage, R. N. *L'Abbaye de Saint-Martin de Troarn*. Caen: 1911.

Searle, Eleanor. 'Fact and Pattern in Heroic History: Dudo of Saint-Quentin.' *Viator* 15 (1984): 75–86.

Searle, Eleanor. 'Frankish Rivalries and Norse Warriors.' *Anglo-Norman Studies* 8 (1986): 198–213.

Searle, Eleanor. *Lordship and Community: Battle Abbey and its Banlieu, 1066–1538*. Toronto: 1974.

Searle, Eleanor. *Predatory Kinship and the Creation of Norman Power, 840–1066*. Berkeley: 1988.

Senne, Félix. *L'Institution des avoueries ecclésiastiques en France*. Paris: 1903.

Shopkow, Leah. 'The Carolingian World of Dudo of Saint-Quentin.' *Journal of Medieval History* 15 (1989): 19–37.

Simonnet, Claude. 'L'Enluminure dans les manuscrits normands.' *Trésors des abbayes nomandes*. Rouen: 1979. 103–62.

Smith, Julia M. H. 'Early Medieval Hagiography in the Late Twentieth Century.' *Early Medieval Europe* 1 (1992): 69–76.

Smith, Julia M. H. *Province and Empire: Brittany and the Carolingians*. Cambridge: 1992.

Soulignac, Robert. *Fécamp et sa campagne à l'époque des ducs de Normandie (911–1204)*. Fécamp: 1987.

Southern, R. W. *Saint Anselm: A Portrait in a Landscape*. Cambridge: 1990.

Southern, R. W. *St. Anselm and His Biographer*. Cambridge: 1963.

Southern, R. W. 'Aspects of the European Tradition of Historical Writing, 1. The Classical Tradition from Einhard to Geoffrey of Monmouth.' *Transactions of the Royal Historical Society* 20 (1970): 173–96.

Soyez, Jeanne-Marie. 'Les Abbayes de Rouen au XIe siécle.' *La Normandie bénédictine au temps de Guillaume le Conquérant*. Ed. J. Daoust and L. Gaillard. Lille: 1967. 69–81.

Spear, David. 'Research Facilities in Normandy and Paris.' *Comitatus* 12 (1981): 40–53.

Spear, David. 'The Norman Empire and the Secular Clergy, 1066–1204.' *The Journal of British Studies* 21 (1982): 1–10.

Stein, Henri. *Cartulaires français ou relatifs à l'histoire de France*. Paris: 1907.

Stenton, Sir Frank. *Anglo-Saxon England*. 3rd edn. Oxford: 1971.

Stenton, Sir Frank. *The Latin Charters of the Anglo-Saxon Period*. Oxford: 1955.

Strayer, Joseph. 'On the Early Norman Charters, 911–1066.' *Medieval Statecraft and the Perspectives of History*. Princeton: 1971. 39–43.

Sullivan, Richard E. 'The Carolingian Age: Reflections on Its Place in the History of the Middle Ages.' *Speculum* 64 (1989): 267–306.

Tabuteau, Emily Zack. *Transfers of Property in Eleventh-Century Norman Law.* Chapel Hill: 1988.

Tardif, Henri. 'La Liturgie de la messe au Mont Saint-Michel aus XIe, XIIe et XIIIe siècles.' *Millénaire monastique du Mont Saint-Michel.* 2 vols. Paris: 1967. 1: 353–77.

Teske, Raymond H. C., Jr, and Bardin H. Nelson. 'Acculturation and Assimilation: a Clarification.' *American Ethnologist* 1 (1974): 351–67.

Thompson, Kathleen. 'Family and Influence to the South of Normandy in the Eleventh Century: the Lordship of Bellême.' *Journal of Medieval History* 11 (1985): 215–26.

Thompson, Kathleen. 'The Norman Aristocracy before 1066: the Example of the Montgomerys.' *Historical Research* 60 (1987): 251–63.

Tobler, Titus, ed. *Descriptiones Terrae Sanctae ex saeculo VIII, IX, XII, et XV.* Leipzig: 1874.

Tour, Imbart de la. 'Des Immunités commerciales accordées aux églises du VIIe au IX siècle.' *Etudes d'histoire du moyen âge dédiées à Gabriel Monod.* Paris: 1896. 71–87.

Tour, Imbart de la. *Les Paroisses rurales du 4e au 11e siècle.* Paris: 1889, rpt. 1979.

Toustain de Billy, René. *Histoire ecclésiastique du diocèse de Coutances.* Rouen: 1874.

Trigan, Charles. *Histoire ecclésiastique de la province de Normandie: avec des observations critiques et historiques.* Caen: 1759.

Valin, Lucien. *Le Duc de Normandie et sa cour (912–1204): étude d'histoire juridique.* Paris: 1910.

Valous, Guy de. *Le Domaine de l'abbaye de Cluny aux X et XI siècles.* Paris: 1923.

van Houts, Elisabeth M. C. 'The *Gesta Normannorum Ducum*: a history without an end.' *Anglo-Norman Studies* 3 (1981): 106–18.

van Houts, Elisabeth M. C. 'Historiography and Hagiography at Saint-Wandrille: the "Inventio et miracula sancti Vulfranni".' *Anglo-Norman Studies* 12 (1990): 233–51.

van Houts, Elisabeth M. C. 'Robert of Torigni as genealogist.' *Studies in Medieval History Presented to R. Allen Brown.* Ed. Christopher Harper-Bill, Christopher J. Holdsworth, and Janet L. Nelson. Woodbridge: 1989. 215–33

van Houts, Elisabeth M. C. 'Scandinavian Influence in Norman Literature of the Eleventh Century.' *Anglo-Norman Studies* 6 (1984): 107–21.

van Houts, Elisabeth M. C. 'The Ship List of William the Conqueror.' *Anglo-Norman Studies* 10 (1988): 159–83.

Vandenbroucke, F. 'Dom Jean Huynes et Dom Thomas Le Roy, historiens Mauristes du Mont Saint-Michel.' *Millénaire du Mont Saint-Michel.* 2 vols. Paris: 1967. 2: 155–67.

Vandeventer, Christiane. 'Bibliographie de la toponymie normande.' *Cahiers Léopold Delisle* 18 (1969): 87–119.

Vaughn, Sally N. *Anselm of Bec and Robert of Meulan: The Innocence of the Dove and the Wisdom of the Serpent.* Berkeley: 1987.

Verdier, P. le. 'Notes inédites relatives à l'abbaye de Saint-Amand de Rouen.' *Almanach liturgique* (1889): 1–11.

Walker, Barbara McDonald. 'The Grandmesnils: A Study in Norman Baronial Enterprise.' Unpublished dissertation, University of California, Santa Barbara: 1968.

Wallace-Hadrill, J. M. 'The Vikings in Francia.' *Early Medieval History*. New York: 1975. 217–36.

Werner, Karl Ferdinand. 'Quelques observations au sujet des débuts du 'duché' de Normandie.' *Droit privé et institutions régionales: Etudes historiques offertes à Jean Yver*. Paris: 1976. 691–709.

Westrup, C. W. 'Le Mariage de trois premiers ducs de Normandie.' *Normannia* 6 (1933): 411–26.

White, Geoffrey H. 'The First House of Bellême.' *Transactions of the Royal Historical Society* 22 (1940): 67–95.

White, G. H. 'The Sisters and Nieces of Gunnor, Duchess of Normandy.' *The Genealogist* 37 (1920): 57–65, 128–32.

White, Stephen D. 'Pactum . . . Legem Vincit et Amor Judicium: The Settlement of Disputes by Compromise in Eleventh-Century Western France.' *The American Journal of Legal History* 22 (1978): 281–308.

White, Stephen D. *Custom, Kinship and Gifts to Saints: The* Laudatio Parentum *in Western France, 1050–1150*. Chapel Hill: 1988.

Williams, Watkin. 'William of Dijon: a Monastic Reformer of the Early XIth Century.' *Downside Review* 52 (1934): 520–45.

Wilmart, A. 'La Complainte de Jean de Fécamp sur les fins derniéres.' *Auteurs spirituels et textes dévots du moyen âge latin*. Paris: 1932. 126–37.

Wormald, C. P. 'The Uses of Literacy in Anglo-Saxon England and its Neighbors.' *Transactions of the Royal Historical Society* 27 (1977): 95–114.

Yver, Jean. 'Autour de l'absence d'avouerie en Normandie.' *Bulletin de la société des antiquaires de Normandie* 57 (1965): 189–283.

Yver, Jean. 'Contribution à l'étude du développement de la compétence ducale en Normandie.' *Annales de Normandie* 8 (1958): 139–83.

Yver, Jean. 'Les Châteaux forts en Normandie jusqu'au milieu du XIIe siècle.' *Bulletin de la société des antiquaires de Normandie* 53 (1957): 28–115.

Yver, Jean. 'Les Premières Institutions du duché de Normandie.' *I Normanni e la loro espansione in Europa nell'alto medioevo*. Spoleto: 1969. 299–366.

Index

The maps on pp. xii–xvi have not been included in this index.